BHUTAN

LAND OF THE THUNDER DRAGON

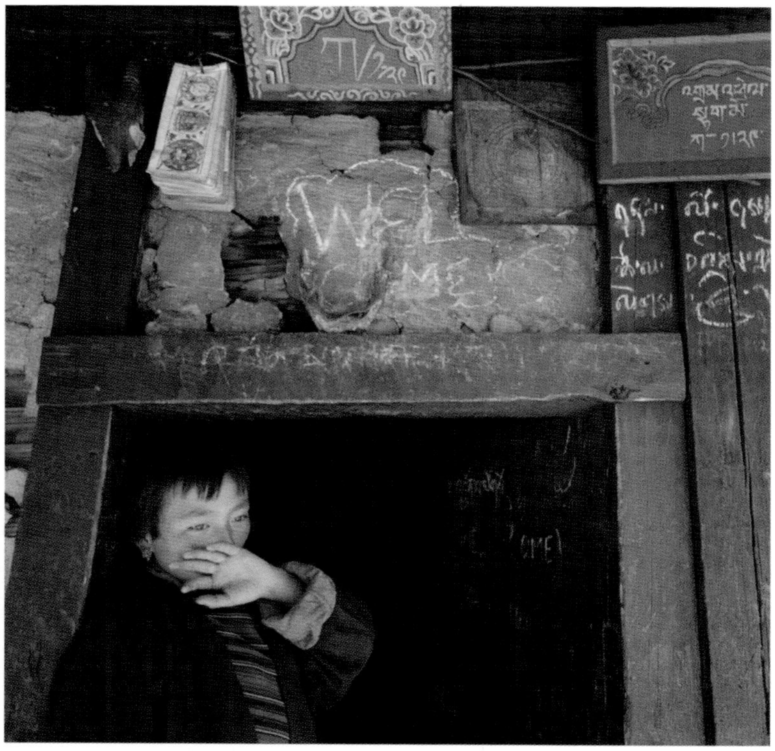

BUDDHISM *and* MONASTIC LIFE

THE OFFICIAL STATE RELIGION of Bhutan, Drukpa Kagyu Buddhism, traces its heritage back to the northern Indian town of Bodhgaya, where Siddhartha Gautama became the Buddha around 500 B.C. After discovering a middle path between asceticism and sensory gratification, Siddhartha overcame numerous inner obstacles to achieve Buddhahood, or full enlightenment.

Known in Bhutan as Shakyamuni, the Buddha traveled widely on the Indian subcontinent and preached that because all beings are driven by selfish desires, a cycle of suffering reincarnation cannot be broken unless one follows the noble eightfold path of ethical behavior, deep meditation, and profound insight. According to Bhutanese legend, Shakyamuni subdued and converted a powerful spirit named Yeshe Goenpo, who then became the principal guardian deity of Bhutan.

Padmasambhava, or Guru Rinpoche, is often called the second Buddha in Bhutan. He is said to have miraculously emerged as an eight-year-old from a blue lotus early in the eighth century. Padmasambhava became an enlightened master of the tantric, or *Vajrayana,* branch of Buddhism and traveled extensively throughout the Himalayan region, spreading the Buddhist teachings. Even though Buddhism had slowly begun to supplant the shamanistic Bon faith centuries before his three visits, Padmasambhava is celebrated for cementing Buddhist ideology in Bhutan and for heroic mediations in remote caves. As a testament to his influence, nearly all temples and monasteries today prominently feature Padmasambhava in the center of the altar.

After Padmasambhava's time, Himalayan Buddhism, which is also known as Tibetan Buddhism, continued to grow and to evolve into the four primary lineages we see today: Nyingma, Kagyu, Sakya, and Gelug. The Drukpa Kagyu Buddhism practiced in Bhutan is one of several traditions within the Kagyu lineage, which descends from Milarepa, Tibet's famous hermit saint. Today, Buddhism permeates nearly all aspects of Bhutanese culture, and it is customary for one son from each family to join the monastic community at an early age. Even though it is not compulsory for Bhutanese monks or nuns to remain as such, many choose to do so, spending their lives in the pursuit of study and meditation. At certain times of the year, they may return to their parents' homes to rest and to help with the responsibilities of maintaining their families' farms.

The central monk body, known as the Dratshang, oversees all religious activity in the country and is led by the highest-ranking lama in the country, His Holiness the Je Khenpo. All monasteries adhere to a strict code that has remained unchanged for hundreds of years. Rising long before dawn, monks and nuns begin group prayers and book study at 4 A.M., continuing until 9 P.M. with breaks for two meals and specific religious duties.

Due to the tremendous complexity of the Drukpa Kagyu beliefs and practices, decades of study are required to master the diverse and extensive teachings. One of the most daunting challenges for monks is a retreat that takes three years, three months, three weeks, and three days during which they do not come into contact with anyone. Once completed, monks will often take a short break and then continue on for an additional two retreats, totaling ten years of isolated meditation.

The Drukpa Kagyu pantheon of saints who have attained enlightenment—Buddhas from the past and future, compassionate guardians known as *bodhisattvas,* and terrifying protective deities—is both extensive and diverse. Although temples, monasteries, and unique holy sites throughout Bhutan differ slightly in content and construction style, they are bound together by the threads of a common religious heritage.

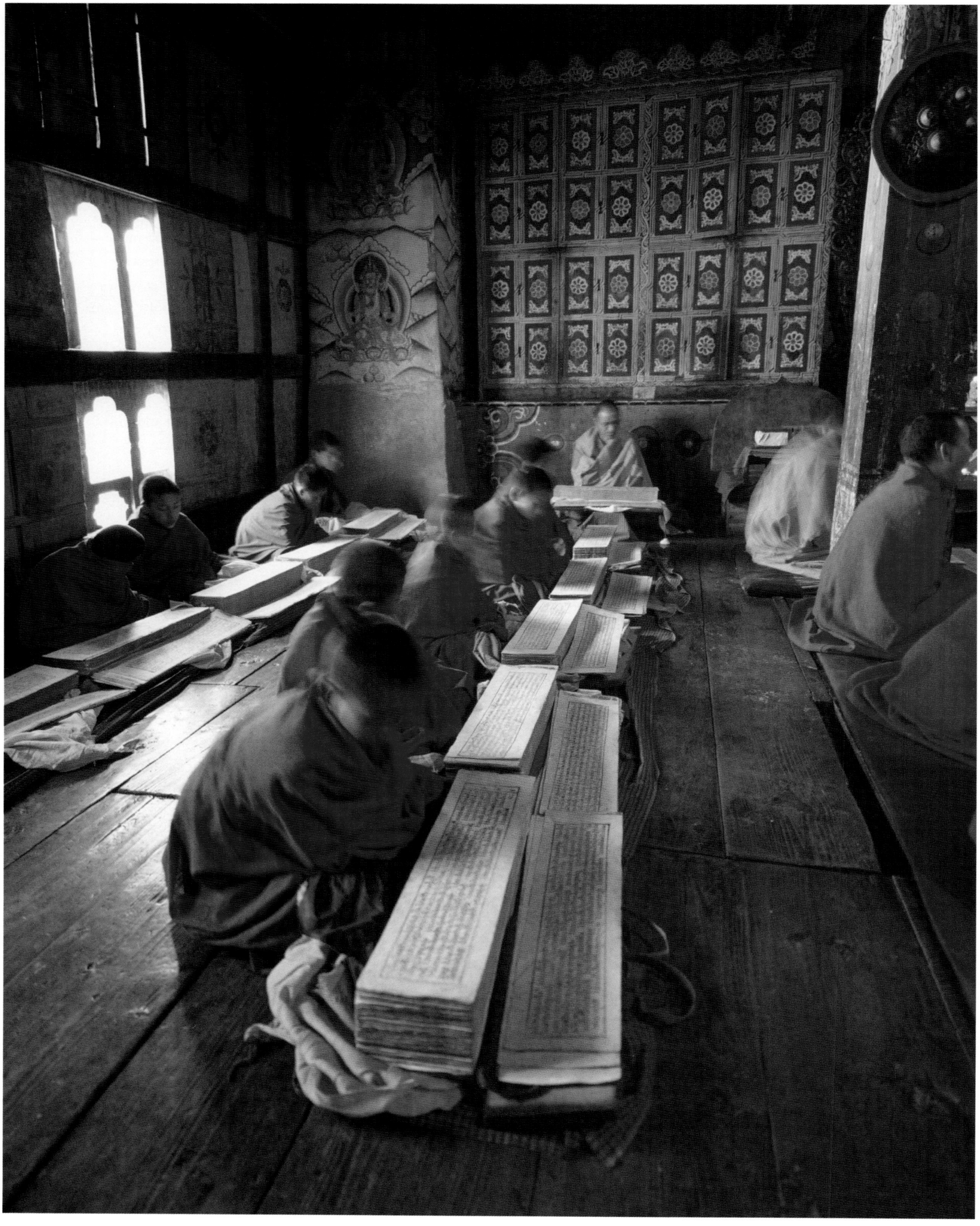

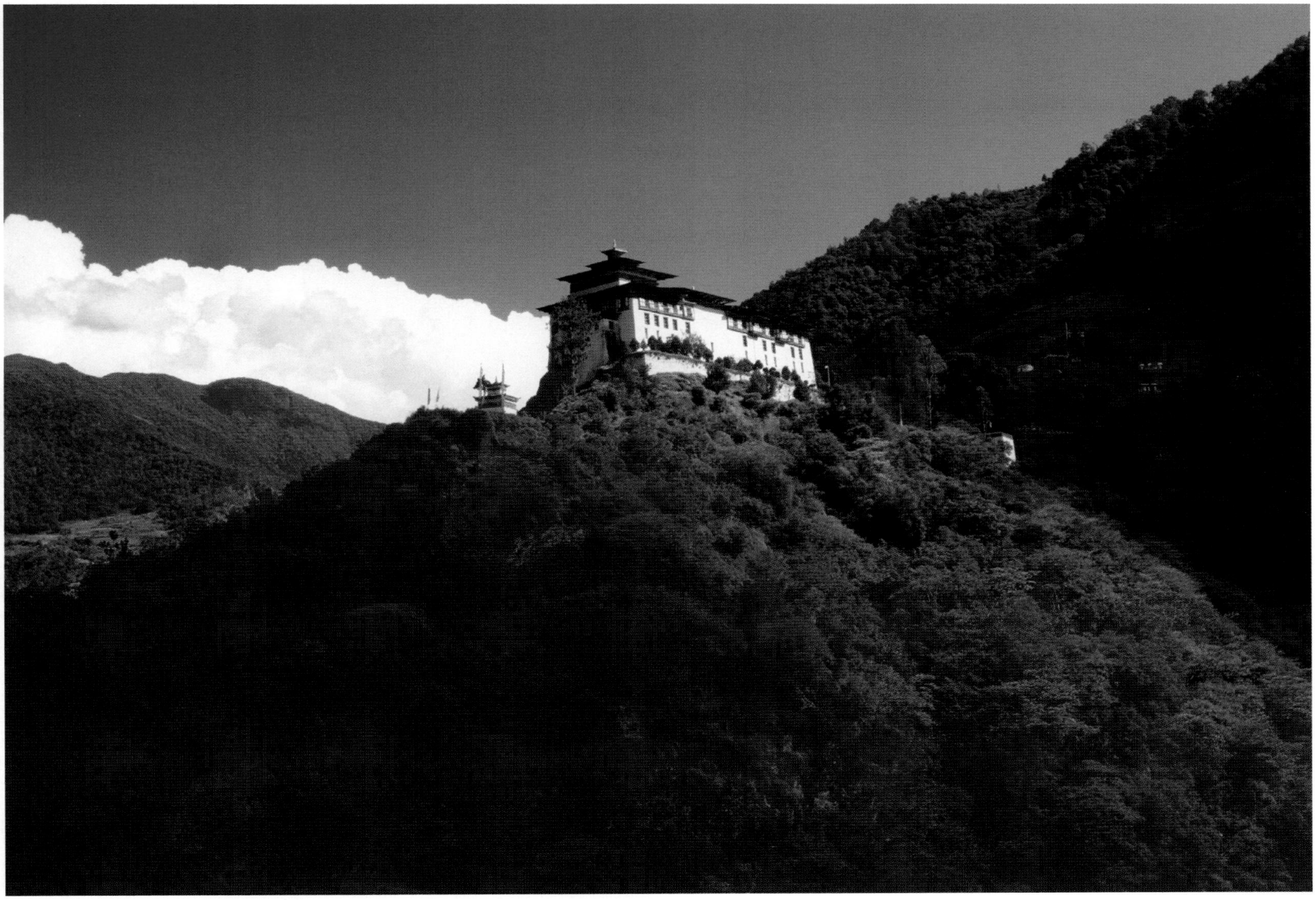

Lhuntsi Dzong was constructed in 1654 on a strategic spur overlooking the Kuri River Valley. Fortress monasteries, known as *dzongs,* built in Bhutan during the seventeenth century needed to command a defensive position to protect the surrounding villages from incursions by Tibetan armies.

Left: Monks from Dagana Dzong, built in 1655, recite their early morning prayers from large books printed on handmade paper. The rigorous monastic schedule that has remained unchanged for generations begins at 3 A.M. when the monks first wake up. Their day is spent studying religious books, participating in group prayers, and sharing the responsibilities of maintaining their residence.

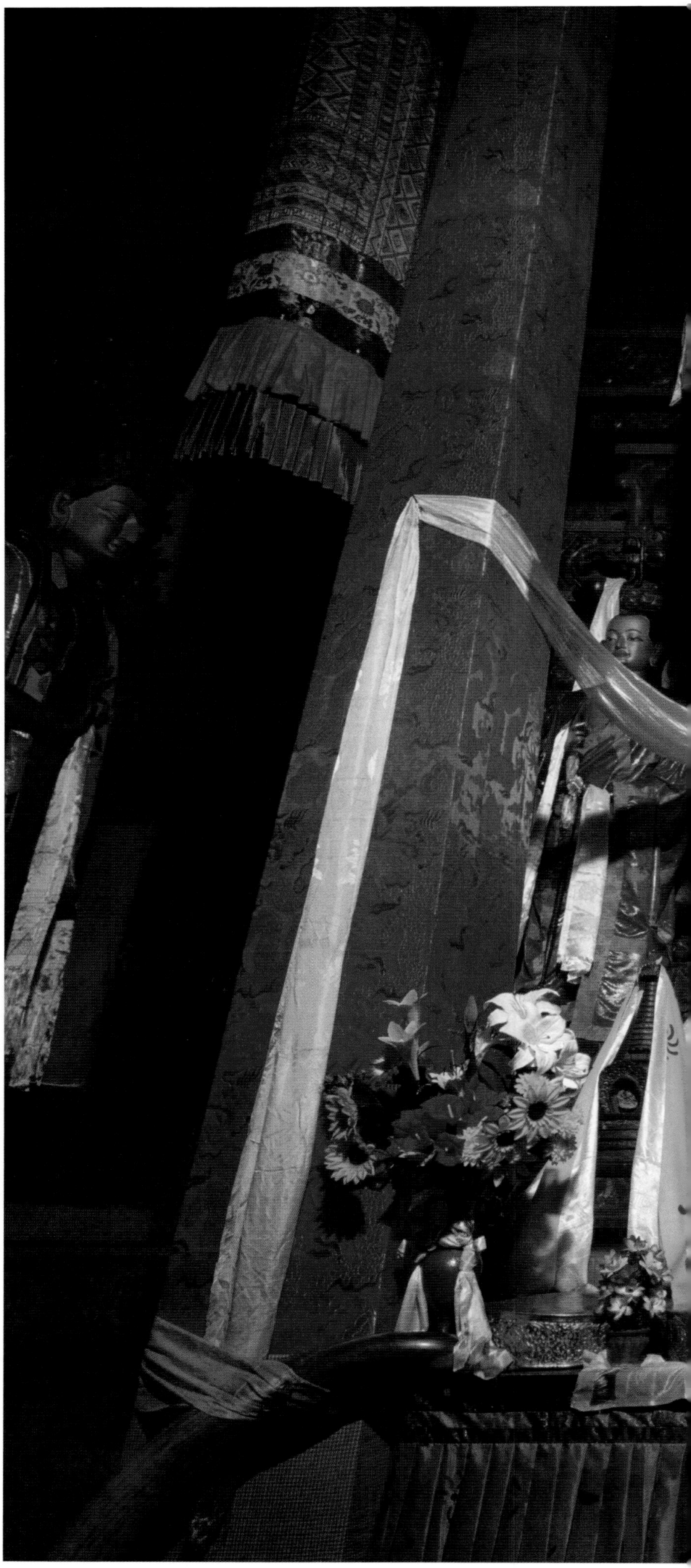

Adjacent to the central prayer hall in Simtokha Dzong is a massive 375-year-old statue of the historic first Buddha, Shakyamuni. The Buddha is flanked by several statues of *bodhisattvas,* disciples who have developed the aspiration to become Buddhas in order to relieve the suffering of all beings.

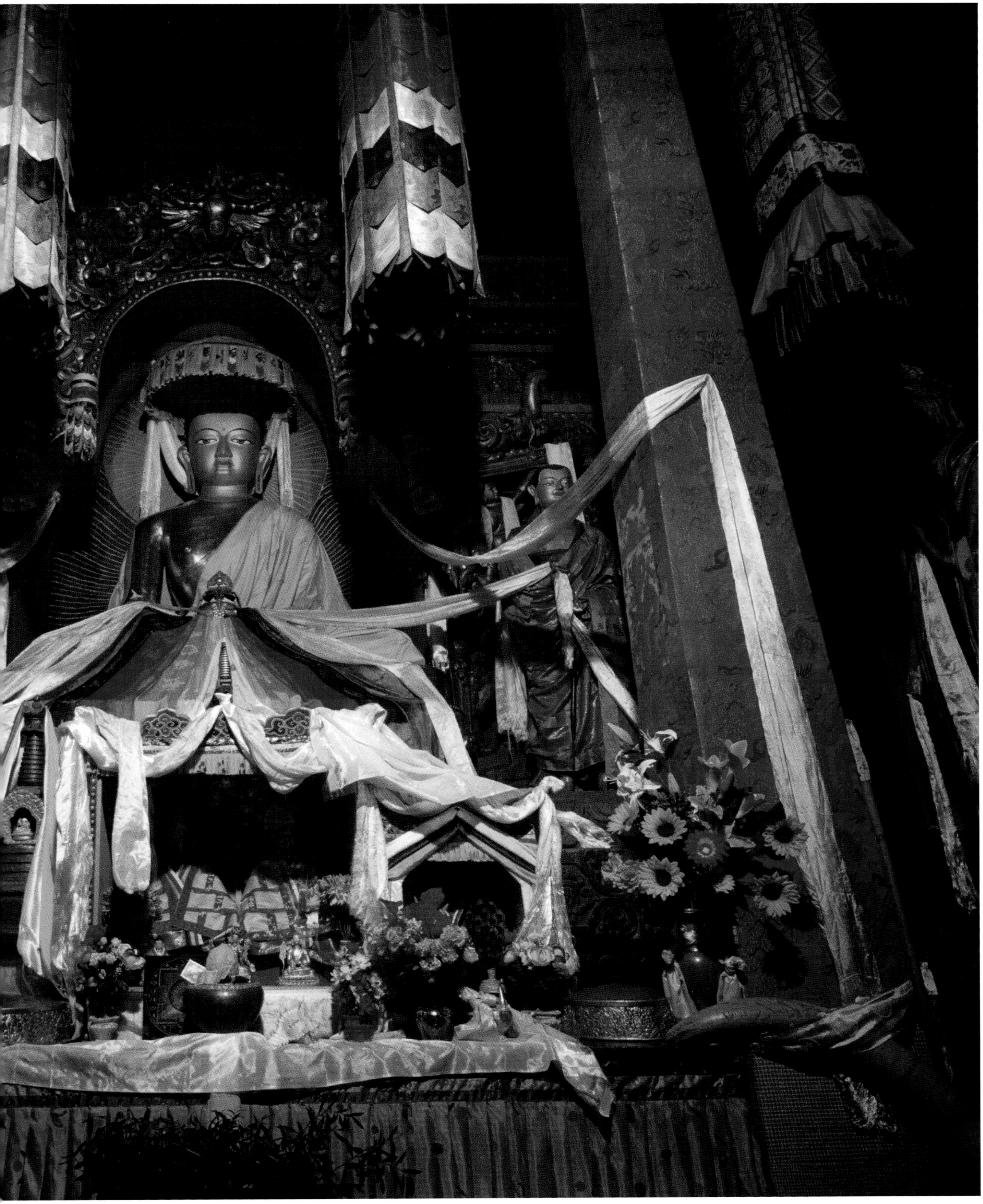

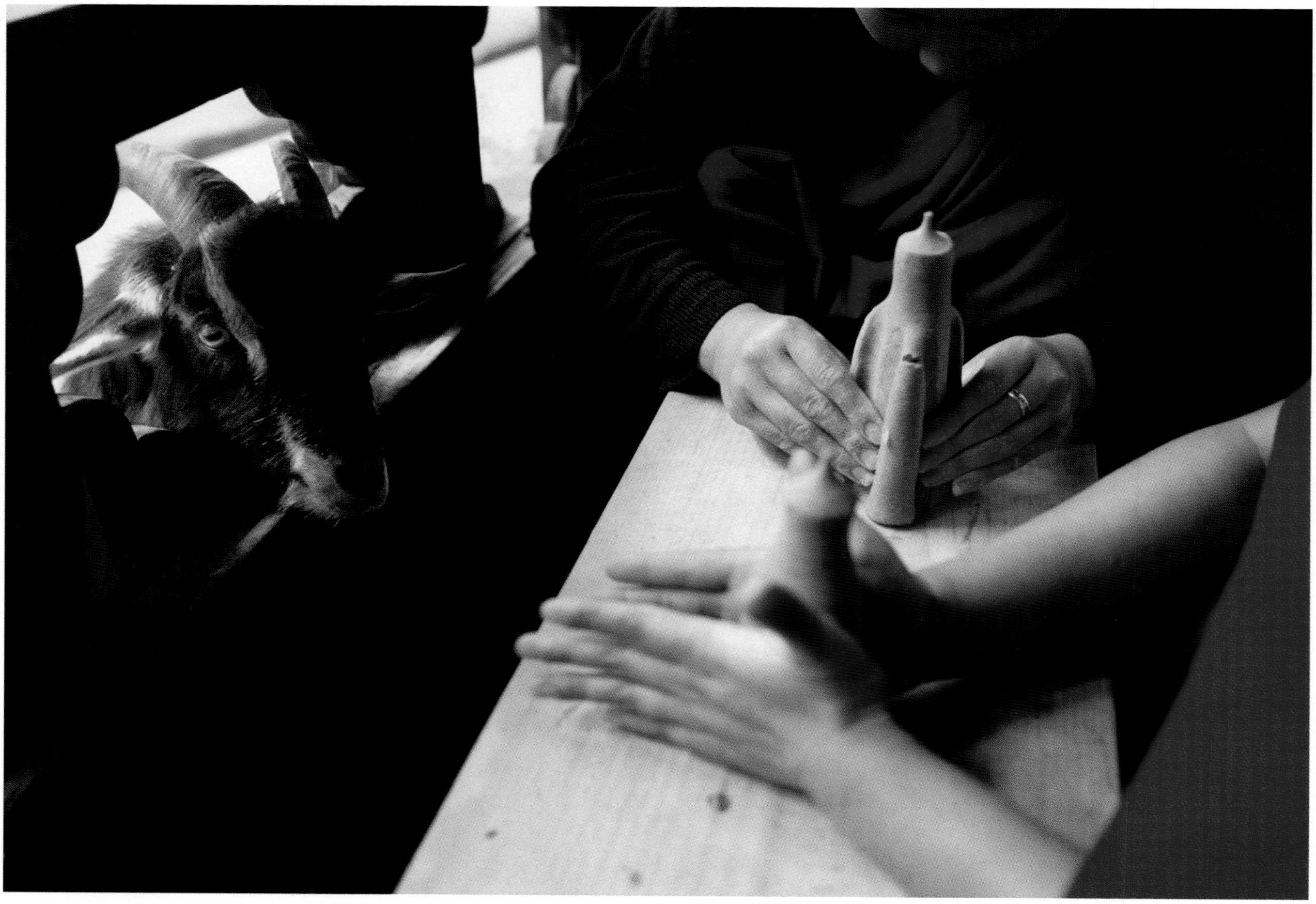

The enticing smell of warm barley flour being molded by nuns from Namsaling Convent into *torma* offerings attracts a hungry goat. Tormas are crafted from a wide variety of ingredients then placed on altars in temples and homes as offerings to Buddhist deities. After a few days, the tormas are destroyed and new ones created.

Right: Nidup Zam, 60, an elderly nun, sits with Kinley Ohm, 11, to her left and Kezang Deki, 11, to her right. Although nuns live in convents separate from monks, they follow a similar lifestyle of study and prayer.

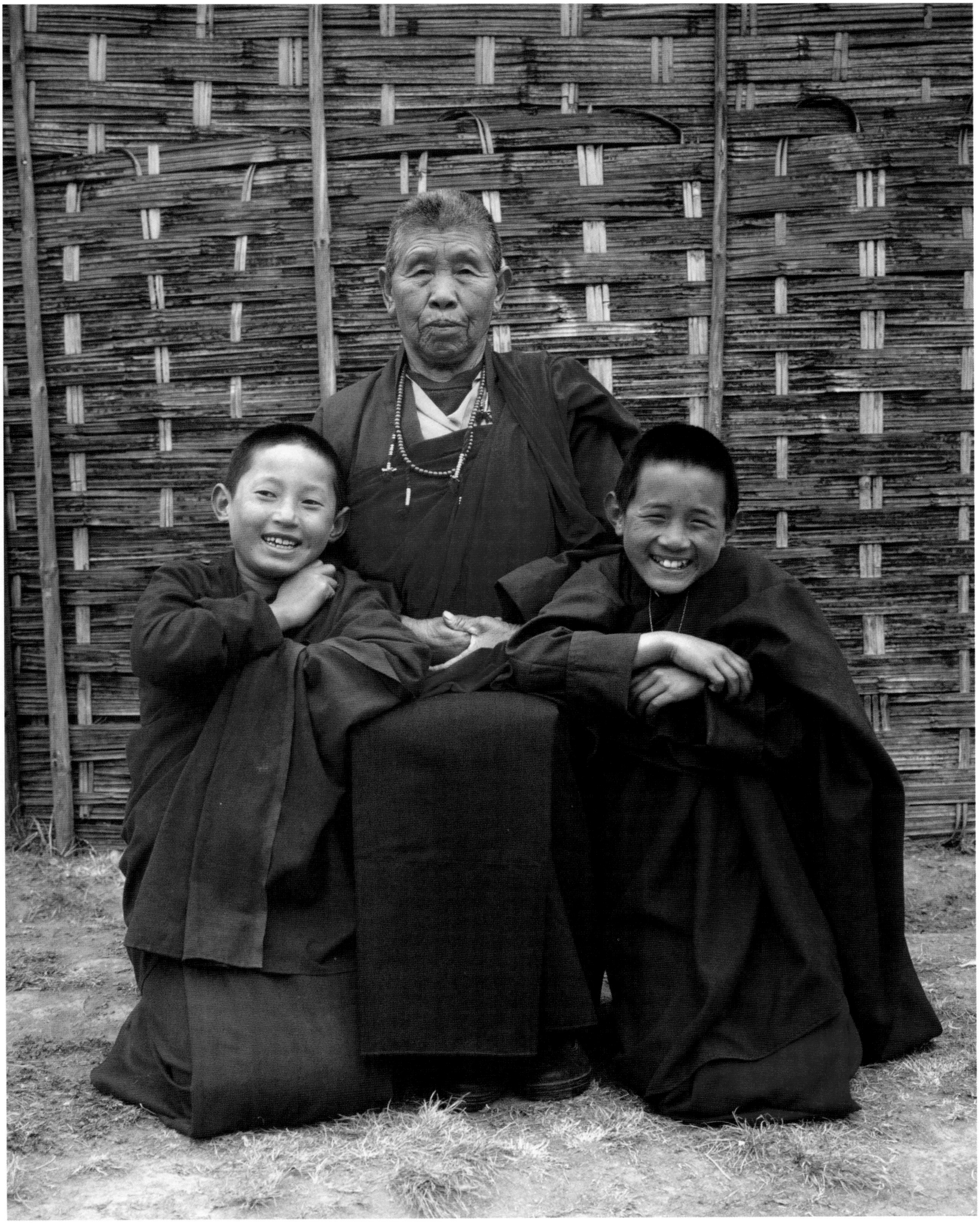

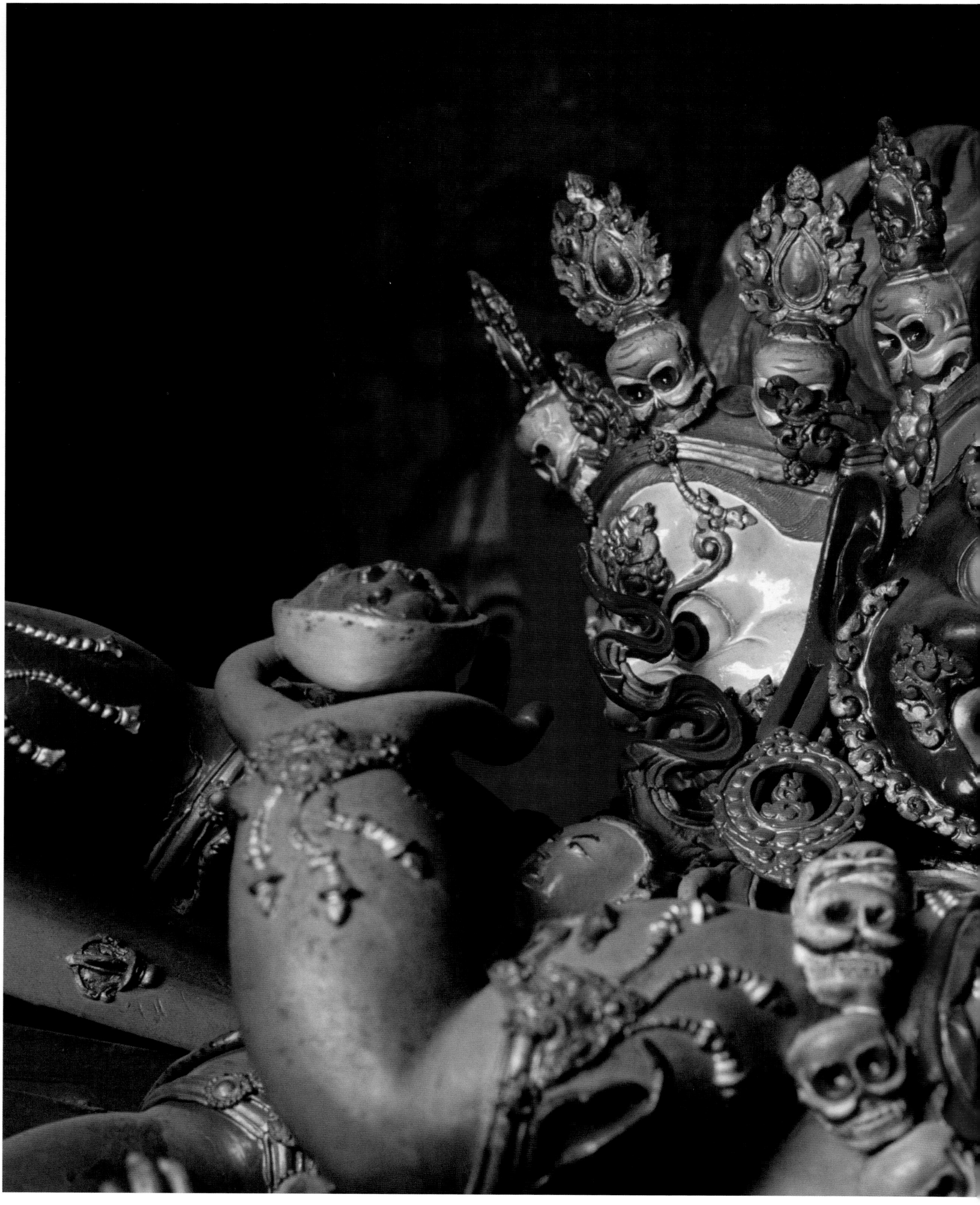

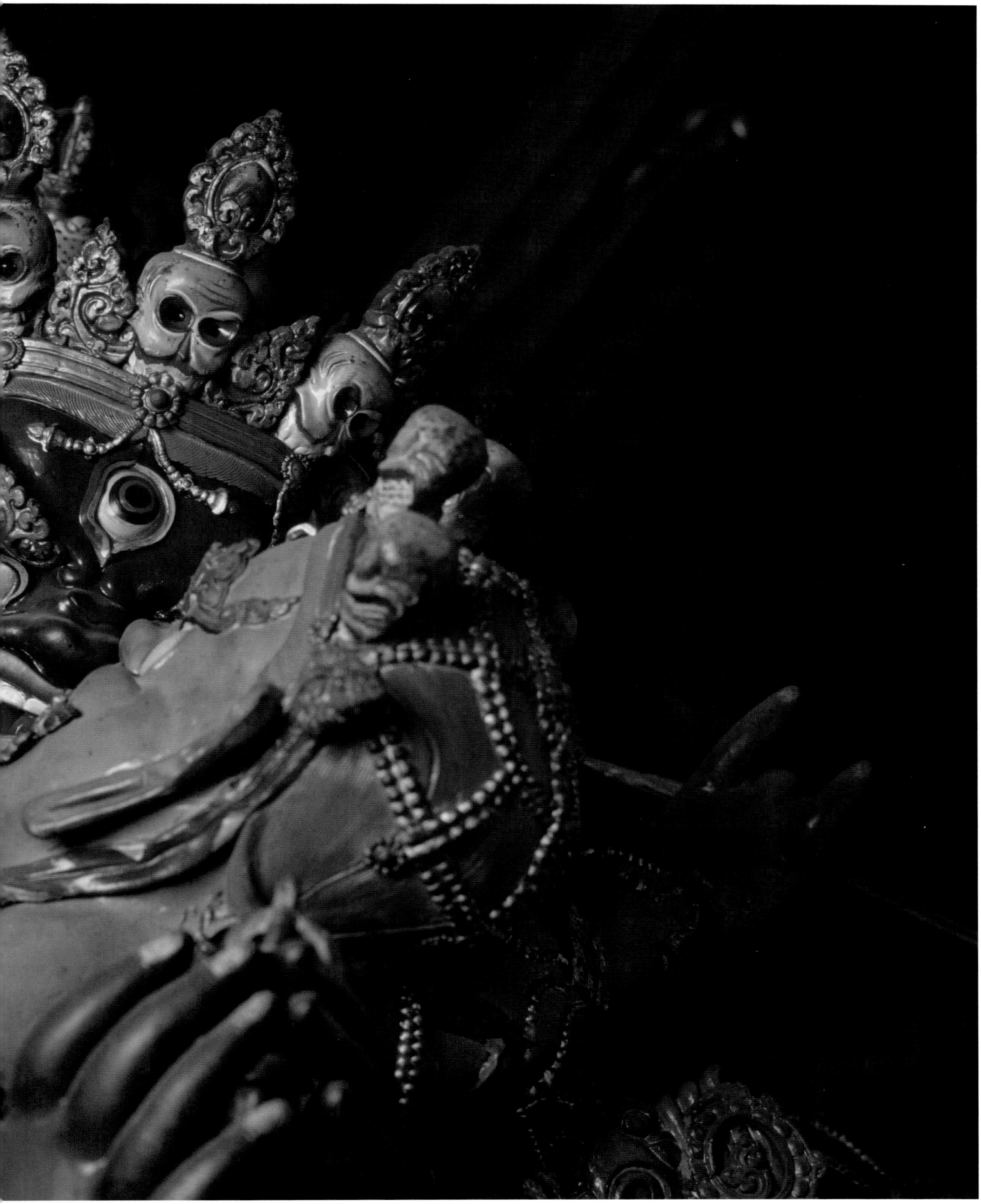

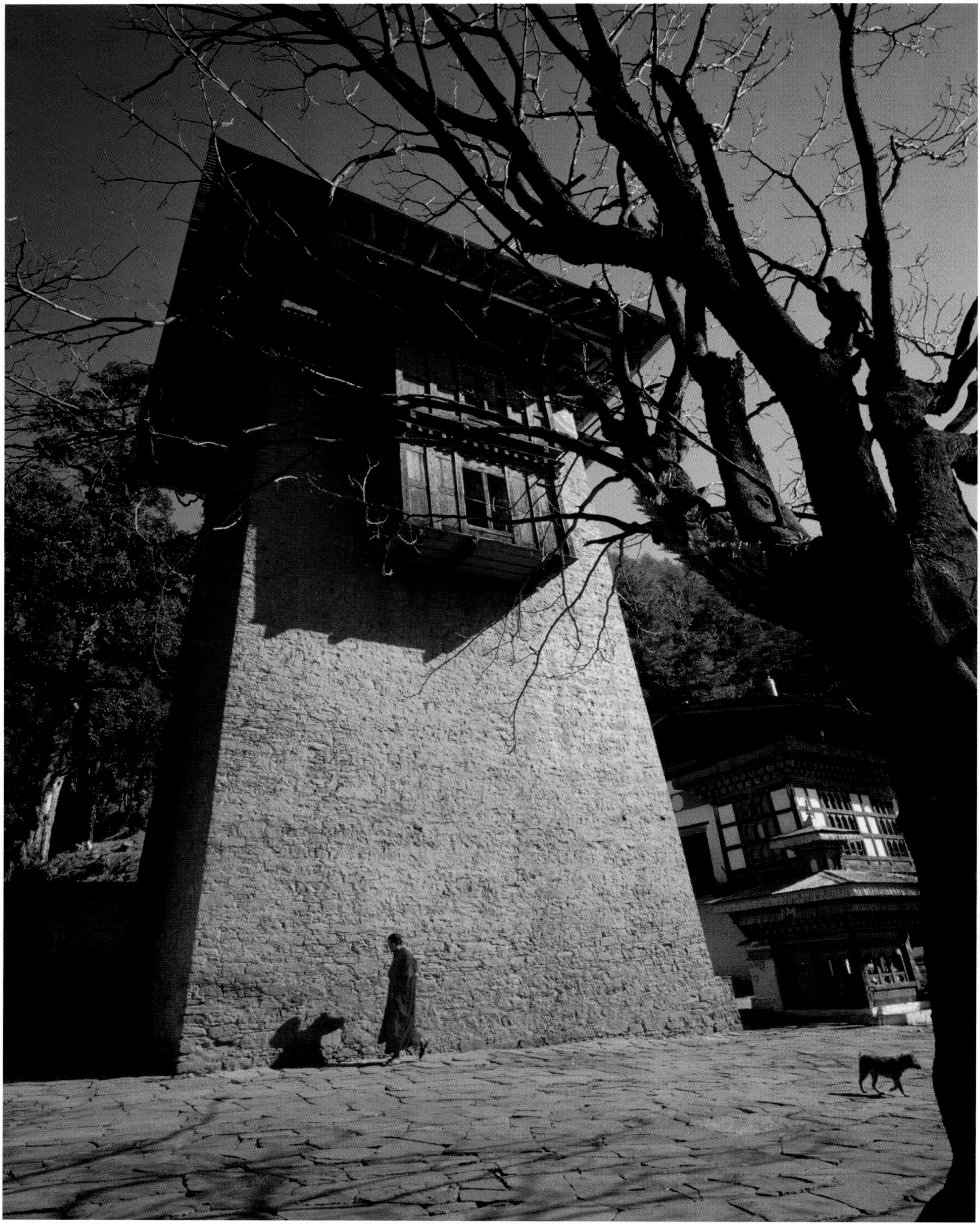

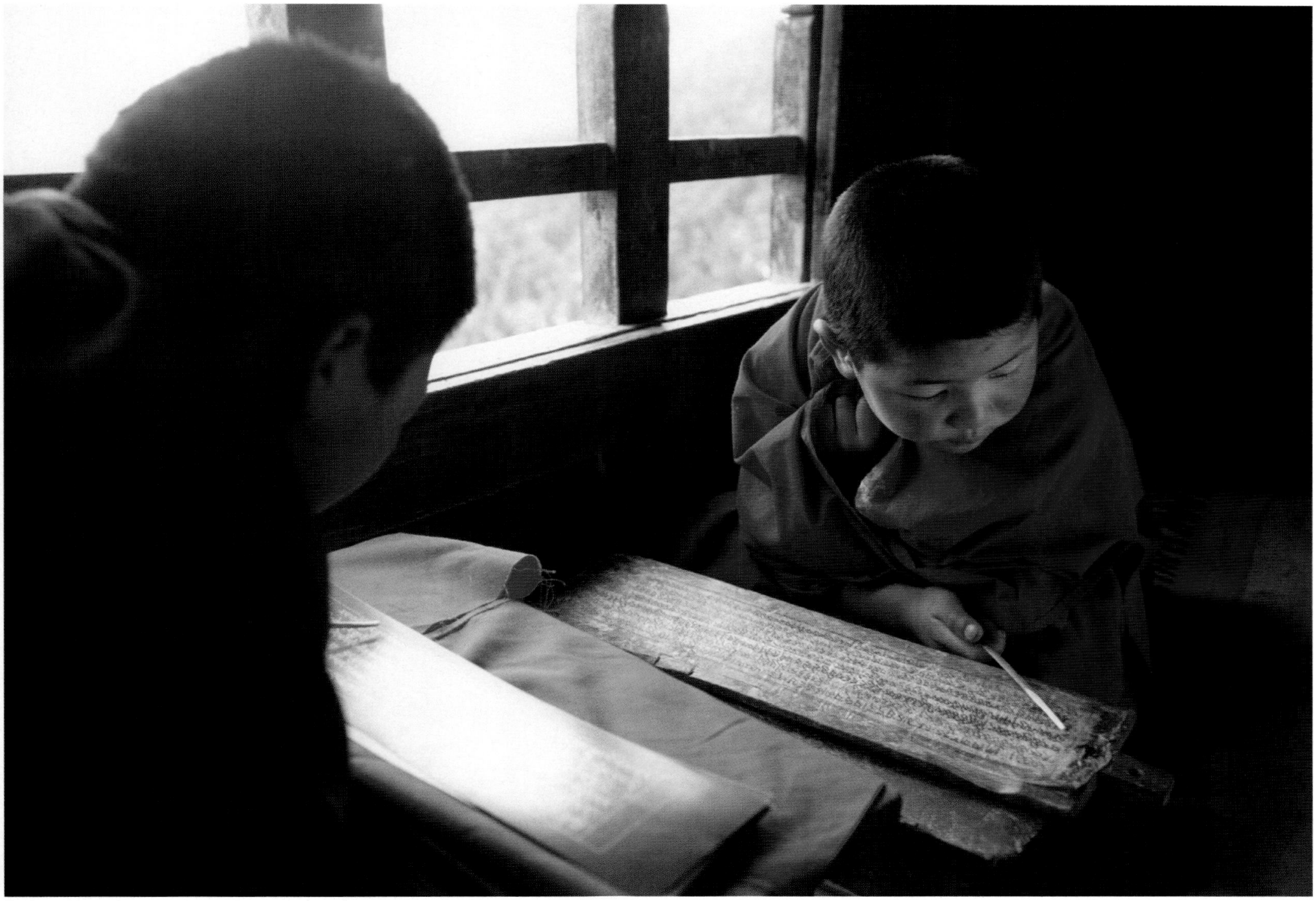

Two nuns from Kilikha Convent, built near the 12,496-foot Cheli Pass, study old religious texts together.

Left: A monk strolls past the imposing tower-shaped Dechenphu temple, known as a *lhakang*. Dedicated to the war god Gyenyen, Dechenphu Lhakhang is believed to protect Bhutanese soldiers from harm and lead them to victory.

Previous spread: A statue inside the Memorial Chorten in Thimphu depicts Phurba Lhatshog, a wrathful Buddha capable of subduing harmful demons.

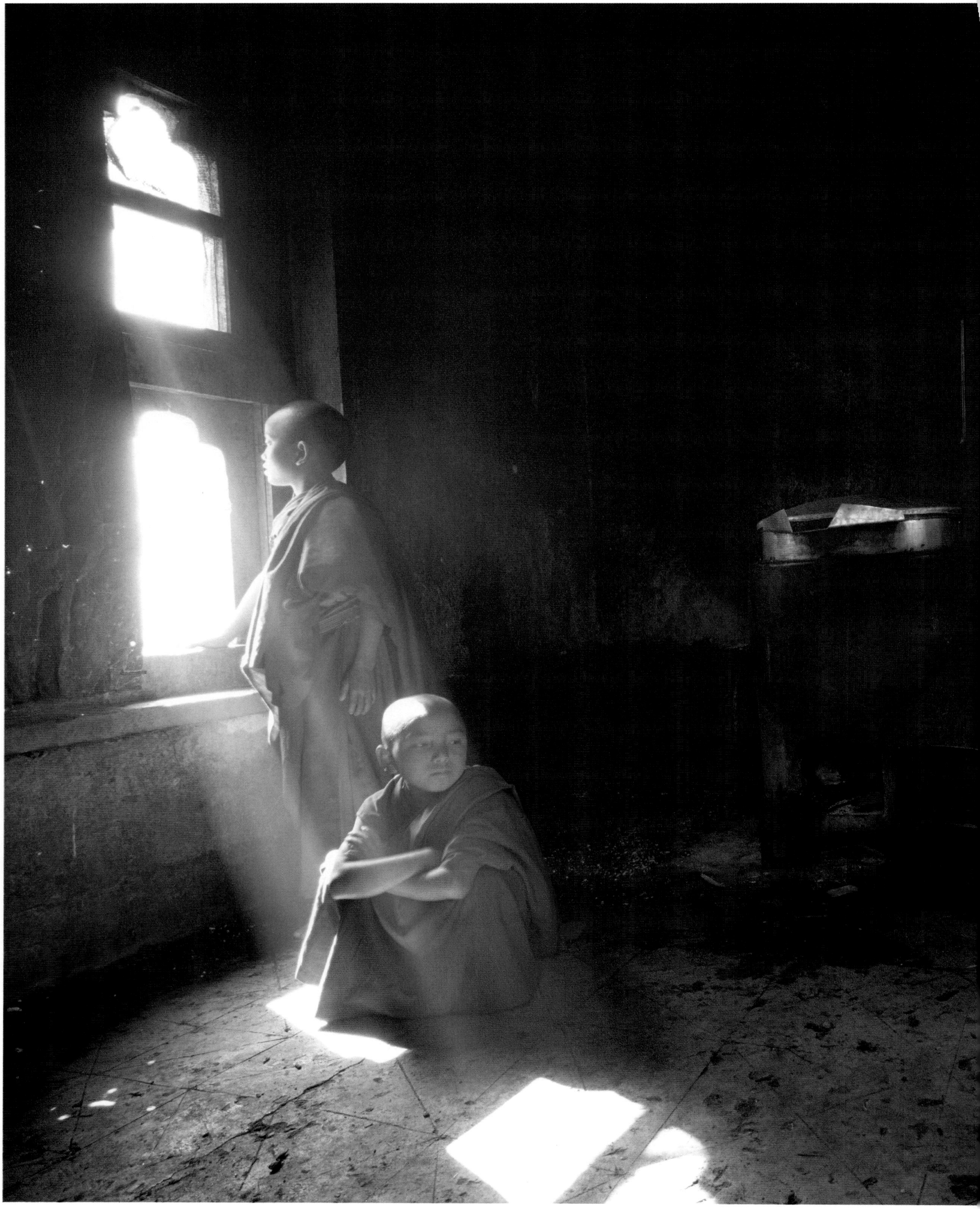

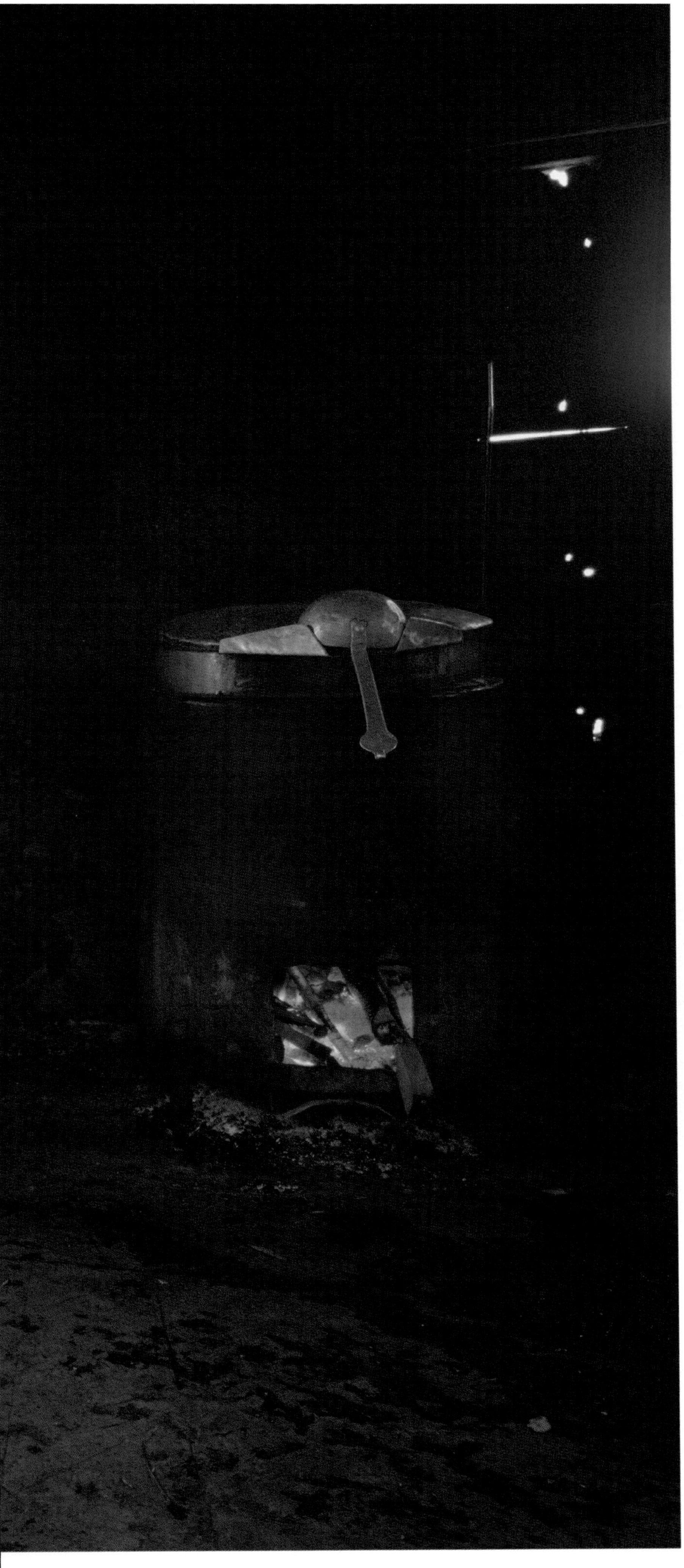

Two monks from Zhemgang Dzong wait patiently for lunch to be served from the monastery kitchen. Using wood fires for cooking is common throughout Bhutan, so kitchens are often smoky.

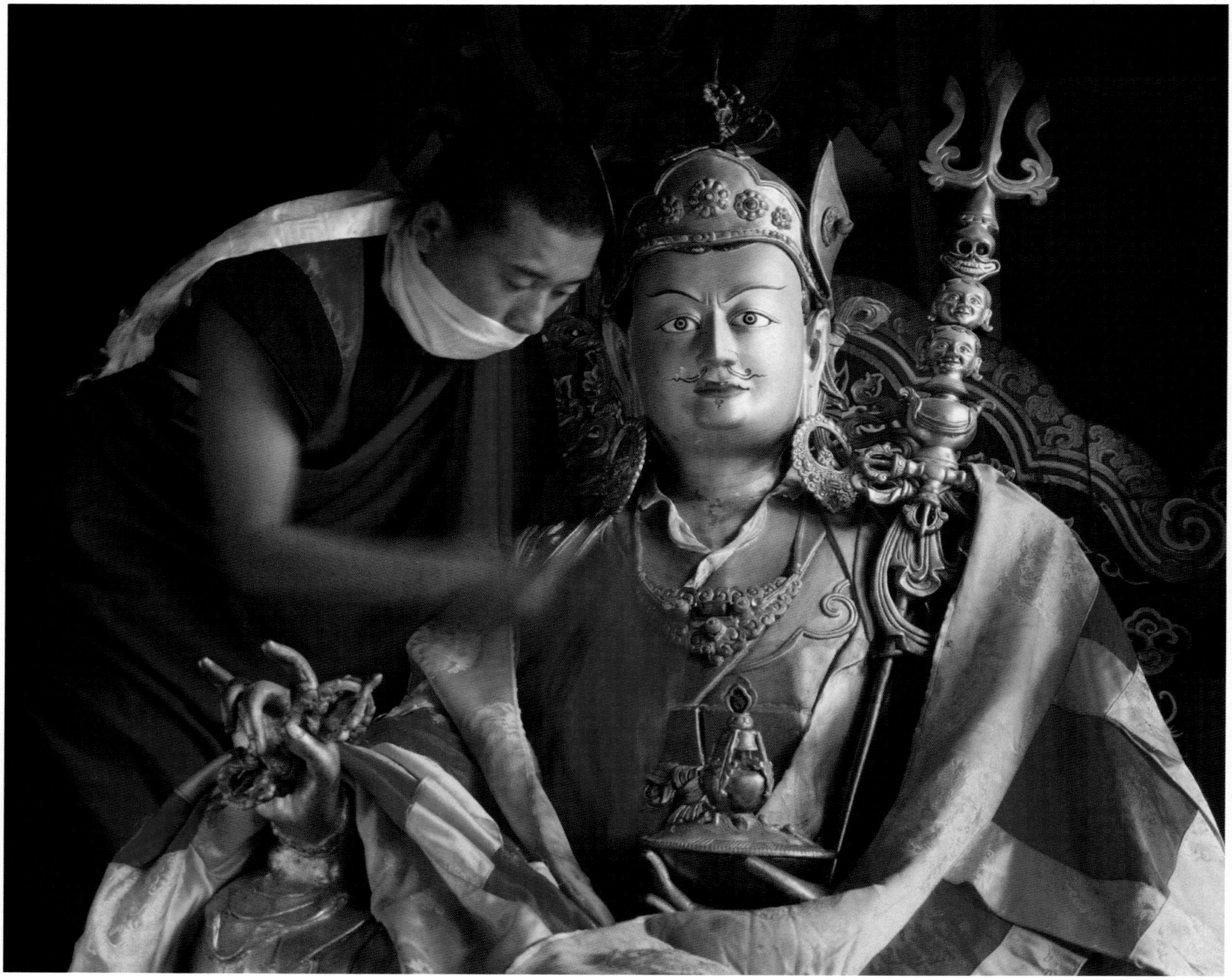

Tshering, 25, wears a silk scarf across his face as a gesture of respect while polishing a statue of Padmasambhava in Gangtey Monastery. Padmasambhava is depicted holding in his right hand a *dorje* or thunderbolt, an implement that helps achieve a mind free from extreme views. In his left hand, he is holding a skull bowl used to hold sacrificial meat or blood to secure the favor of protective deities. Leaning against his chest is a staff of supernatural powers that is decorated with two miniature human heads and a skull.

Right: A painting inside Trashi Yangste Lhakhang depicts a group of lamas presenting gifts and offerings, including a bowl of colored torma and a jug used to hold holy water.

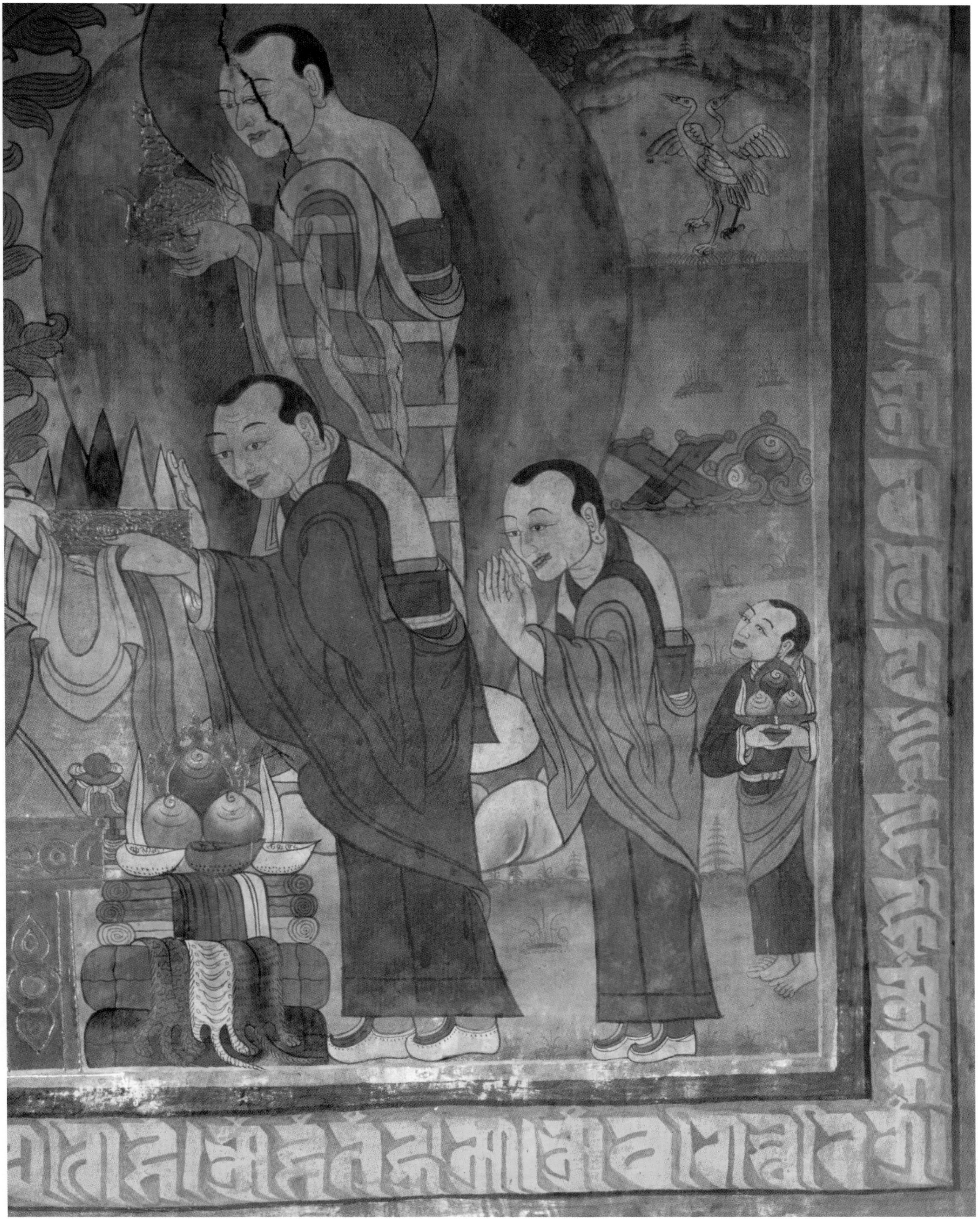

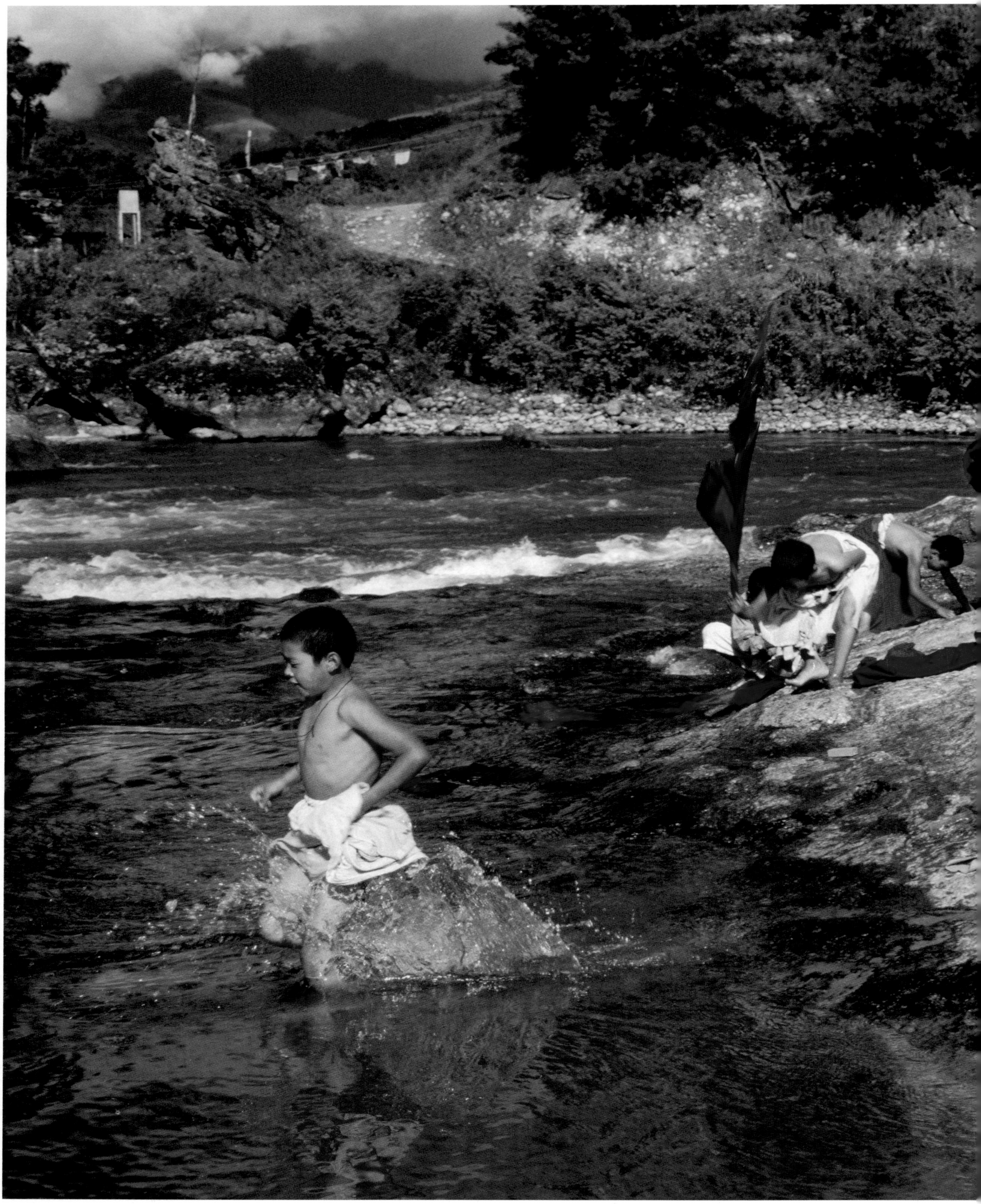

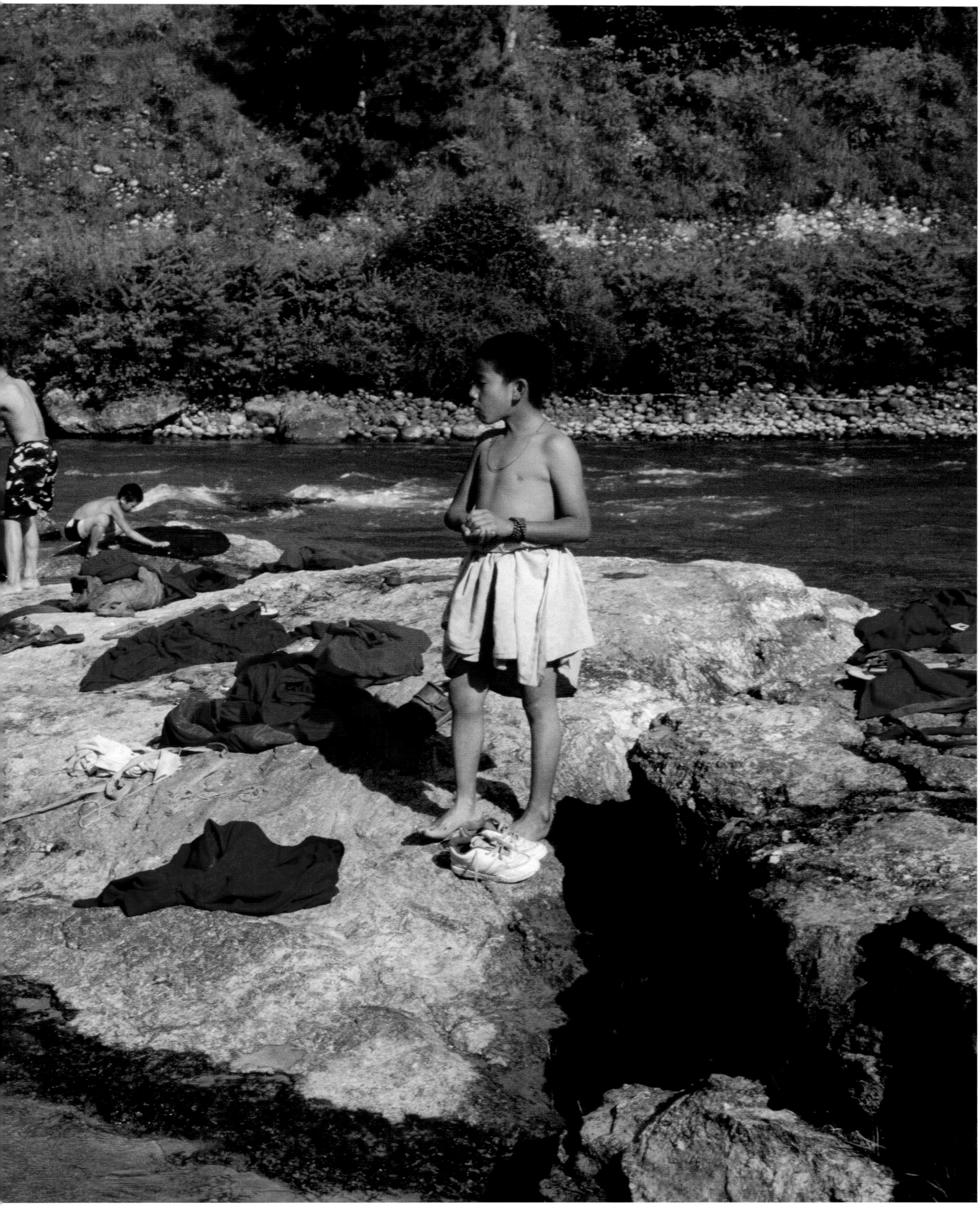

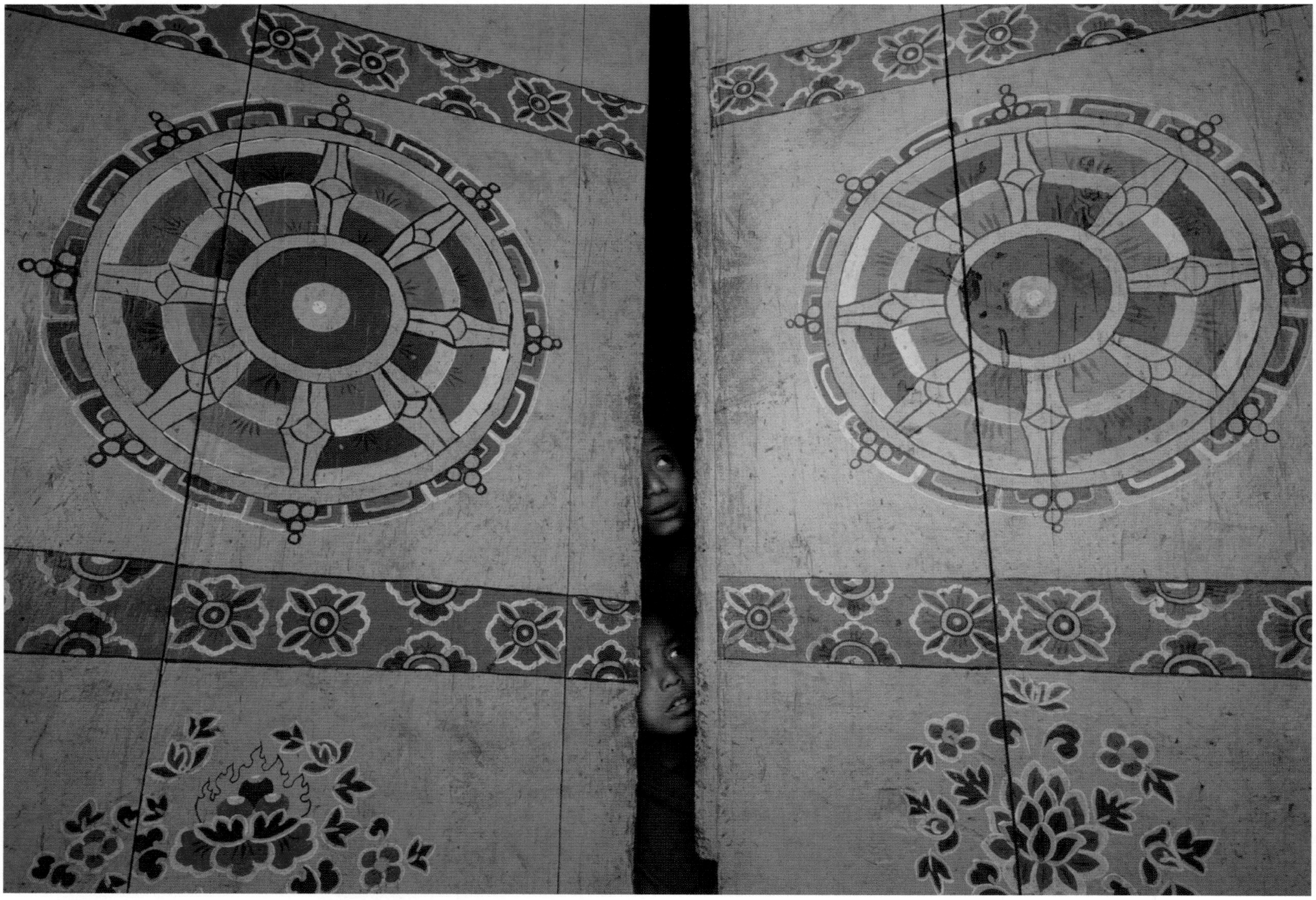

Sonam, 9, and Ugyen, 12, cast a wary gaze through the two partially open doors of Zhemgang Dzong. The large circles on the doors represent the wheel of dharma, a cycle of eternal rebirth that cannot be broken unless the teachings of the Buddha are followed.

Right: Head lama Singye Rinchen, 47, instructs a group of novice monks during prayers at Guru Lhakhang located high above the Paro Valley. Managing the financial requirements for the lhakhang are somewhat difficult, because many of the young monks are orphans who cannot depend on relatives for help.

Previous spread: A group of young monks wash their crimson robes and brave a chilly dash into the Bumthang River.

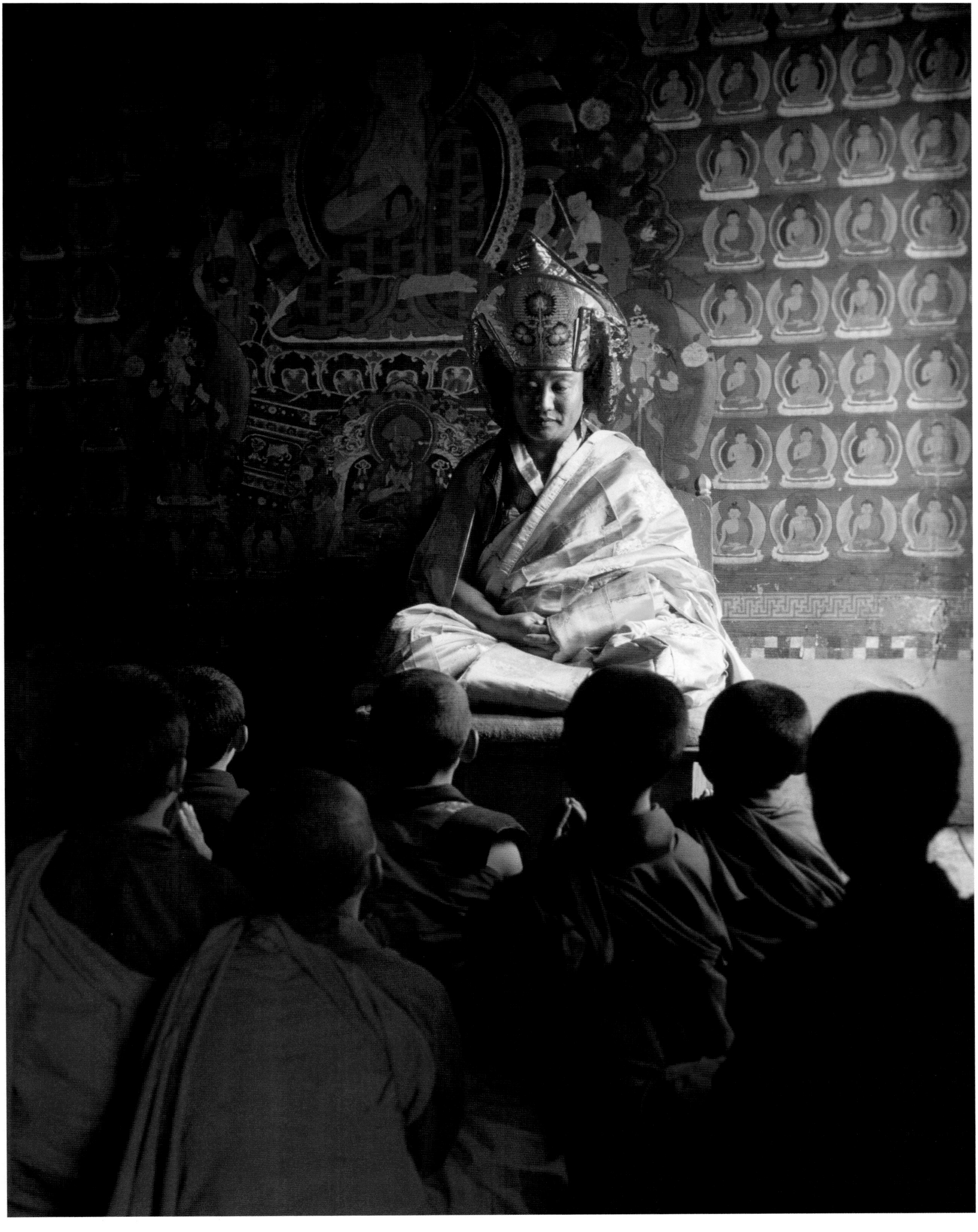

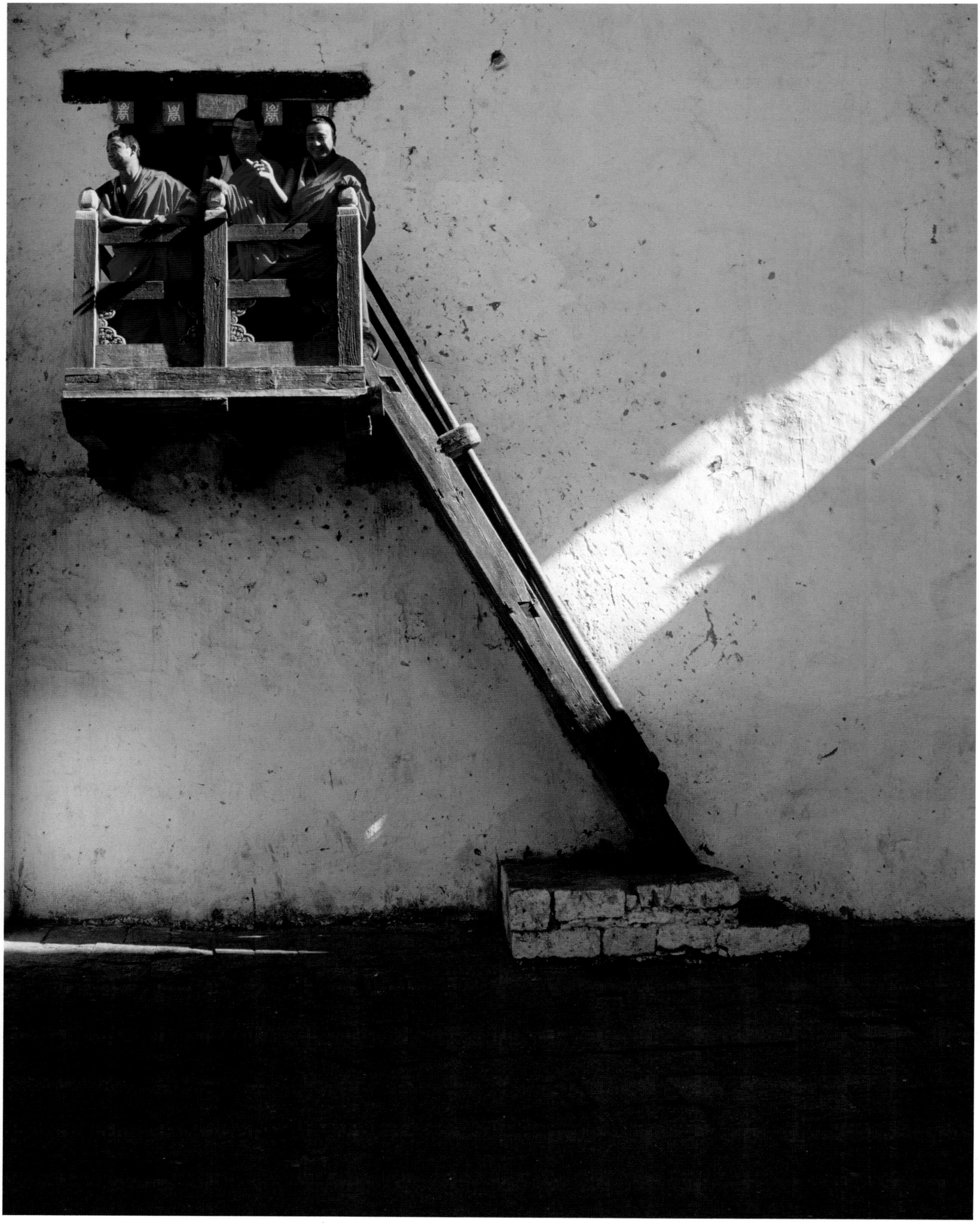

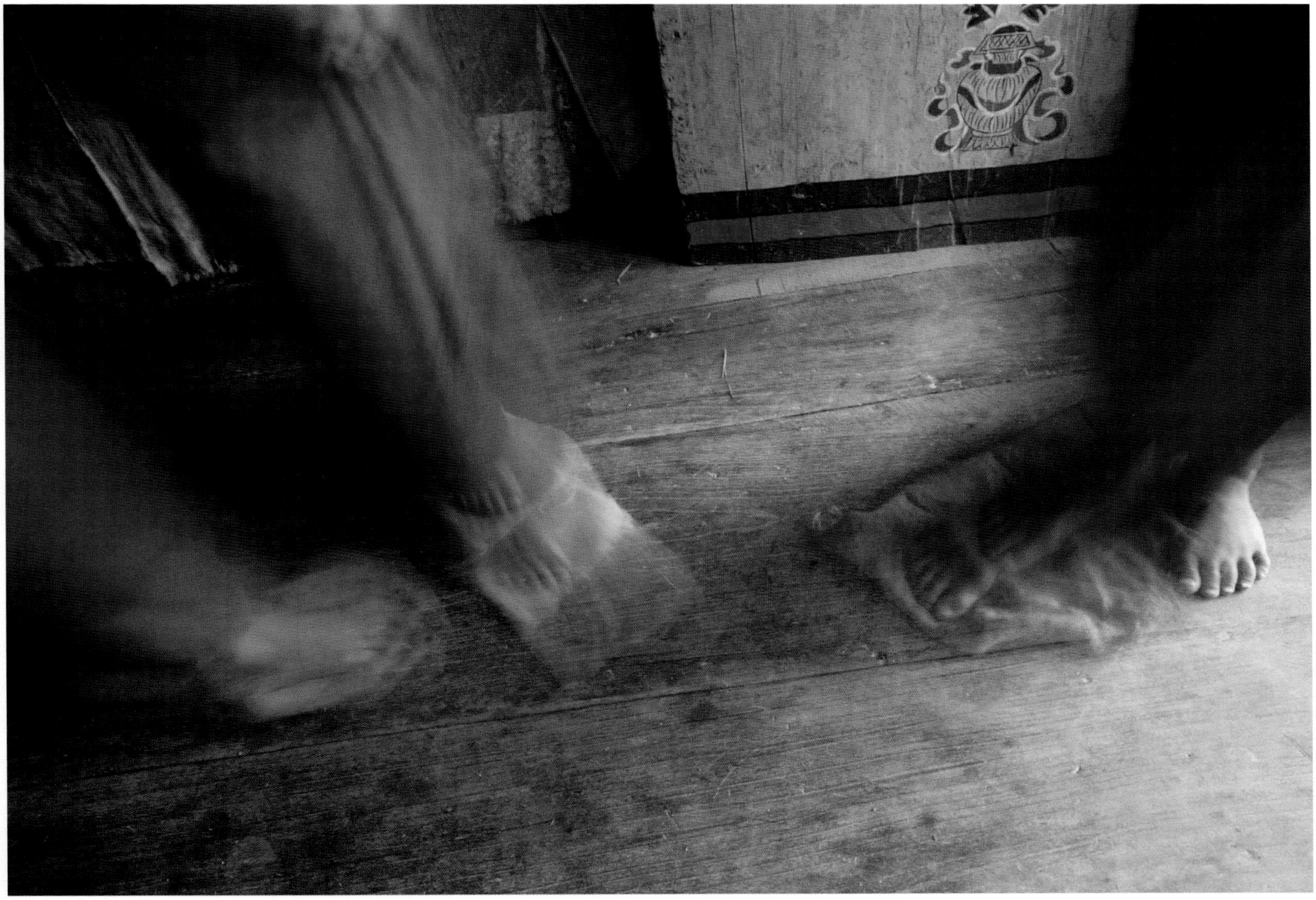

One of the duties monks from Zhemgang Dzong are responsible for is to clean and polish by foot the hardwood floors of the central prayer room with soft pieces of cloth.

Left: Three monks share a laugh inside the courtyard of Dagana Dzong. Interior courtyards of dzongs were originally designed for optimal defense against attack, such as this deck that features a removable staircase in the event of an enemy incursion.

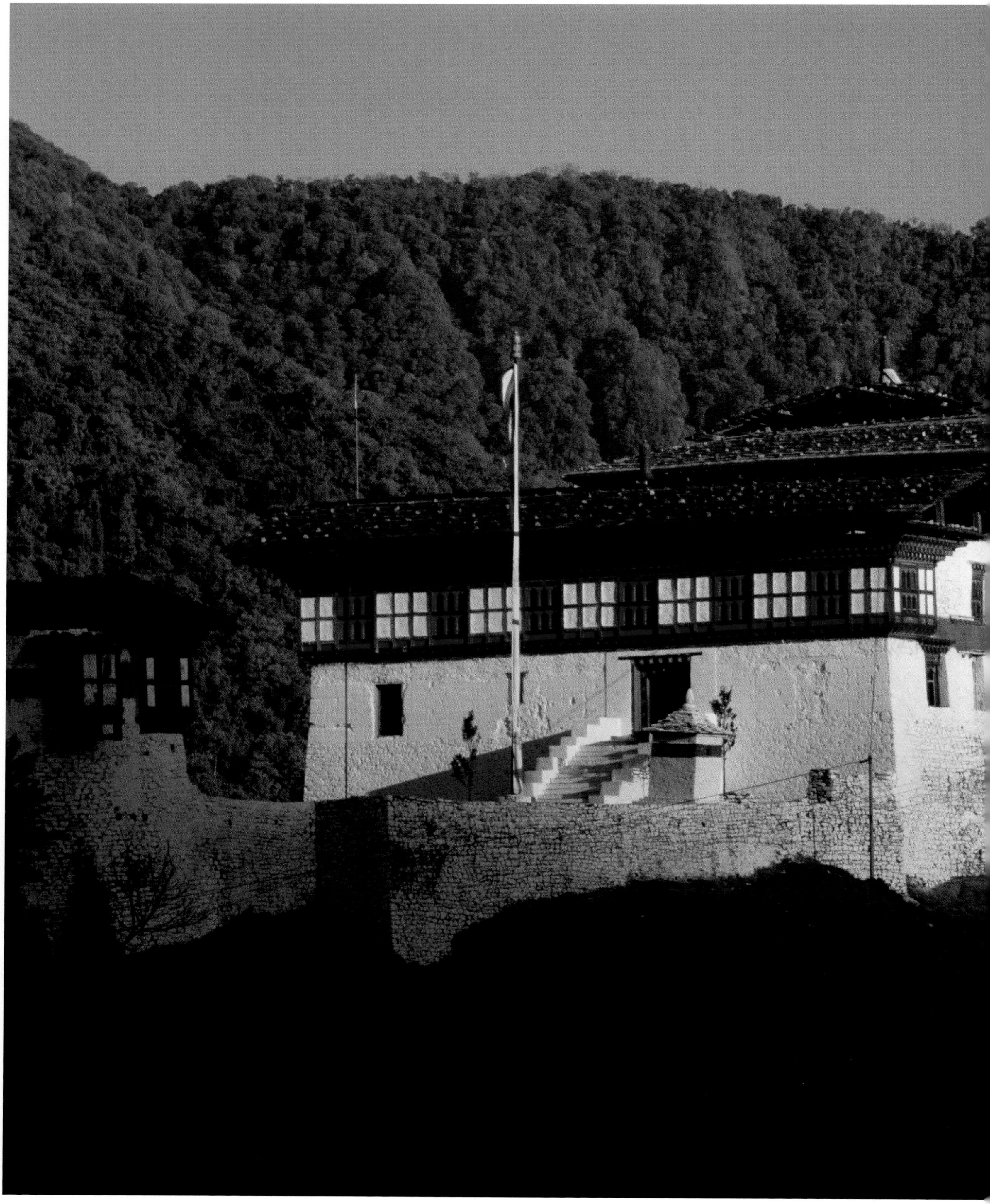

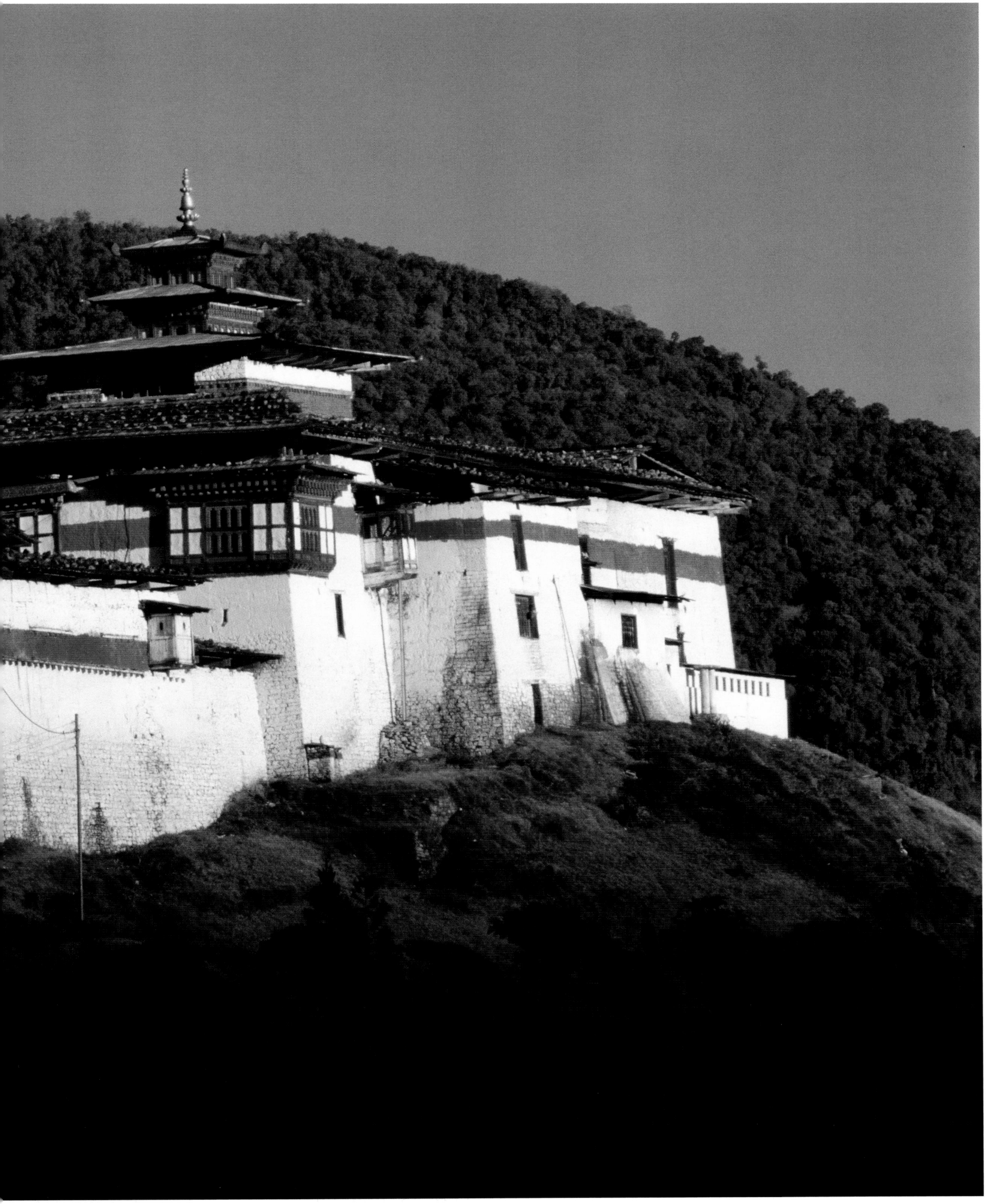

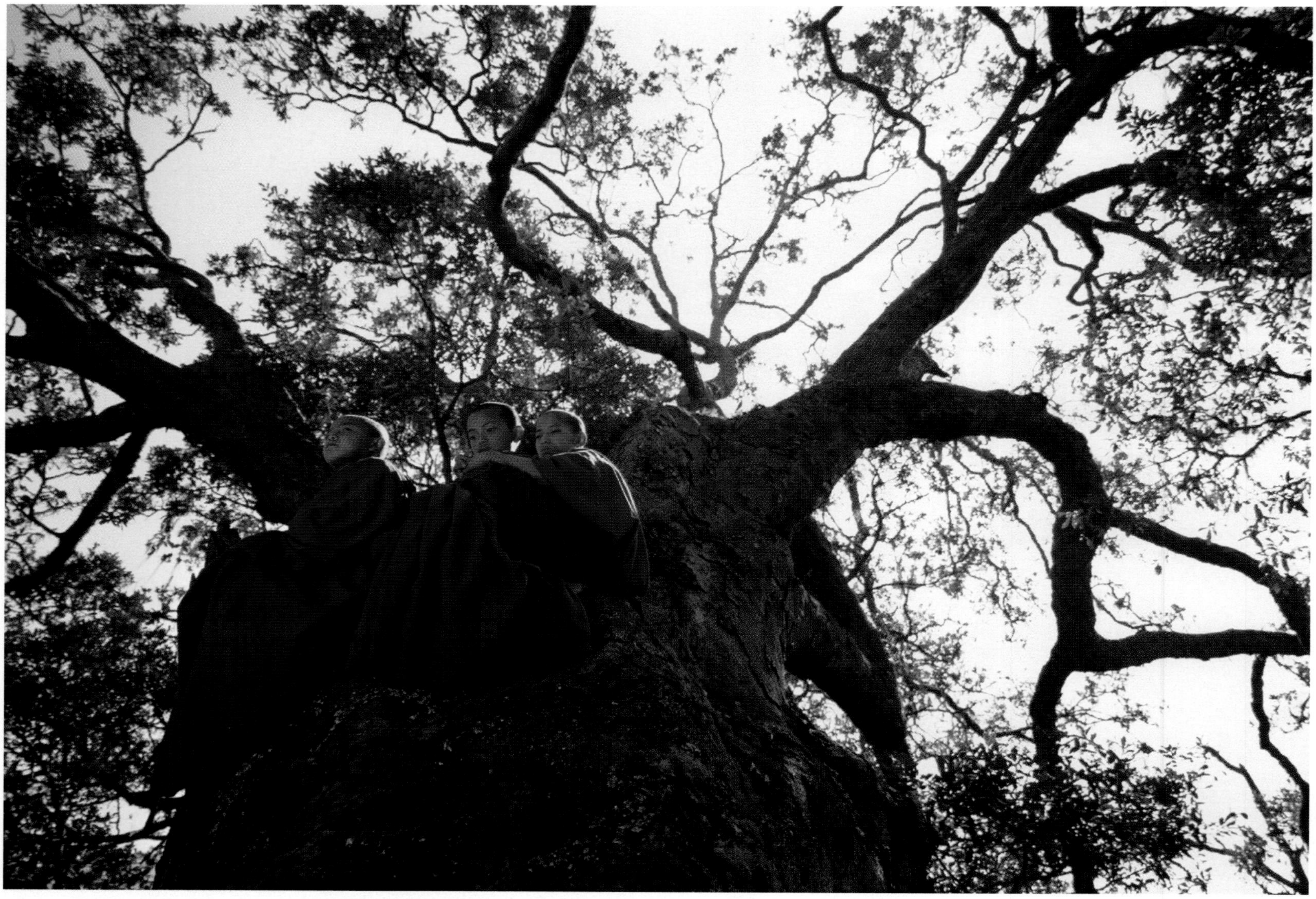

Three novice monks from Zhemgang Dzong relax in an oak tree during a break from their studies and prayers. Nearly all Buddhist parents in Bhutan aspire to continue the ancient tradition of sending one of their sons to a monastery to become a monk for life.

Right: Taktshang Monastery is built onto a sheer cliff face at an altitude of 10,299 feet. Legend relates that in 746 A.D., Padmasambhava flew to the site on the back of a flying tigress and meditated in a nearby cave for three months. In 1692 the regional governor ordered the primary temple to be built, but it was badly destroyed in an accidental fire in 1998. Though the temple was rebuilt five years later, several priceless treasures were lost.

Previous spread: Sunset falls on Dagana Dzong.

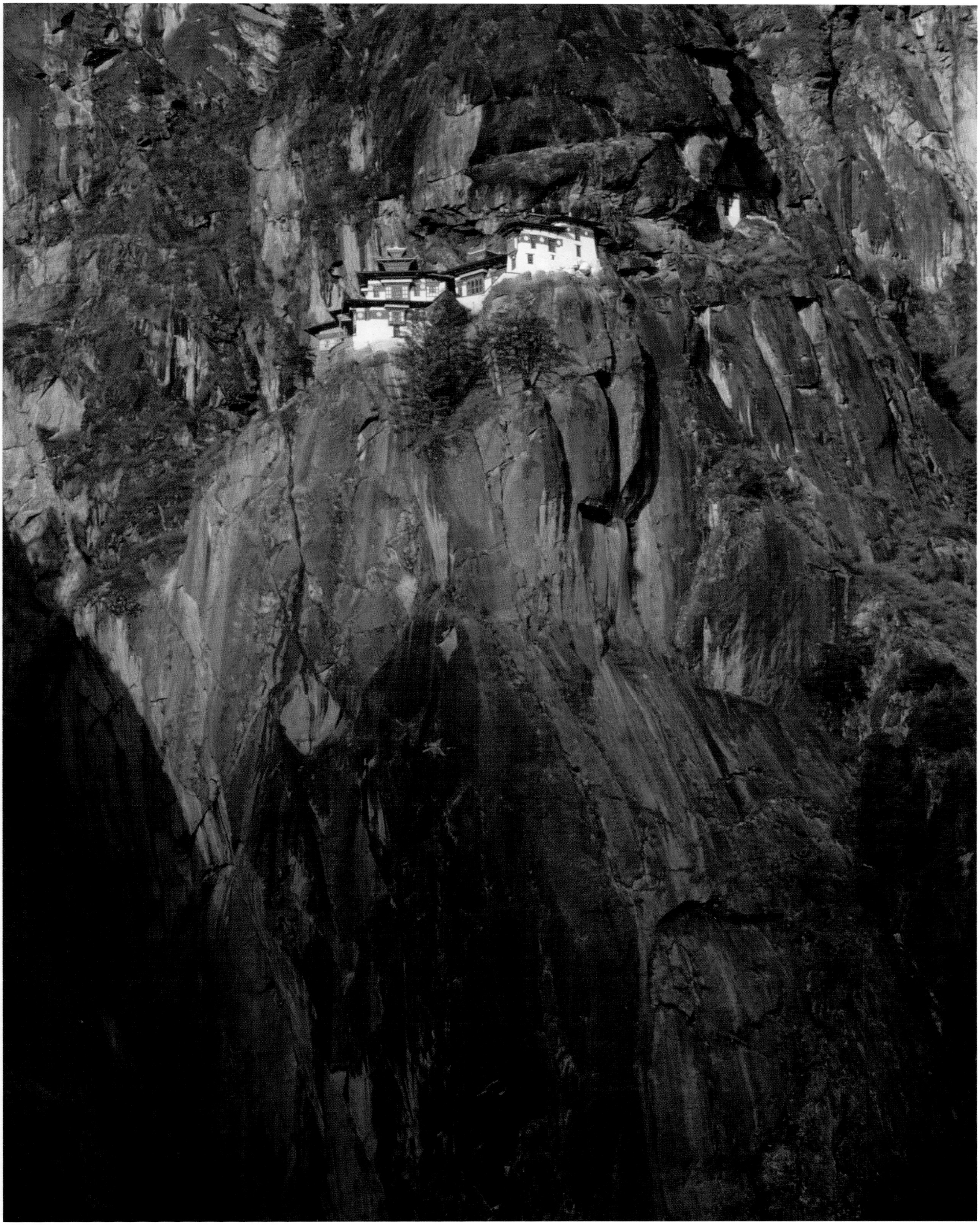

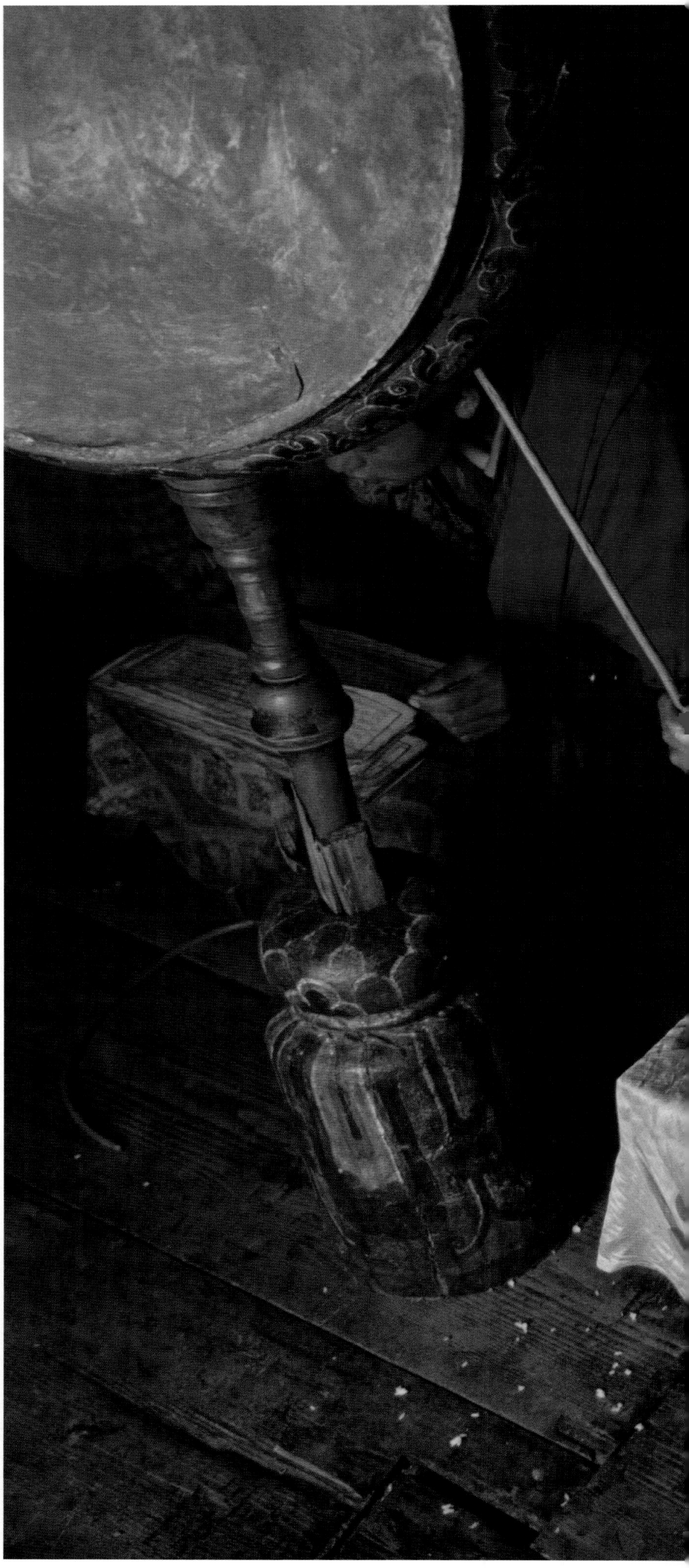

Two lay religious practitioners, known as *gomchens,* help perform an eight-hour ceremony at Towada Lhakhang. Though gomchens have not taken monastic vows, they are essential in the maintenance of religious duties at small monasteries and temples that cannot support a fulltime monastic clergy.

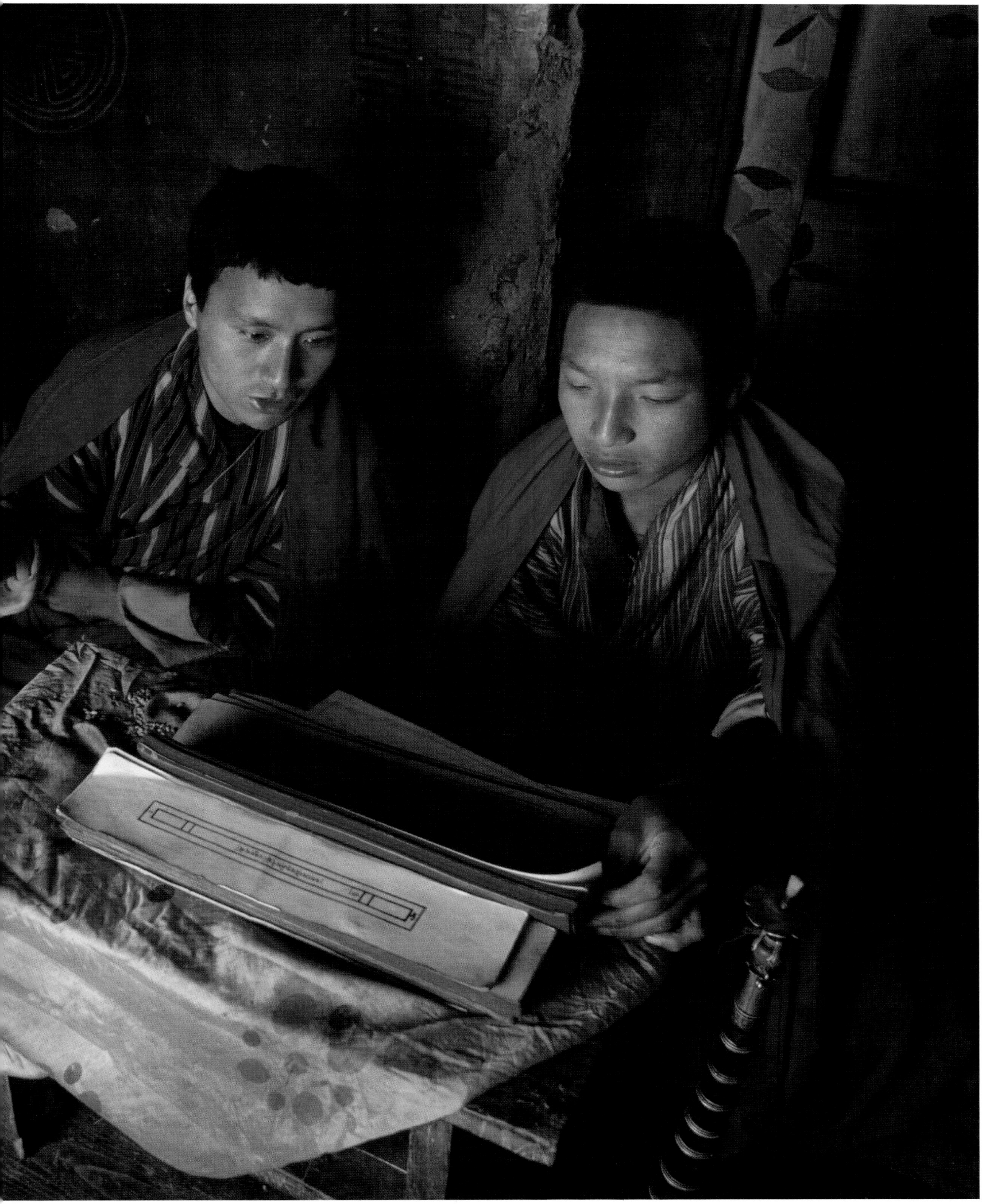

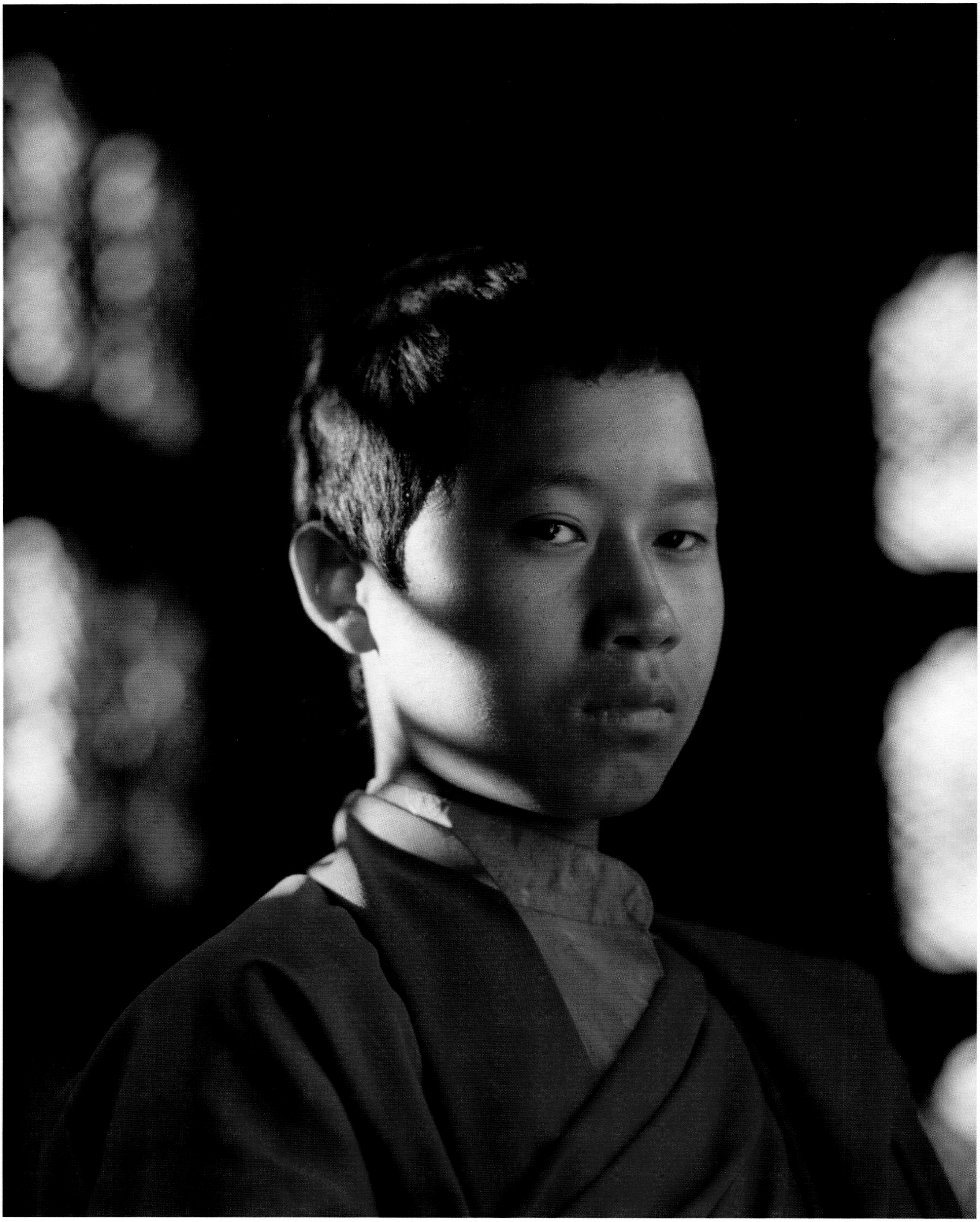

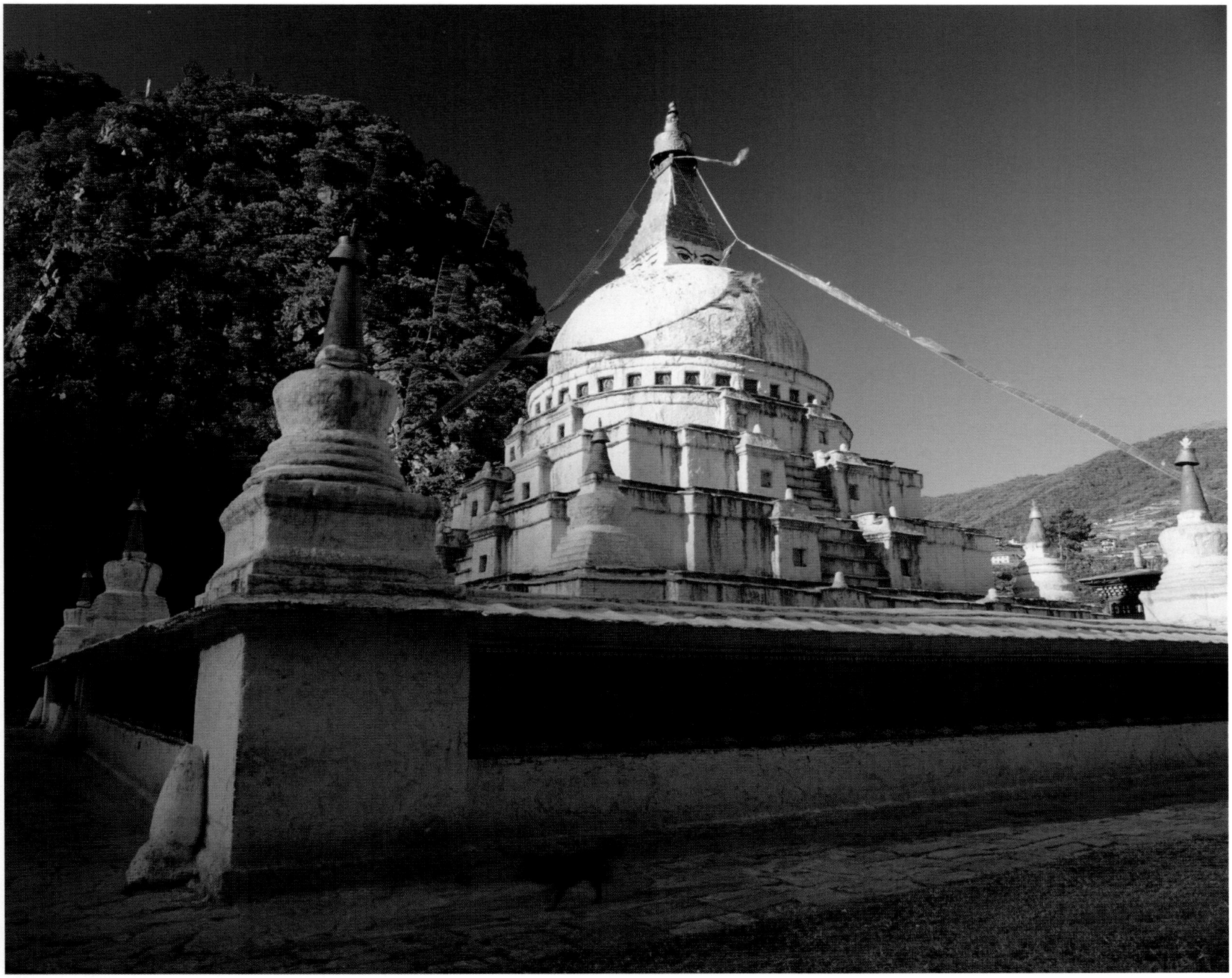

Chorten Kora was erected as a religious monument in 1740 to subdue evil spirits and provide an opportunity for local villagers to meditate and practice Buddhism.

Left: Gyeltshen, 13, is the caretaker for the main temple at Kharbandi Monastery near Phuntsholing.

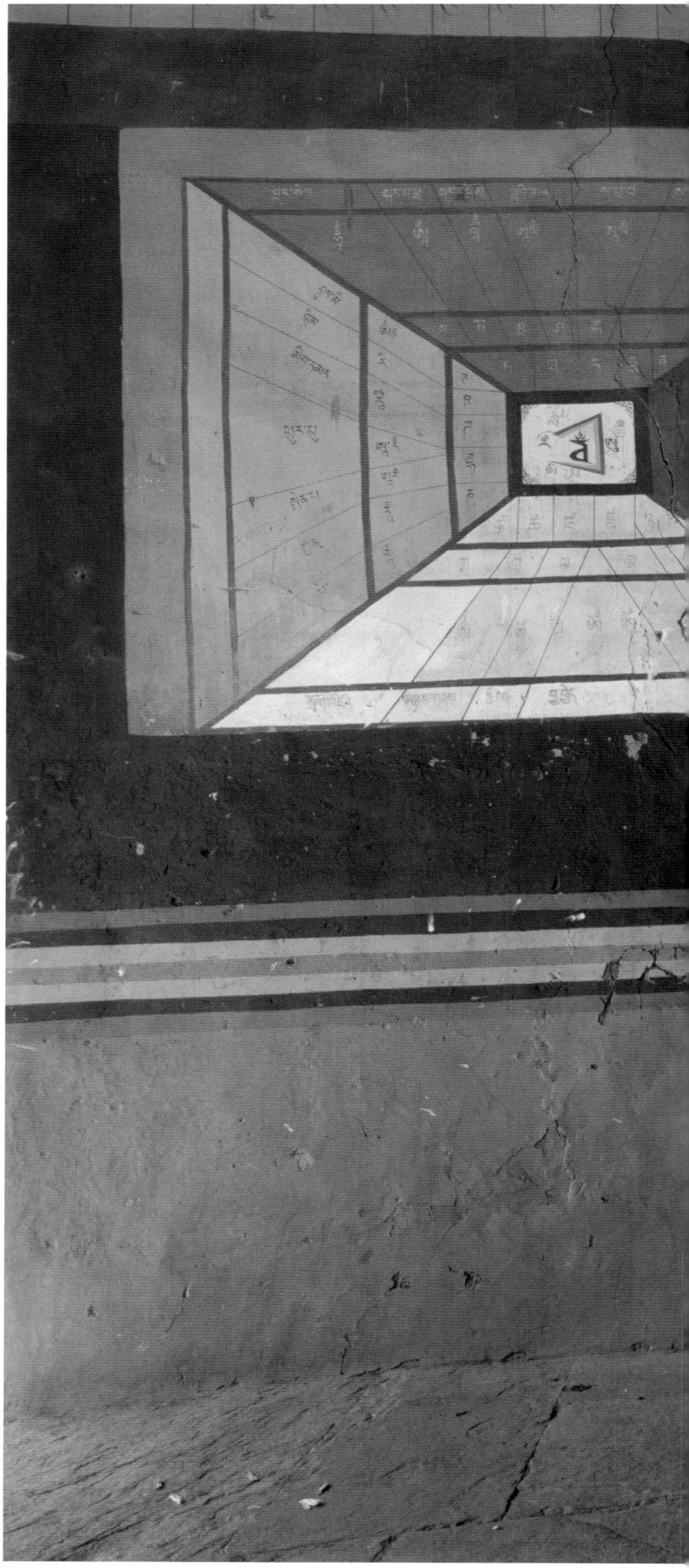

Three nuns stand beside a cosmic mural depicting the universe near the entrance of Punakha Dzong.

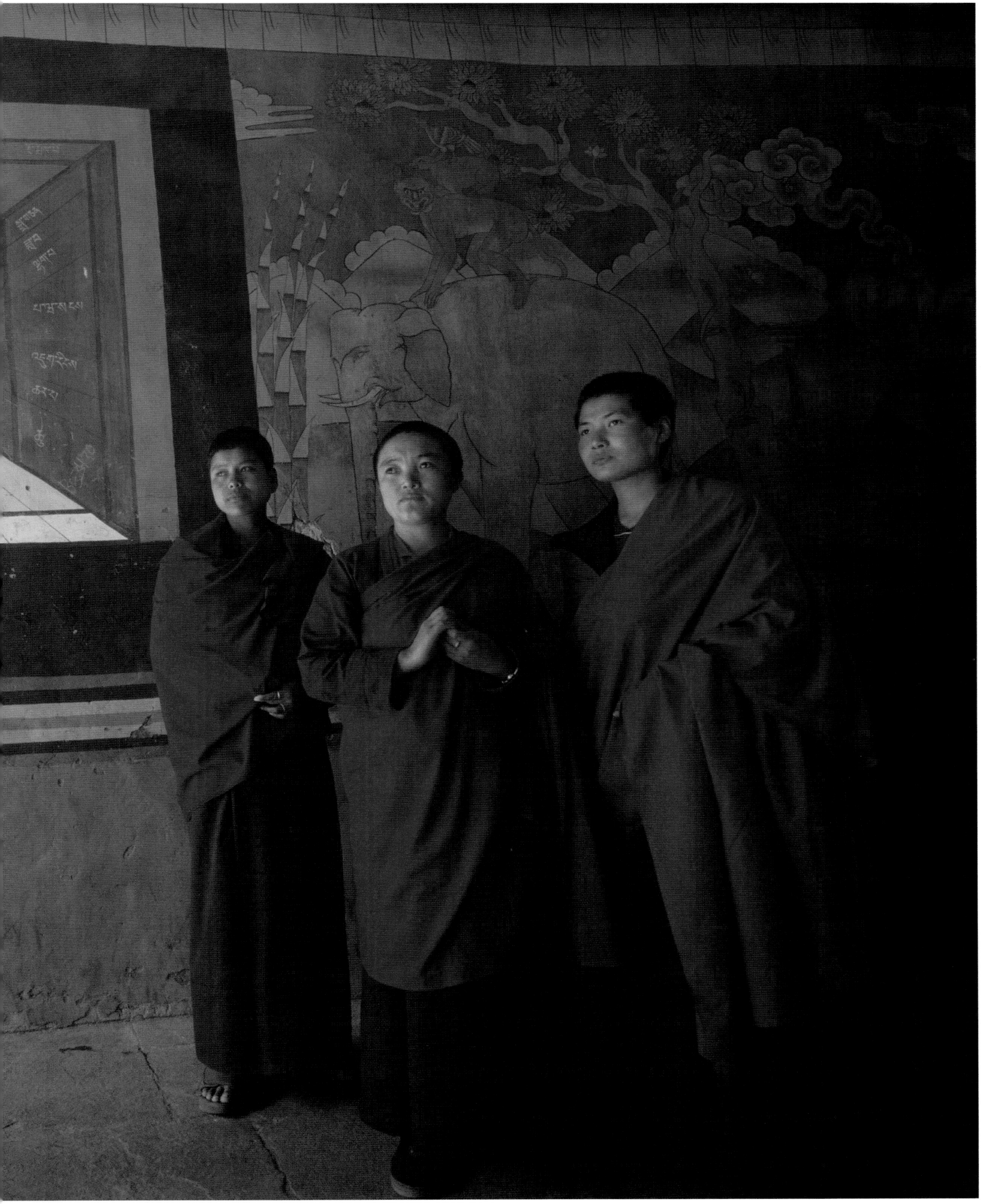

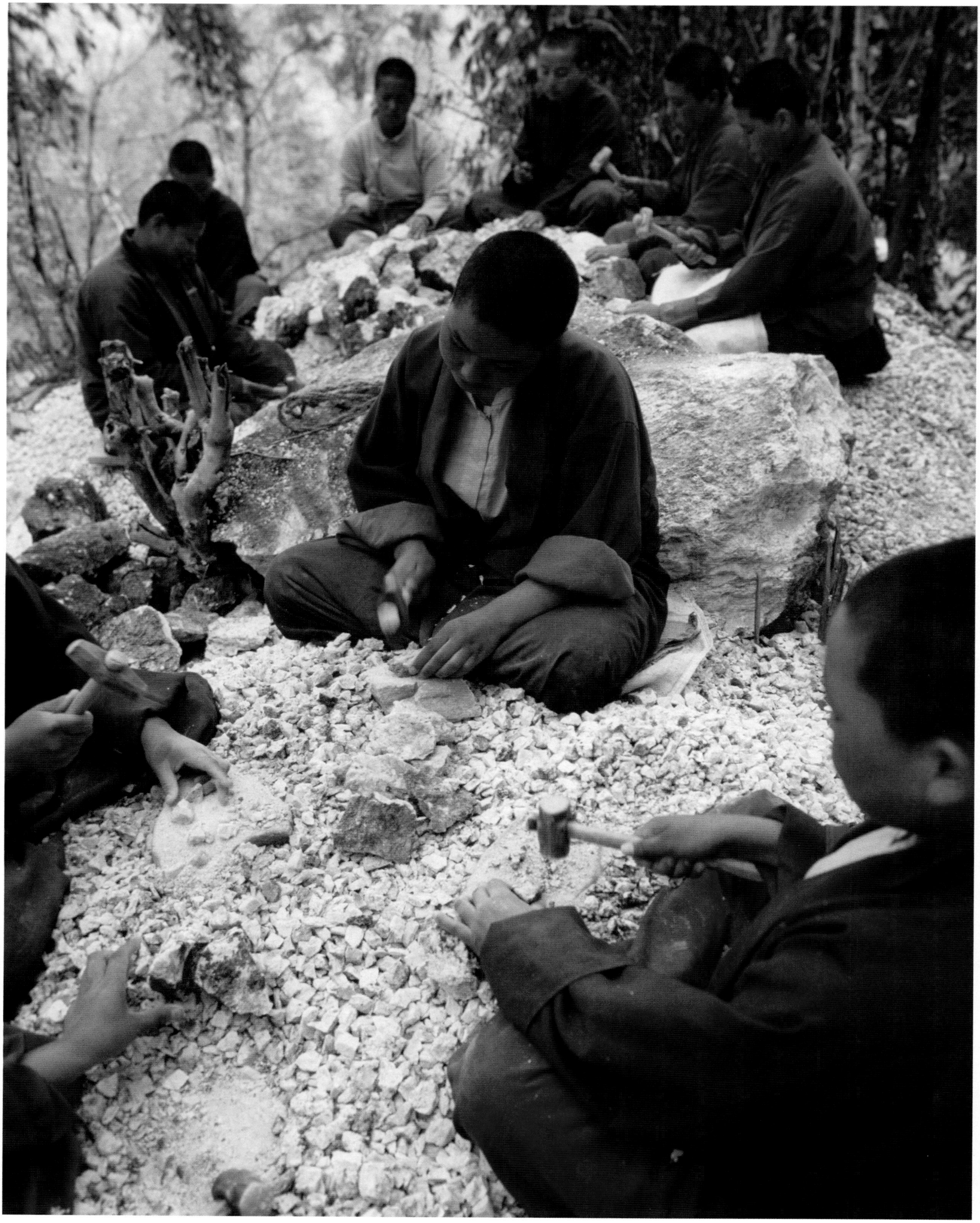

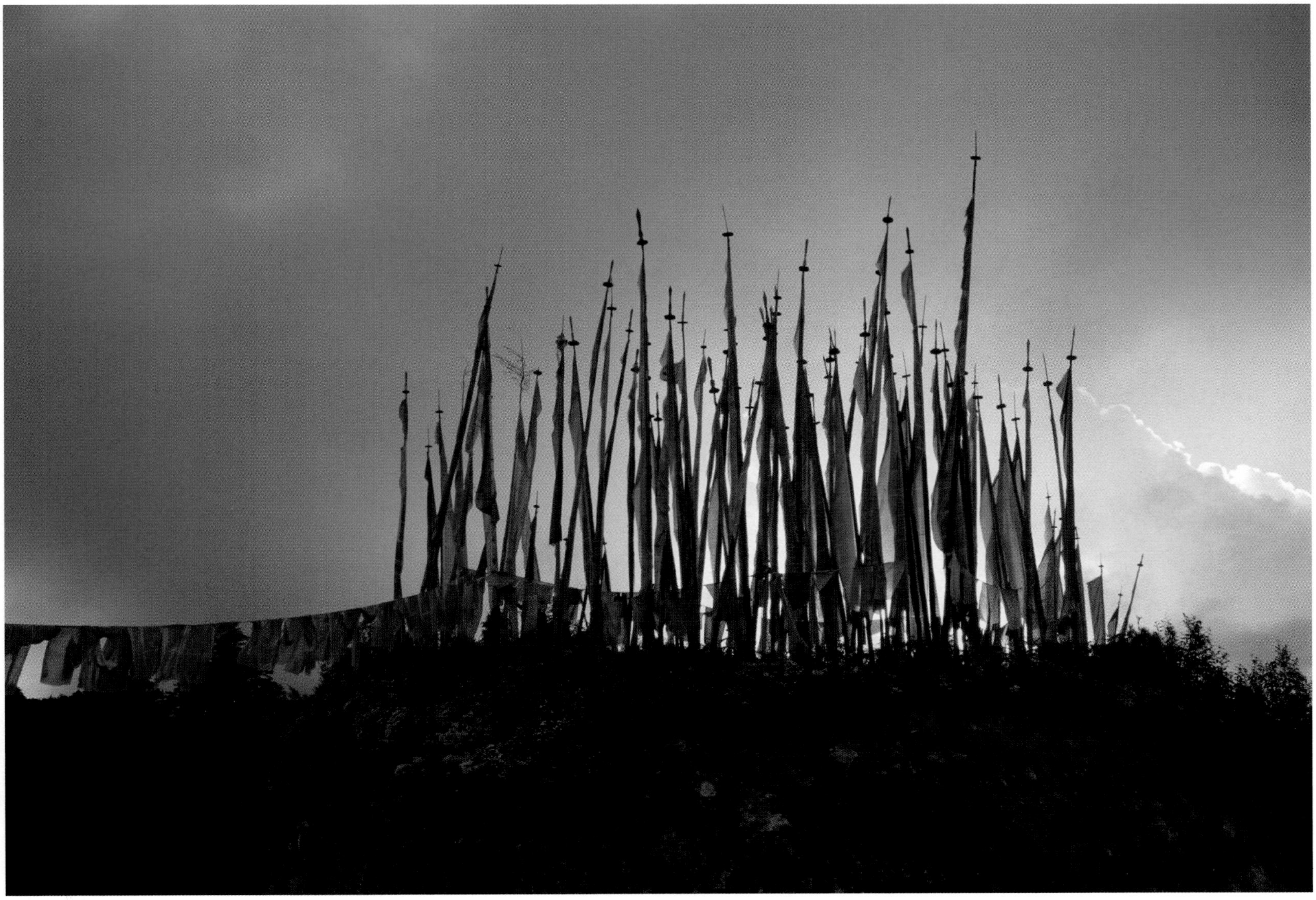

Prayer flags such as these near Dochu Pass are ubiquitous in Bhutan. They are created in five symbolic colors: blue for water, green for wood, red for fire, yellow for earth, and white for iron. Most flags are erected on a hill overlooking a river, enabling the prayers imprinted on them to float with the wind to the river for a long journey onward.

Left: A group of nuns from Khardung Dratsang Convent near Rhadi breaks rocks into small stones, which they need for constructing a retaining wall around their recently restored convent.

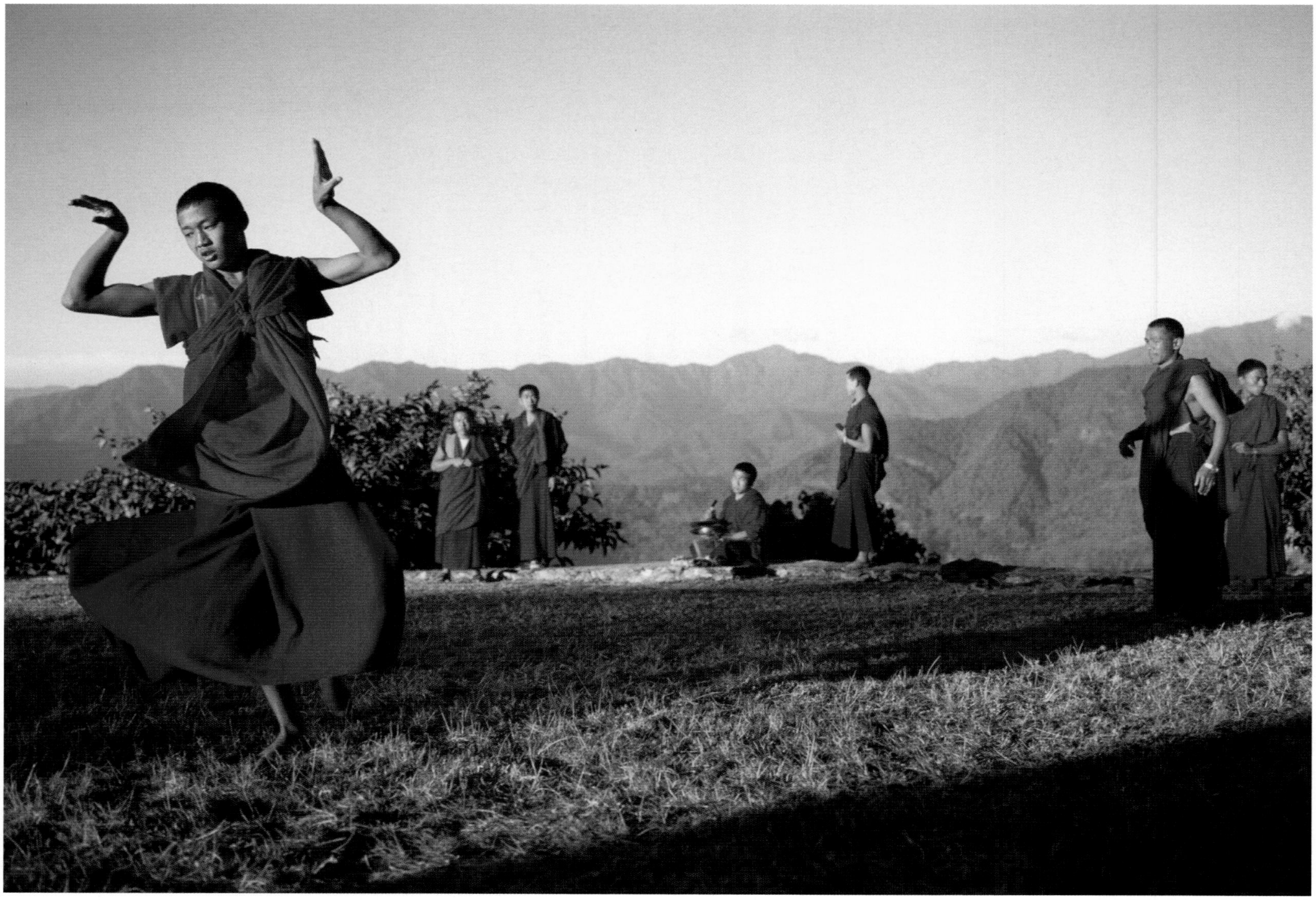

At sunset, monks from Damphu Lhakhang practice the dances to be performed for their annual winter festival.

Right: The terrifying protector deity Rahu greets all visitors near the entrance of Gangtey Monastery.

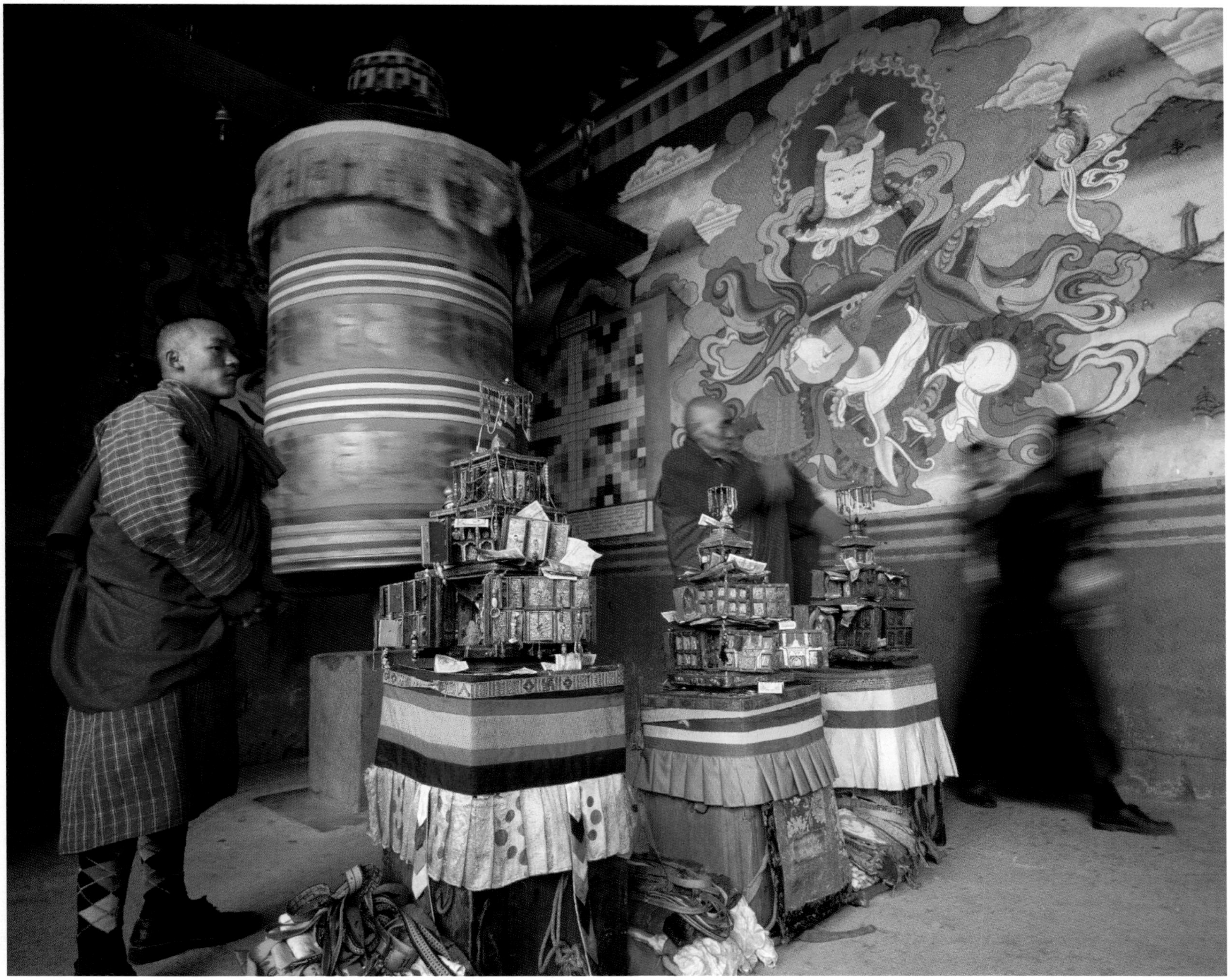

Portable shrines called *tashigomos* are often brought to major festivals by gomchens. These shrines contain tiny statues of Buddhist deities housed in small compartments that become packed with donation money by the end of a festival.

Left: Gomchen Wangdi, 71, is well known around Punakha village for his boisterous and charismatic personality. As with many Bhutanese, his teeth are darkly stained from chewing betel-nut.

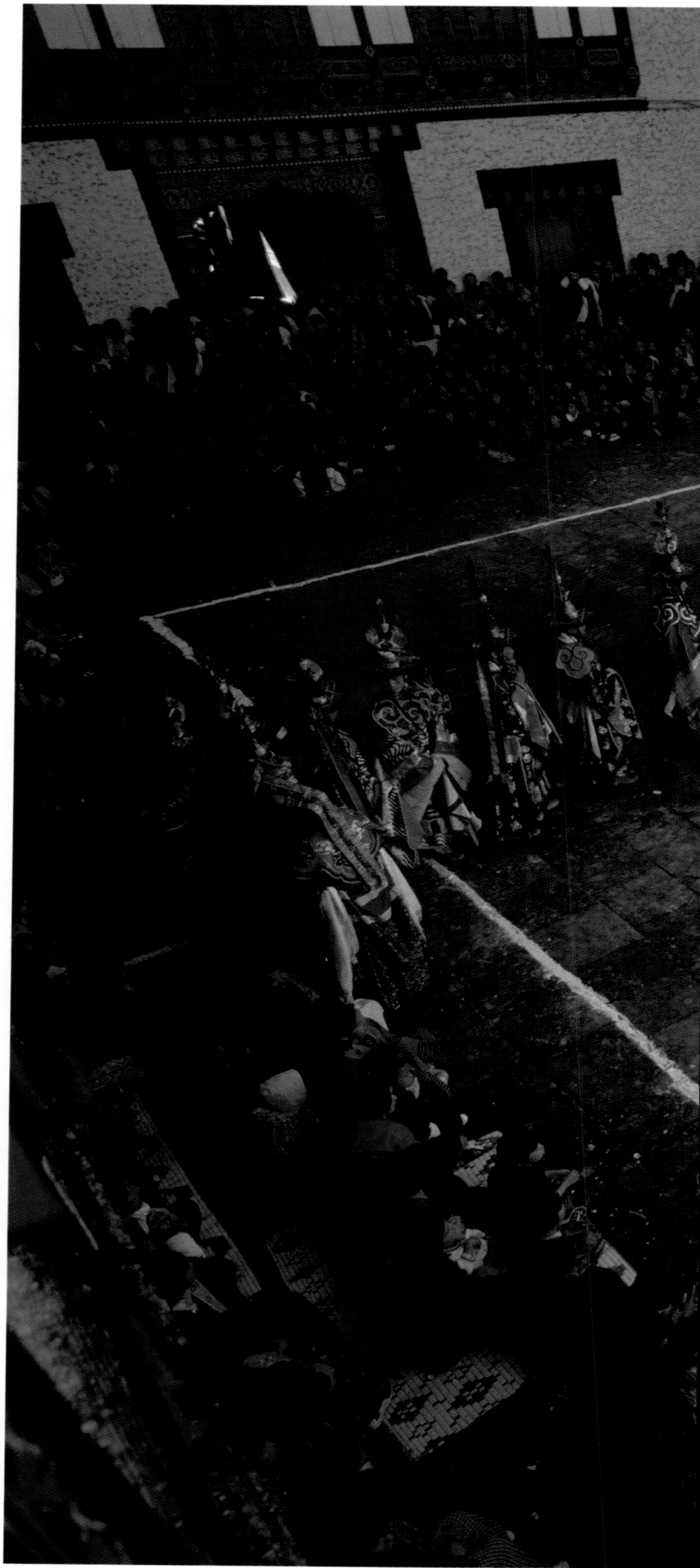

The black hat dance called *shana* is always performed on the opening day of the Trashigang tsechu. While wearing special brocade robes and wide-brimmed hats, the monks take on the appearance of powerful tantric masters capable of protecting the earth from evil demons.

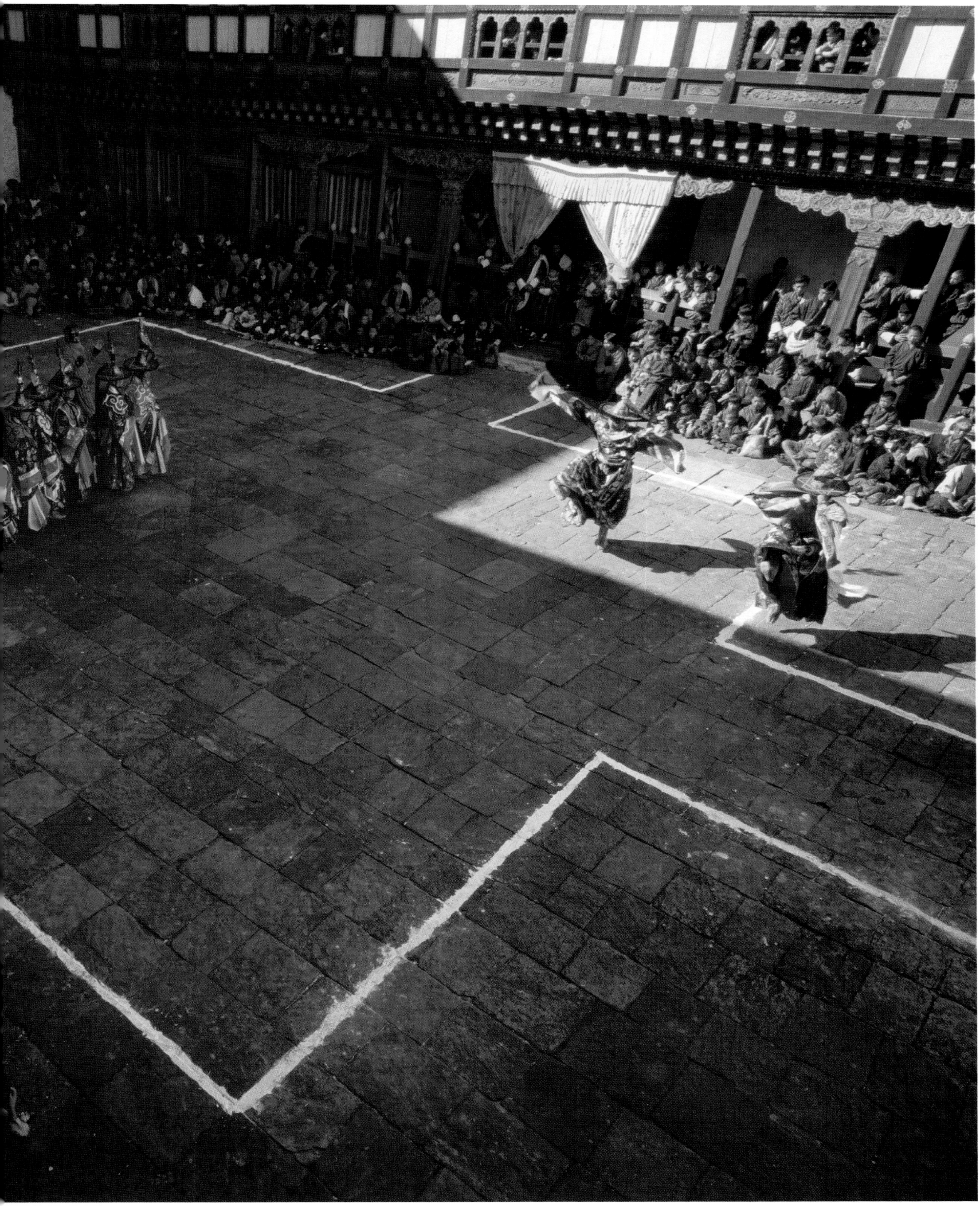

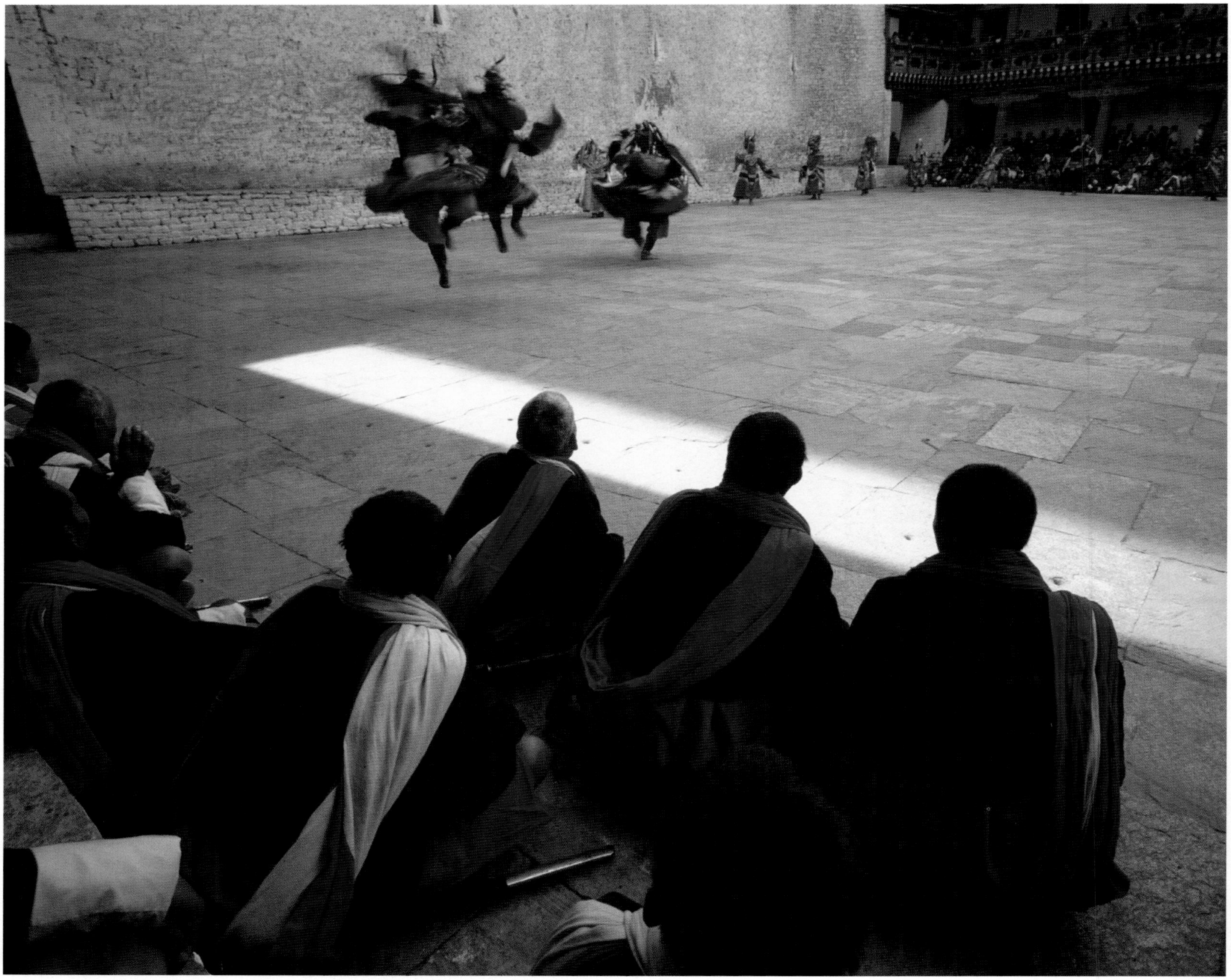

A group of *pazaps,* men from western Bhutan who are elected by their villages to participate in the Punakha dromche, watch the masked dances being performed in the main courtyard of Punakha Dzong. The original pazaps fought to protect Bhutan from invading Tibetans in the seventeenth century.

Right: Continually spinning and twisting, monks who perform the black hat dance must possess a great deal of stamina to avoid becoming dizzy and to maintain group synchronization.

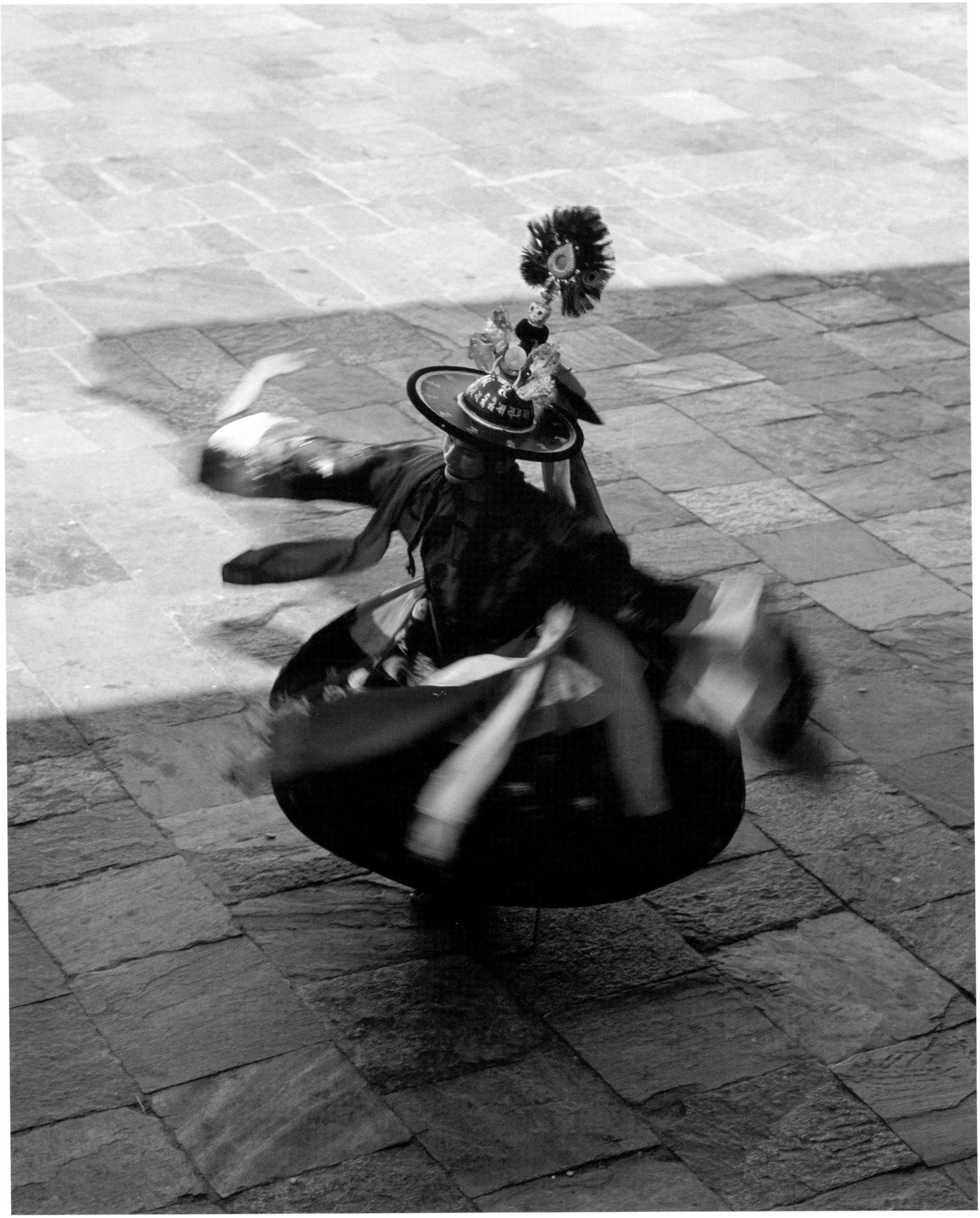

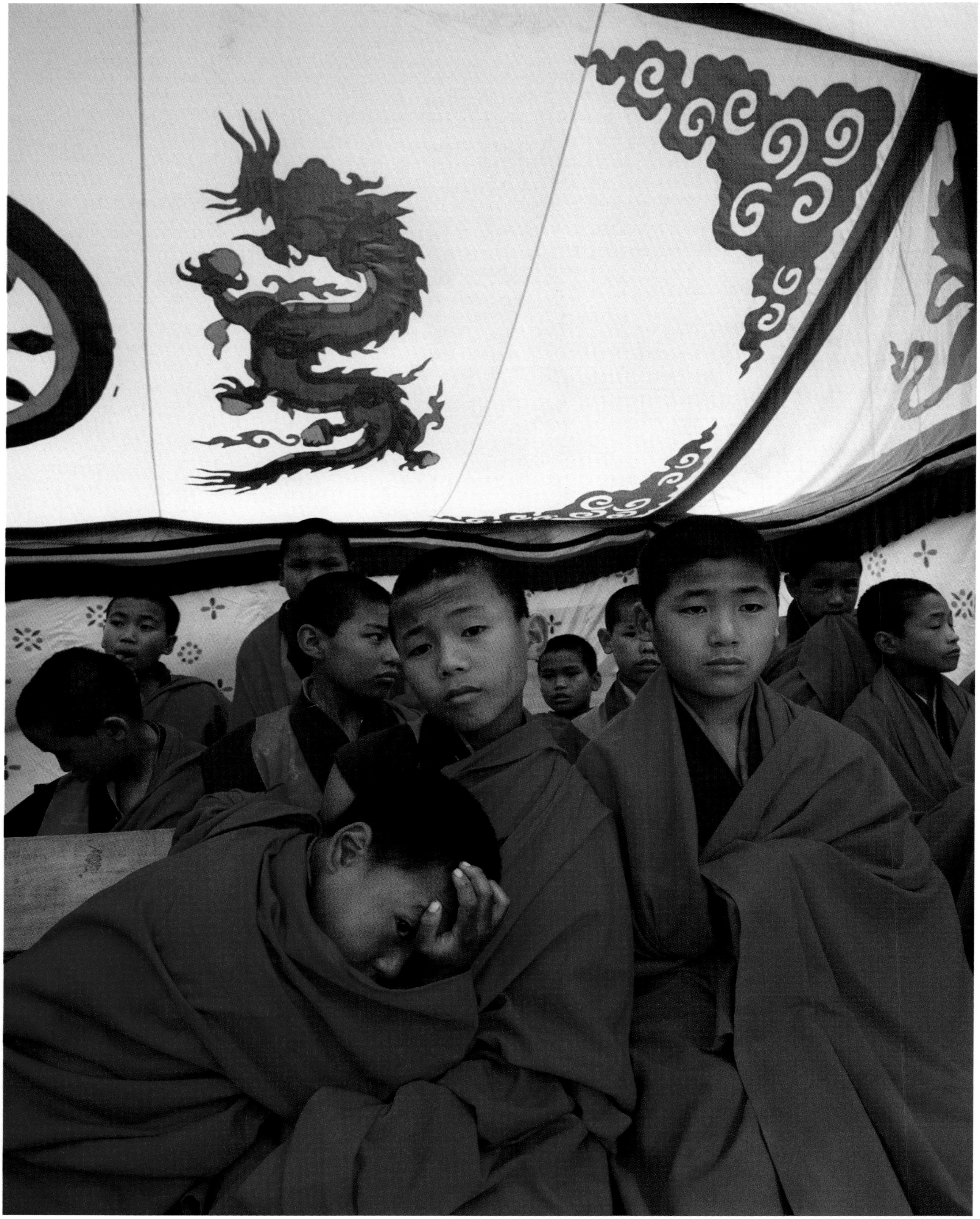

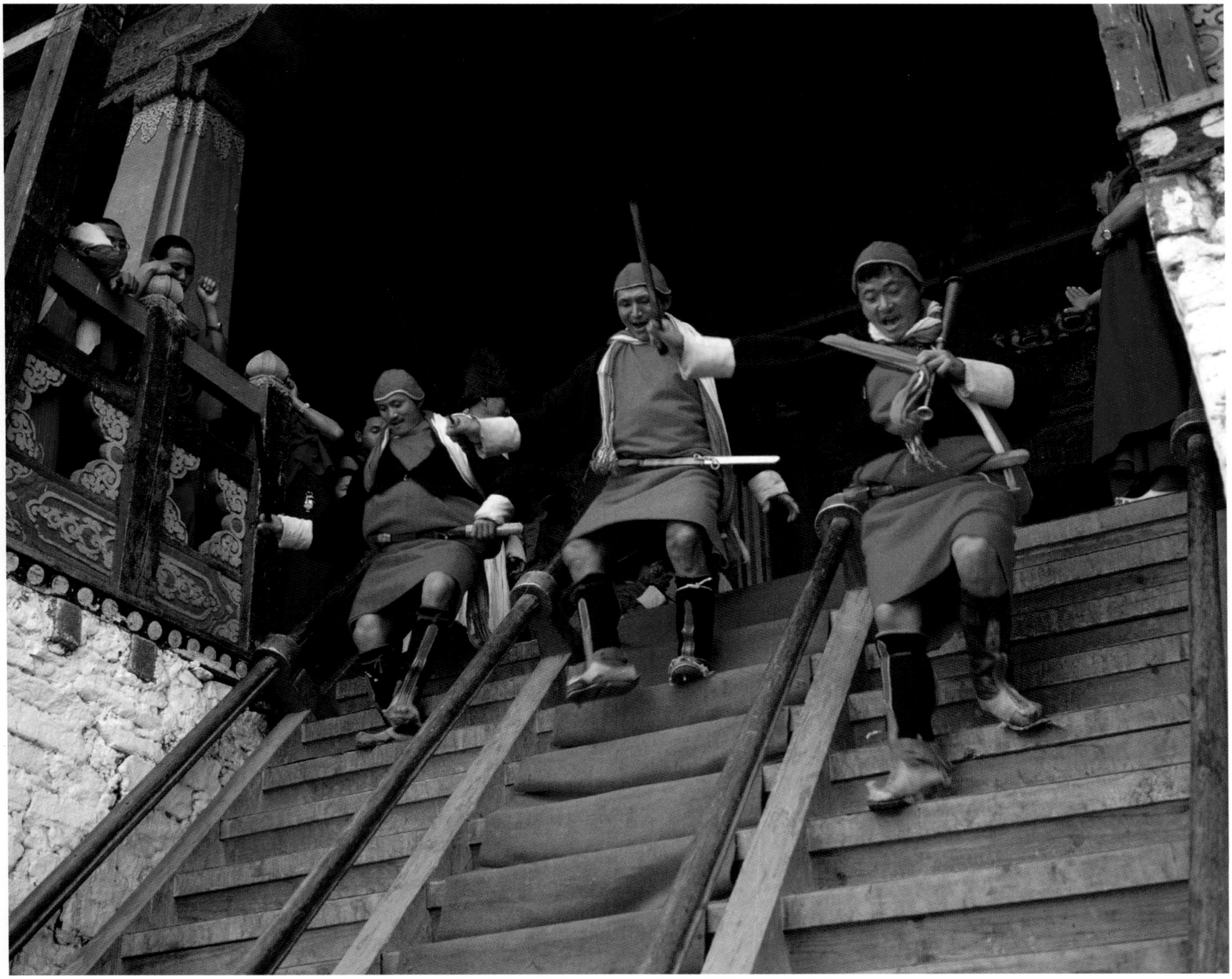

Amid the loud bang of firecrackers, three pazaps with swords drawn run quickly down the stairs of Punakha Dzong to recreate a centuries-old battle charge.

Left: By midafternoon, young novice monks from Dagana Dzong grow tired and restless after having woken up at 3 A.M. for early morning prayers before the tsechu dances begin.

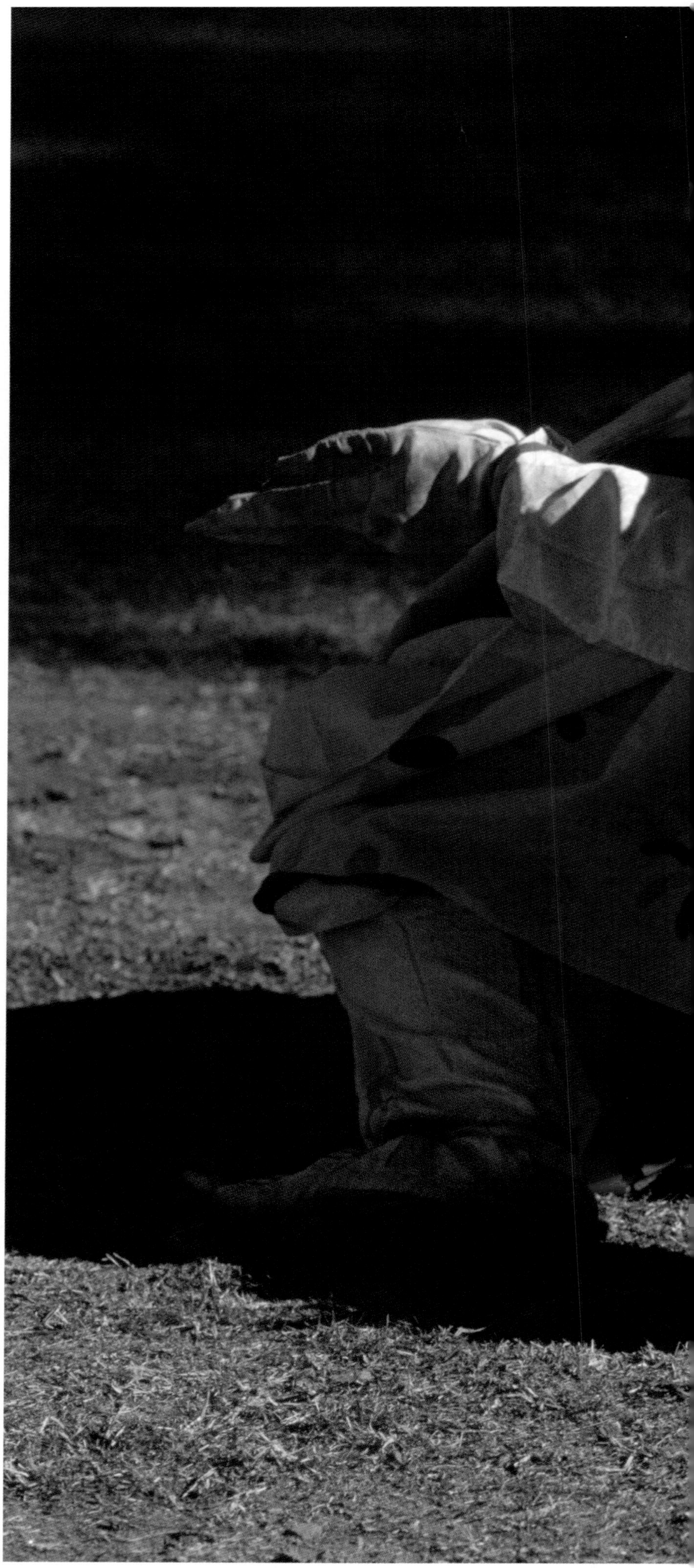

During the Dagana tsechu, a monk dressed as a skeleton performs a dance called *durdag* to drive away evil spirits from the sacred Mount Sumeru, the legendary center of the Buddhist cosmos.

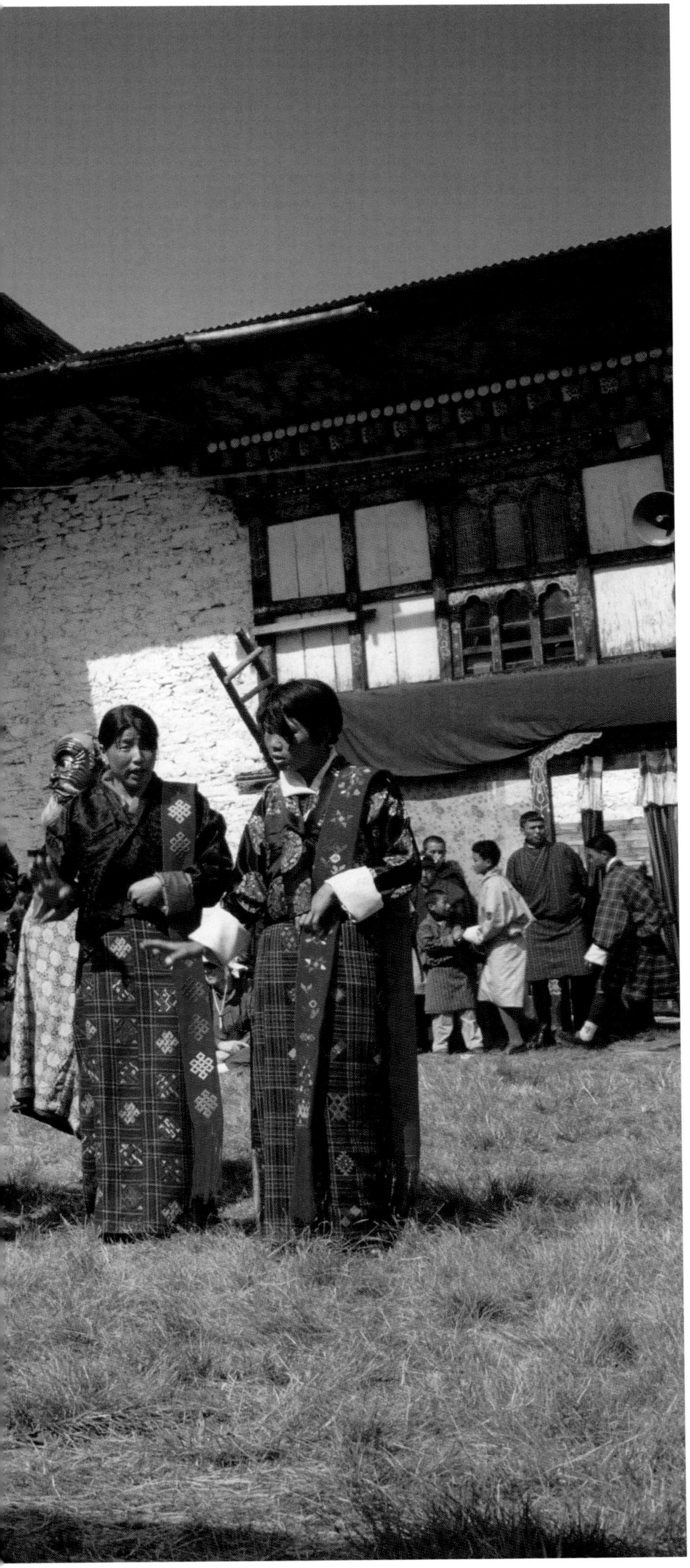

Women from the upper Bumthang Valley perform a dance during the Jambay tsechu around a monk pretending to be dead. Dressed all in white, the monk assumes the appearance of a powerful demon. Known as a *shawley,* the demon harms villagers by making them sick and causing their crops to die. At the conclusion of the dance, the shawley is killed with a three-bladed ritual dagger by other dancers.

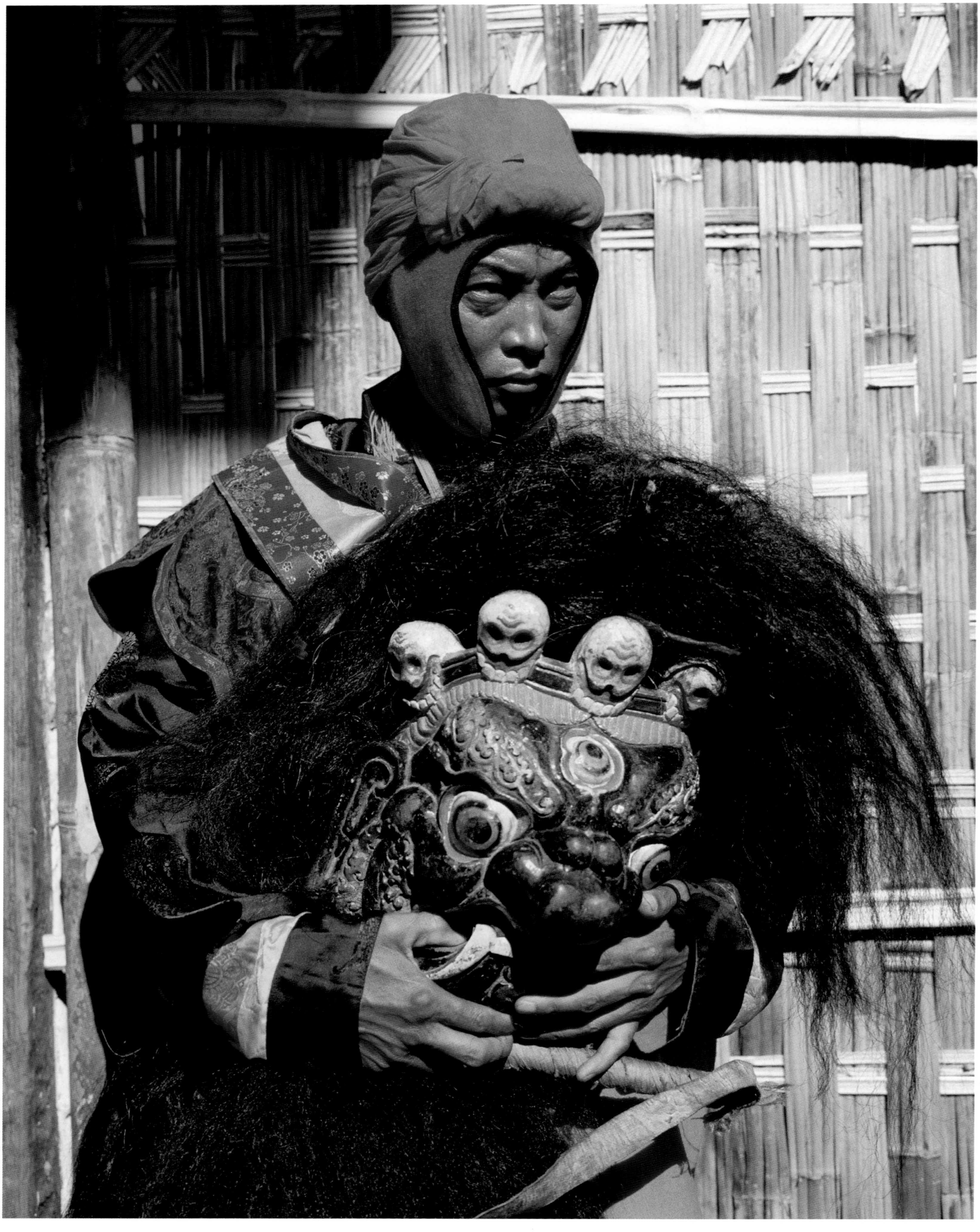

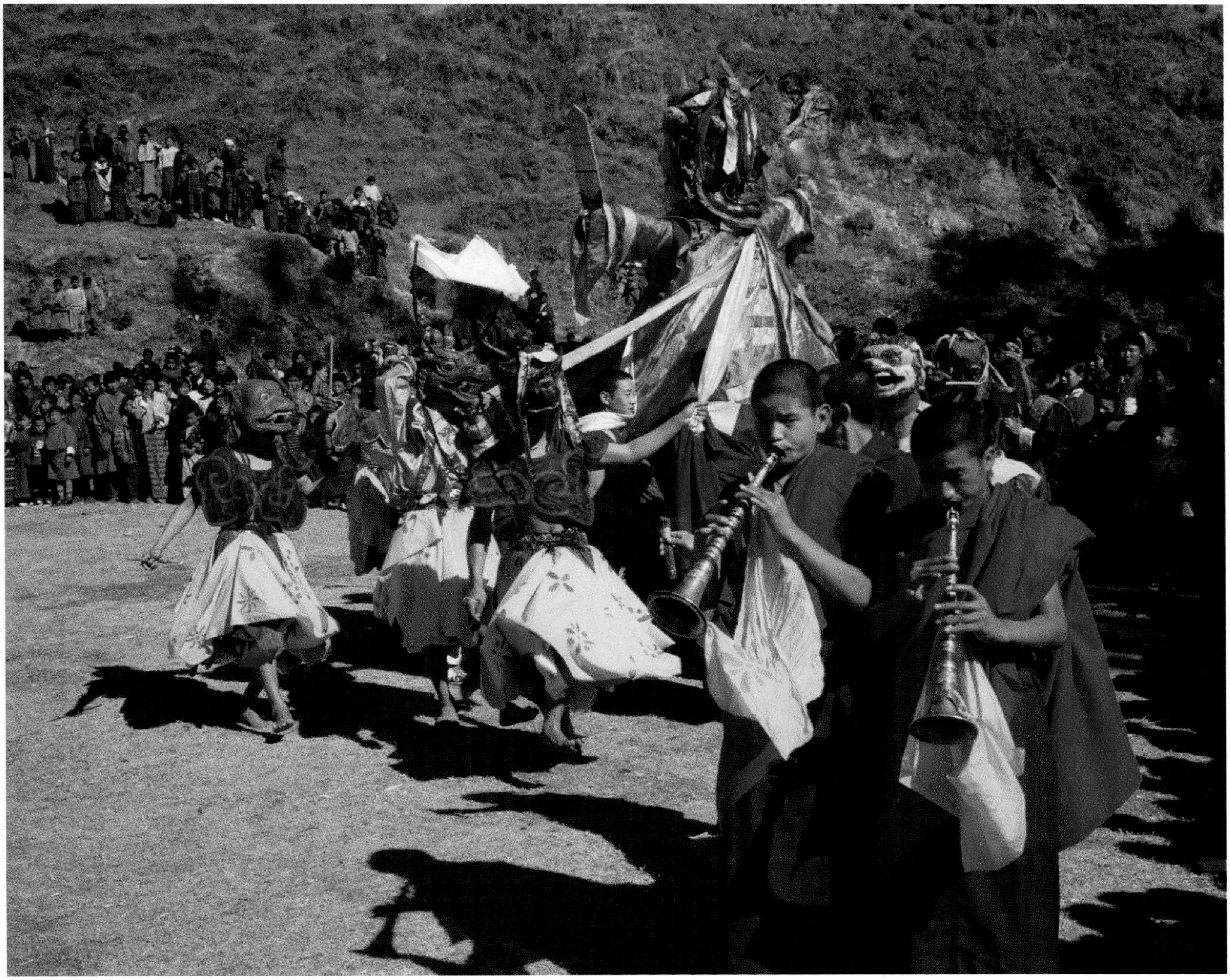

Leading the procession with loud trumpets, a group of monks from Dagana Dzong wear animal face masks as they celebrate the arrival of Shinje Chogyal, known as the Lord of Death. When beings die they first enter an intermediate state to be judged by Shinje Chogyal as worthy to proceed to a higher rebirth or damned to suffer in hell.

Left: Dodam, 36, rests after performing a dance as Danakpo, the black demon. Before being judged by Shinje Chogyal, all beings during their lifetimes are subjected to the evil influence of Danakpo as well as the pious influence of Lhakarpo, the white god.

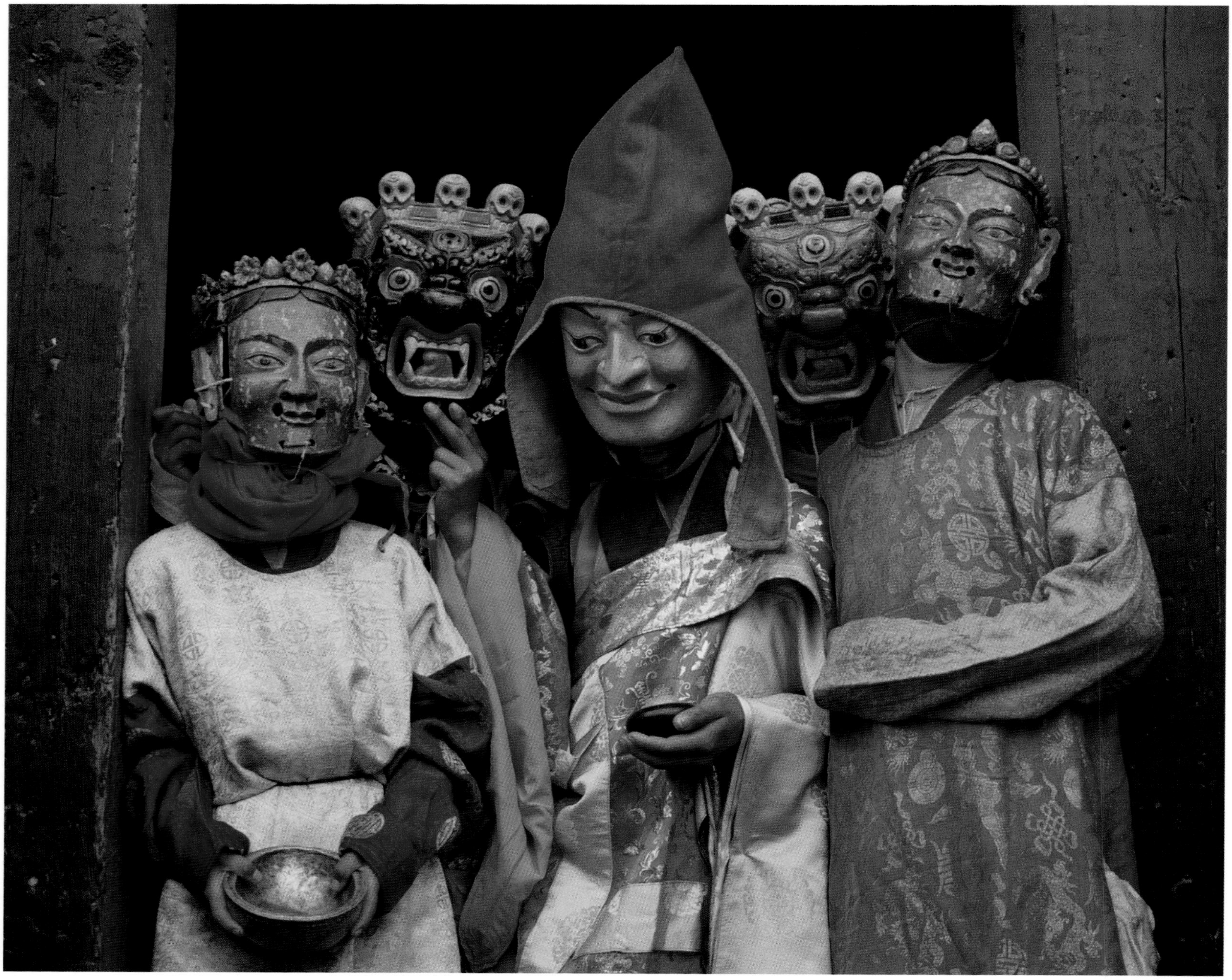

A group of monks pose by the Dagana Dzong dressing room prior to the final dance of the annual tsechu. The monk in the center is dressed as a smiling manifestation of Padmasambhava known as "Pemajuney," surrounded by two terrifying deities and two peaceful disciples.

Right: Two monks and a dignitary help to roll up the large *thongdrel* from Dagana Dzong featuring Buddha Shakyamuni in the center. Thongdrels provide protection from bad rebirths to all the villagers and attendees who have come to view it.

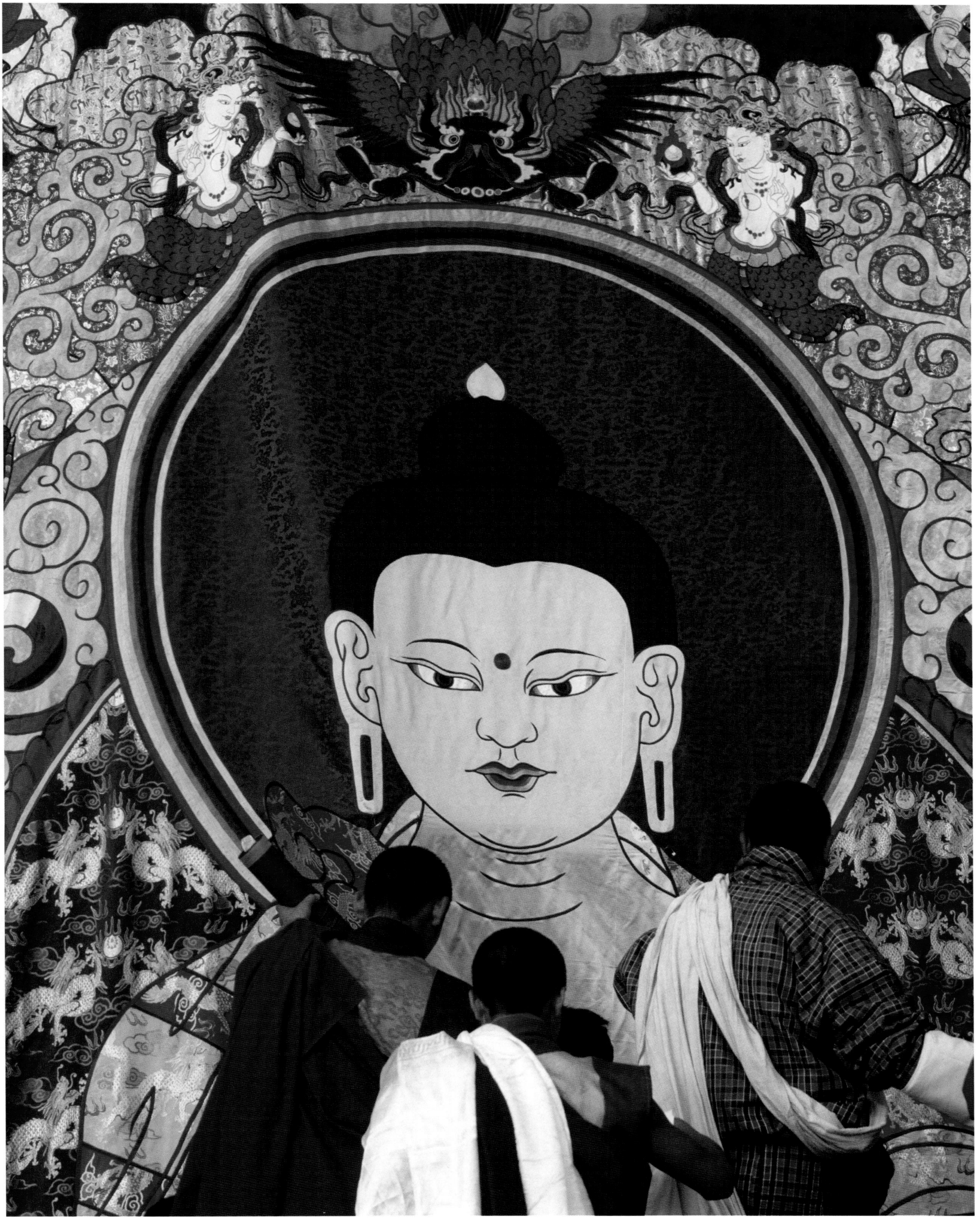

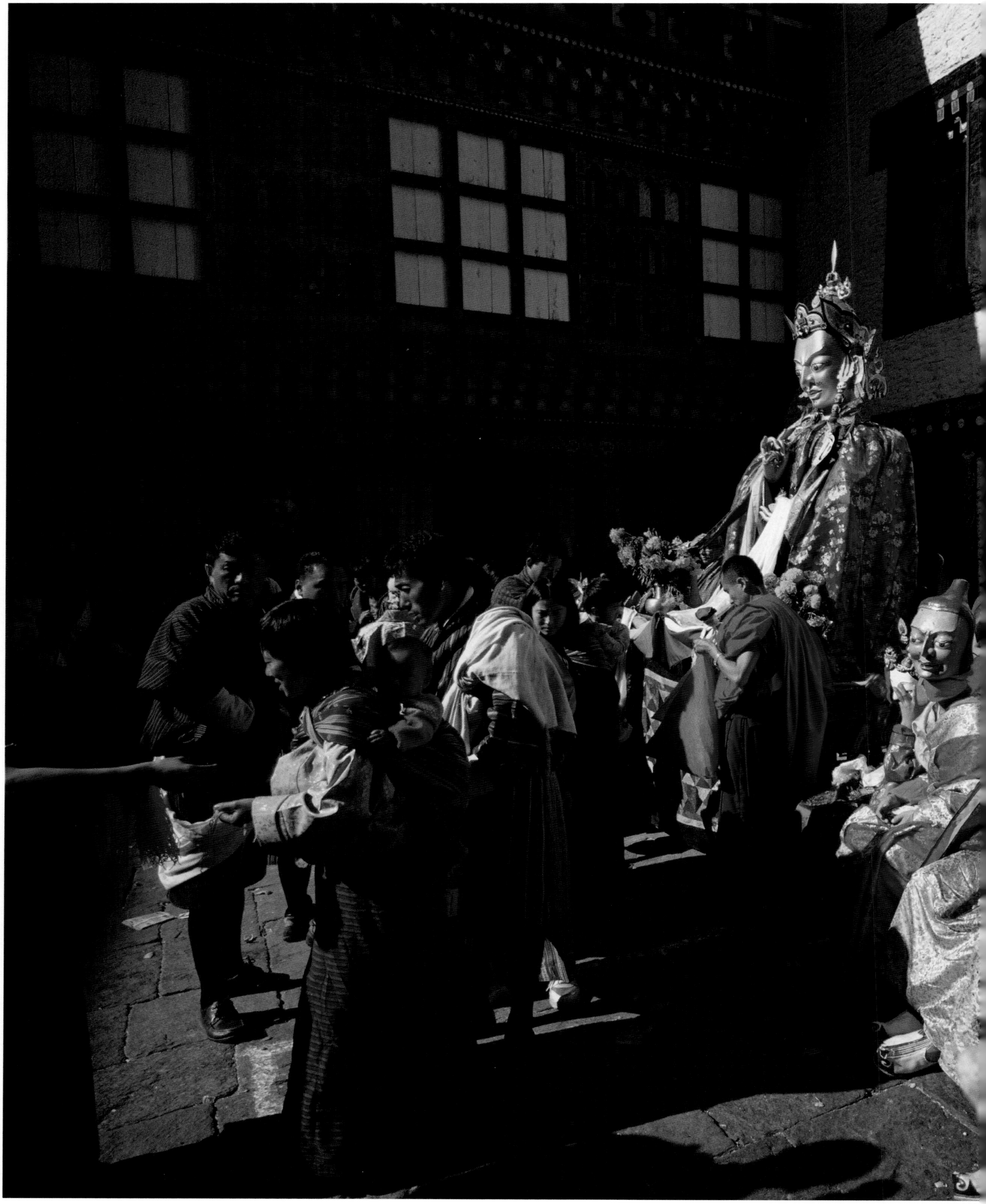

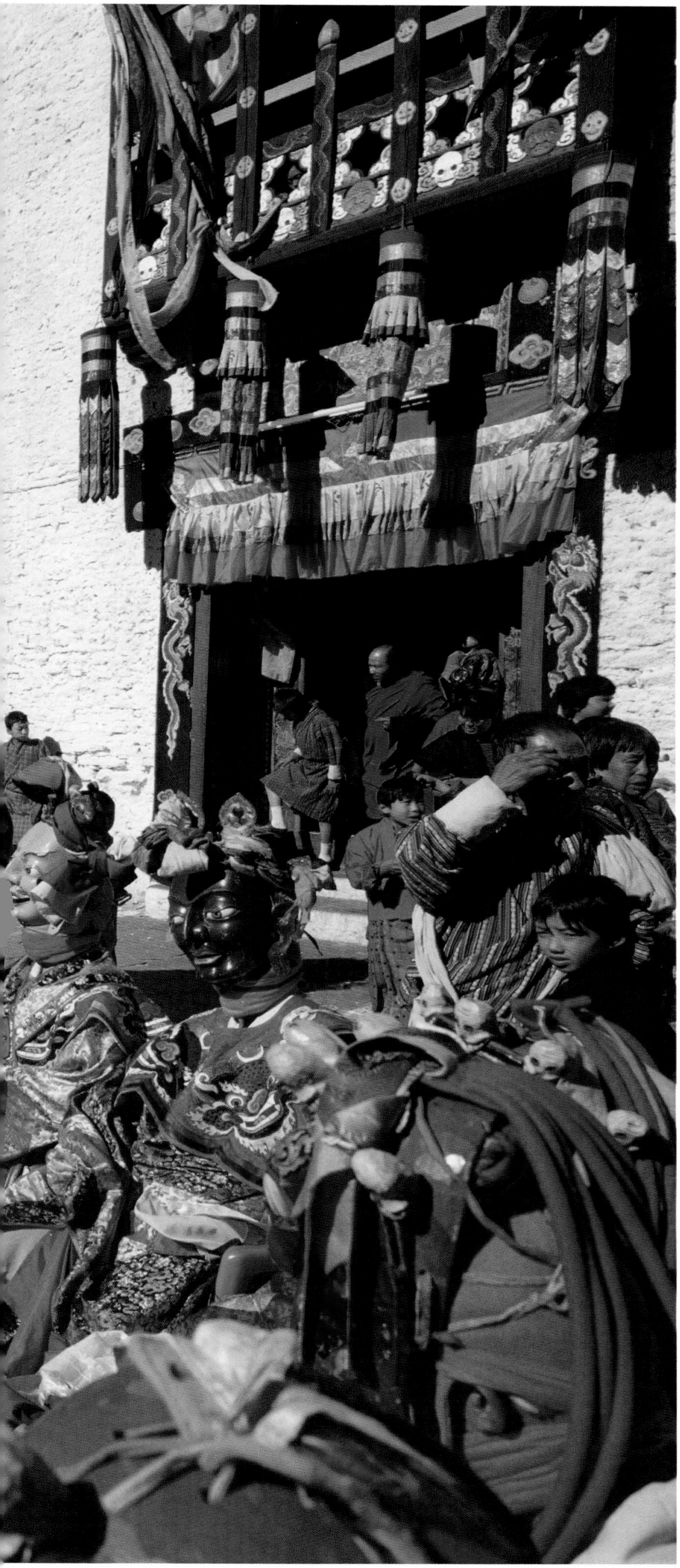

On the final day of the Trashigang tsechu, a tall statue of Padmasambhava is taken outside the dzong, while monks dressed as his different manifestations perform a dance to honor him. When finished, the dancers sit beside Padmasambhava as villagers file past to receive a blessing and a special thread necklace known as a *sunki*.

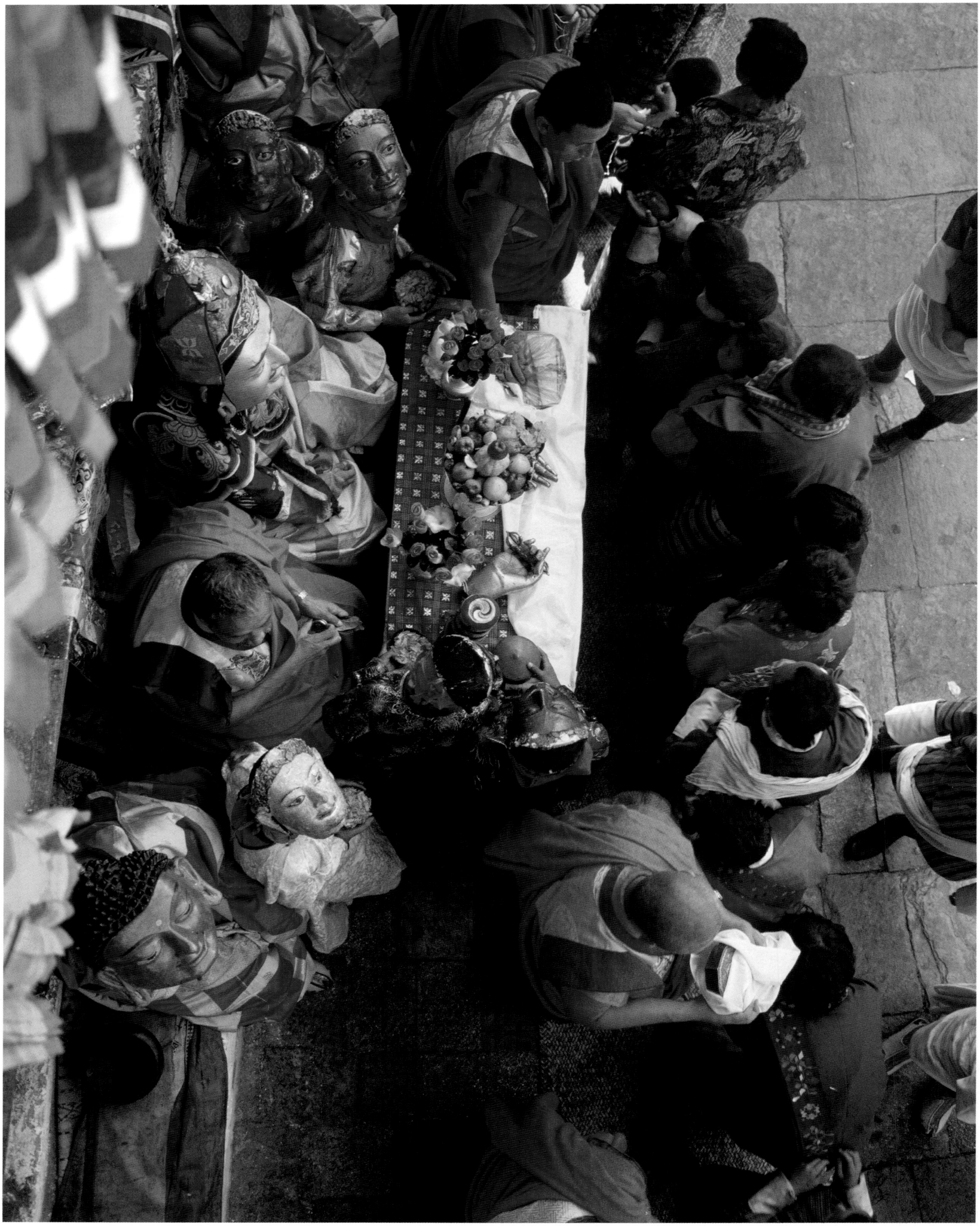

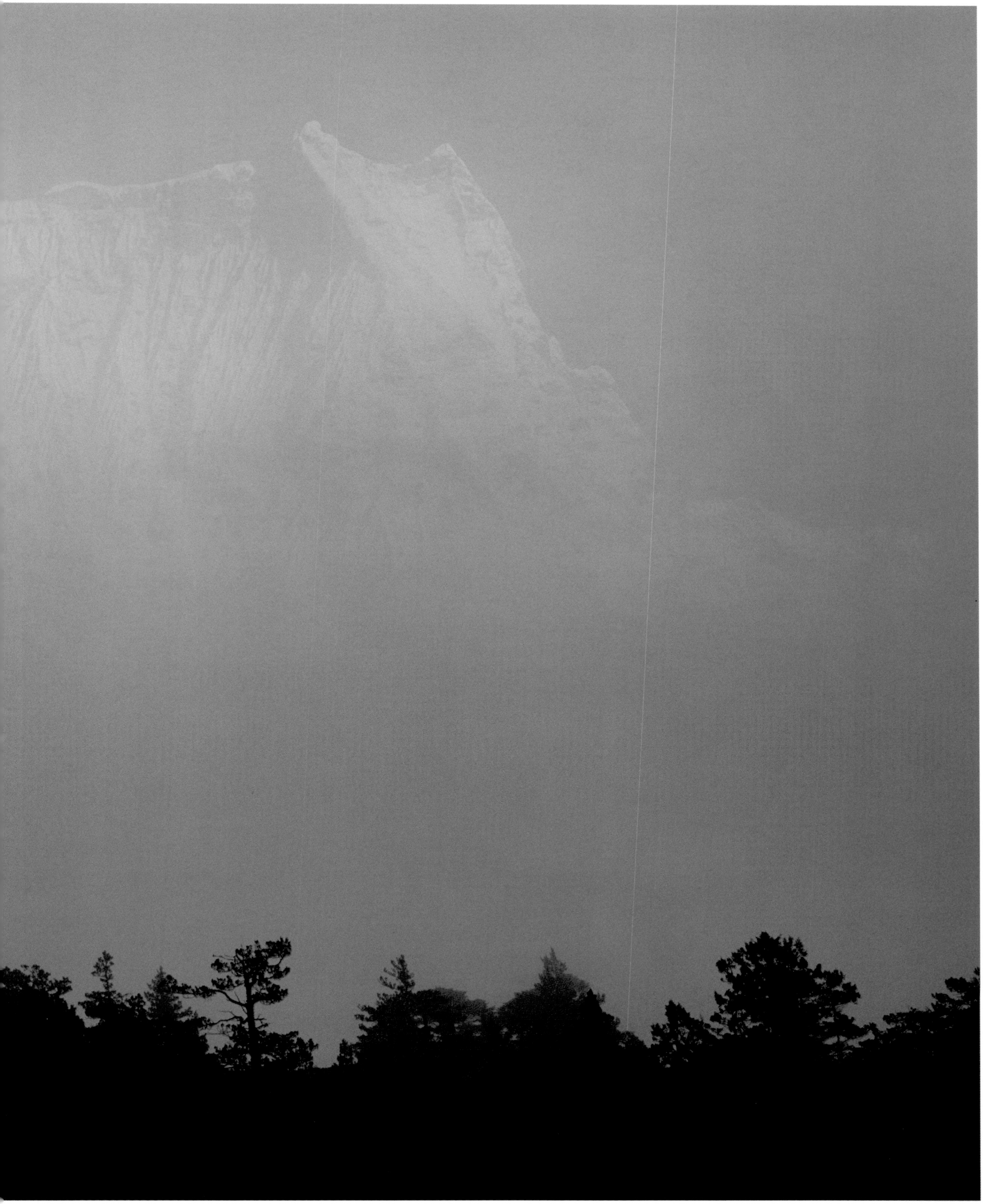

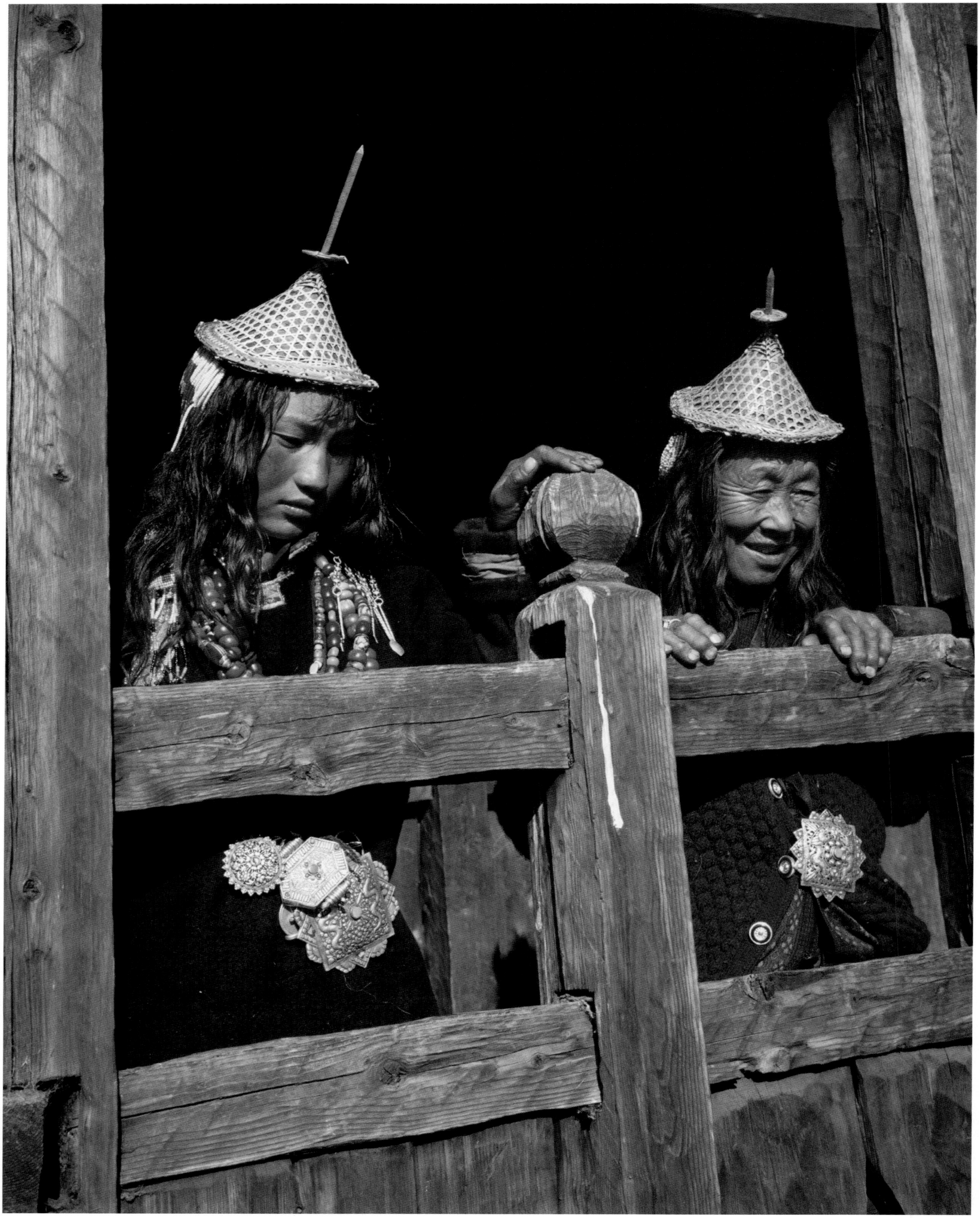

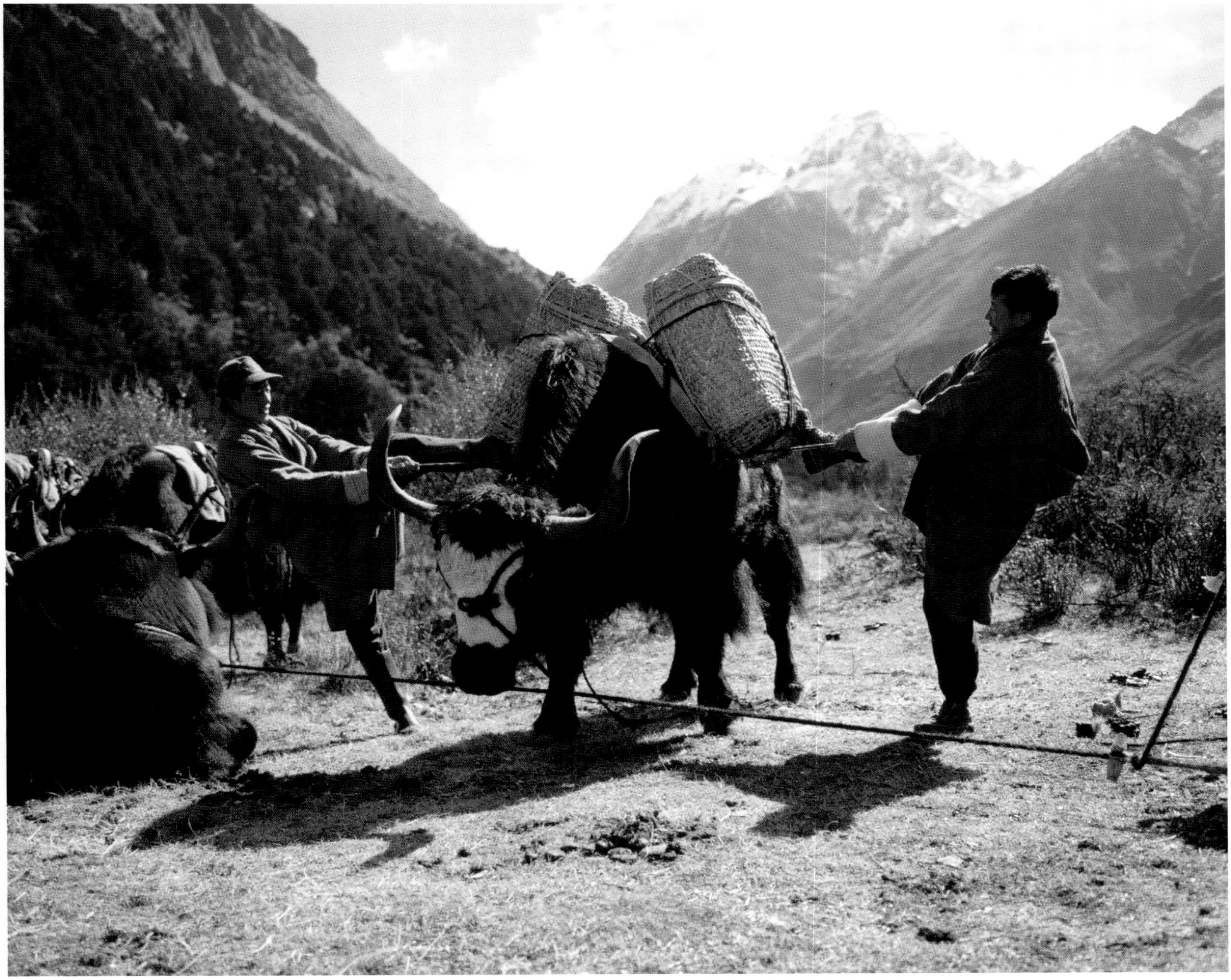

Two villagers from Lingshi struggle to secure hand-woven baskets on the back of a yak at a campsite near Laya.

Left: Deki, 22, and her neighbor, Sangay, 47, stand on the porch of a house in Laya.

Previous spread: The 22,435-foot peak of Gangchenta Mountain is partially obscured by fog at dawn. Translated as "tiger mountain," Gangchenta features a distinctive pair of peak-shaped "ears" and a curved "back."

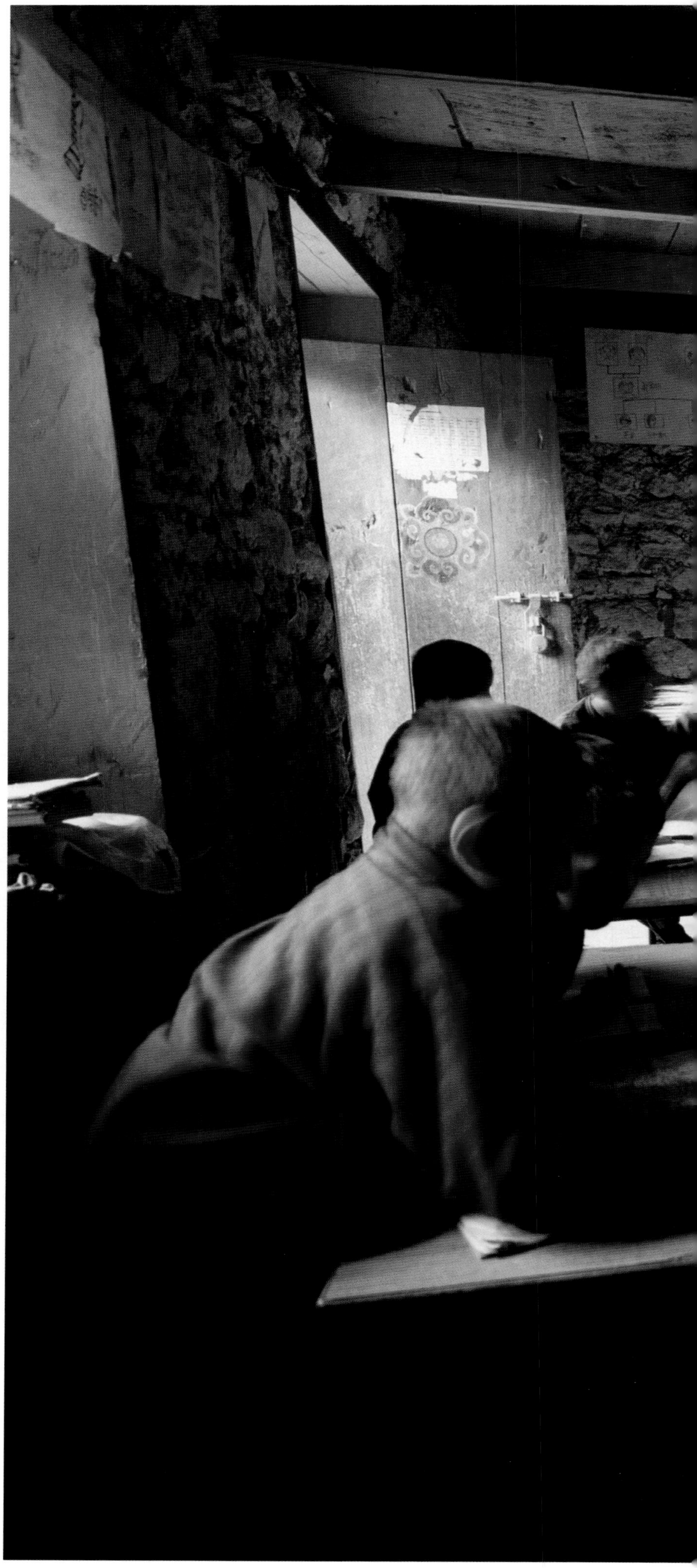

Students from the Laya primary school work on class assignments together under the watchful eye of their teacher. Even though northern Bhutan is sparsely populated, several schools have been built to provide a free education for the local children.

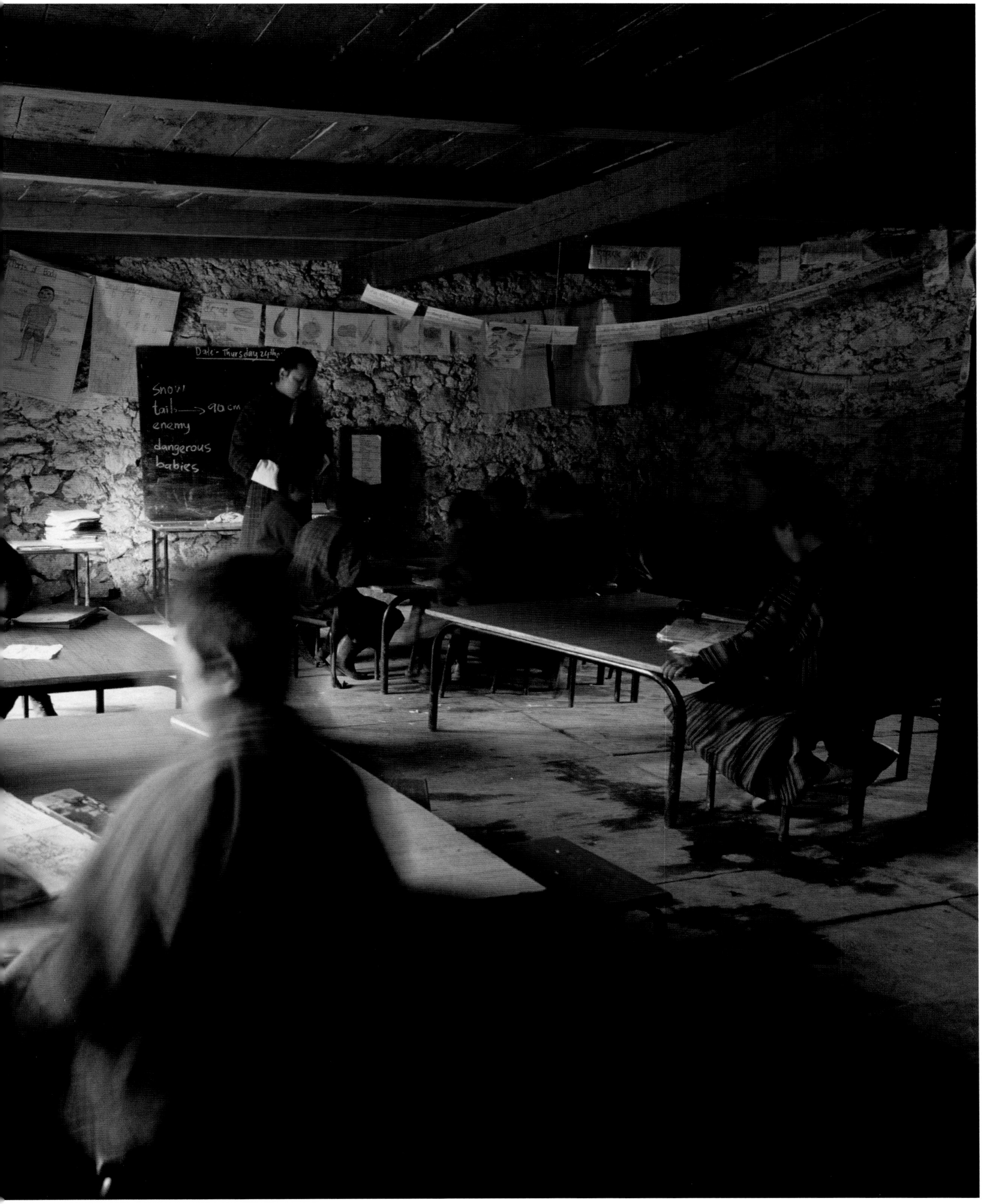
snow
tail → 90 cm
enemy
dangerous
babies

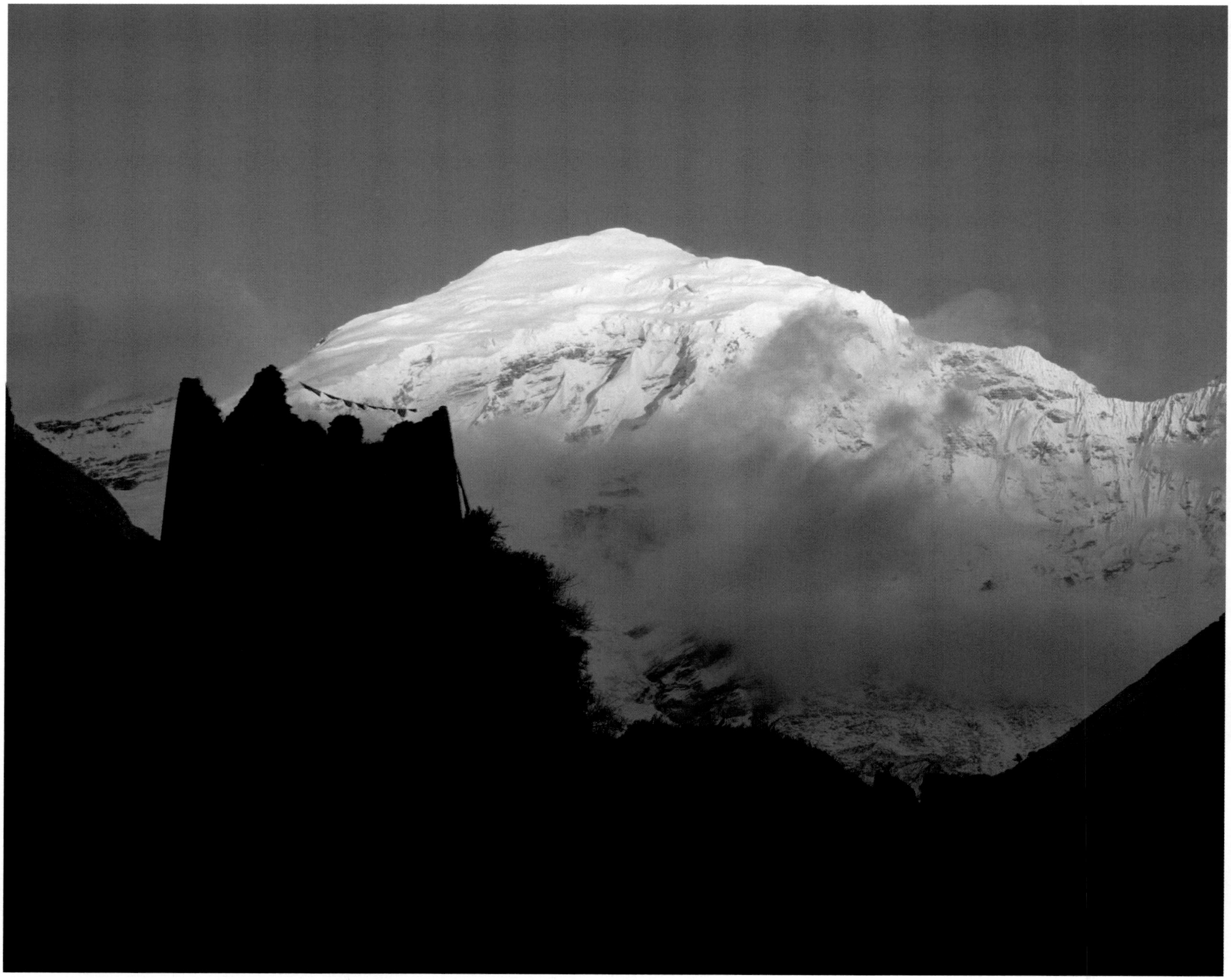

The upper summit of 23,989-foot Jhomo Lhari Mountain casts a pink hue for a few moments at sunrise.

Right: Namgay, 58, spends the entire year living alone while taking care of a small temple near the base of Jichu Drakey Mountain. He complains that ghosts occasionally disturb the otherwise peaceful retreat.

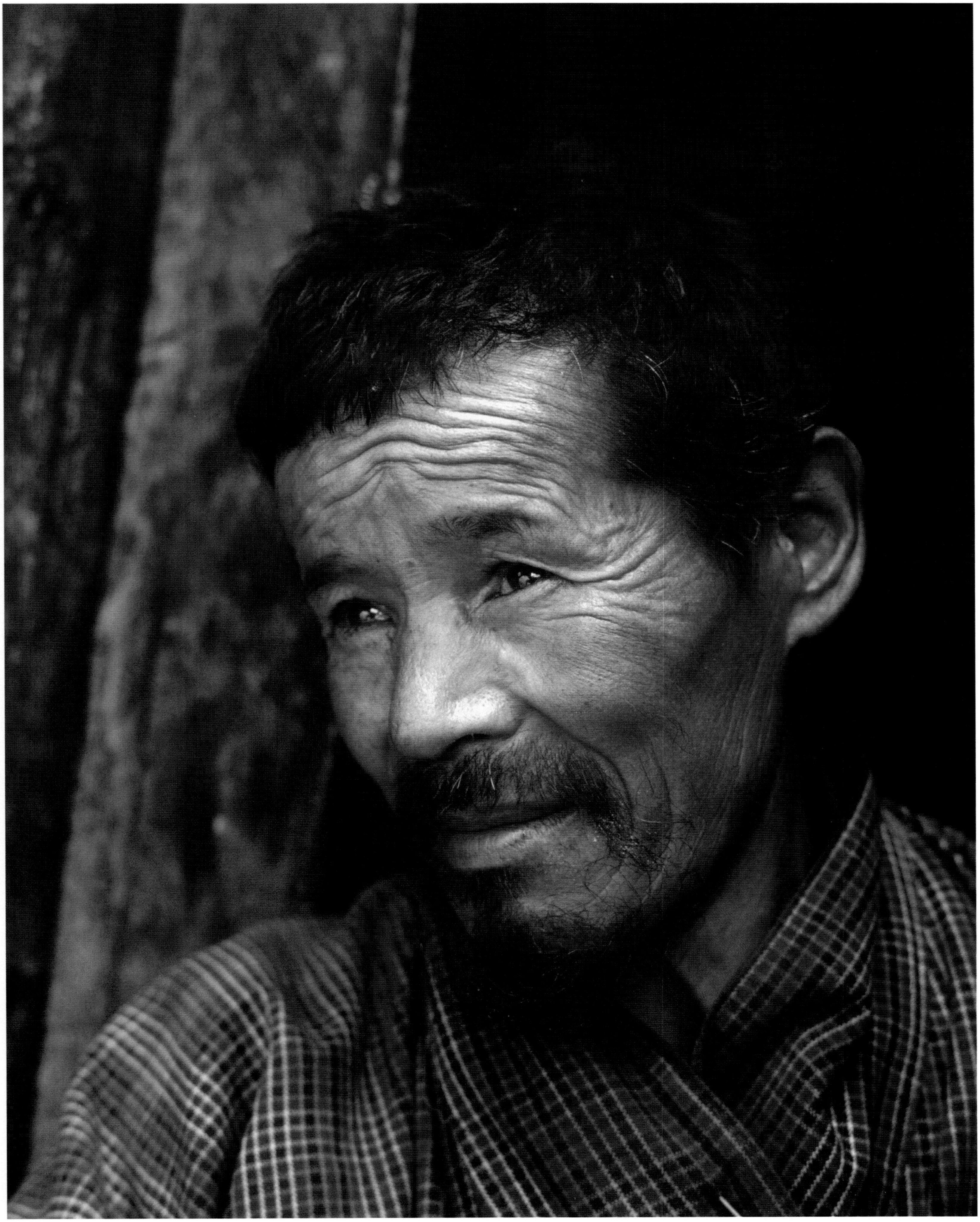

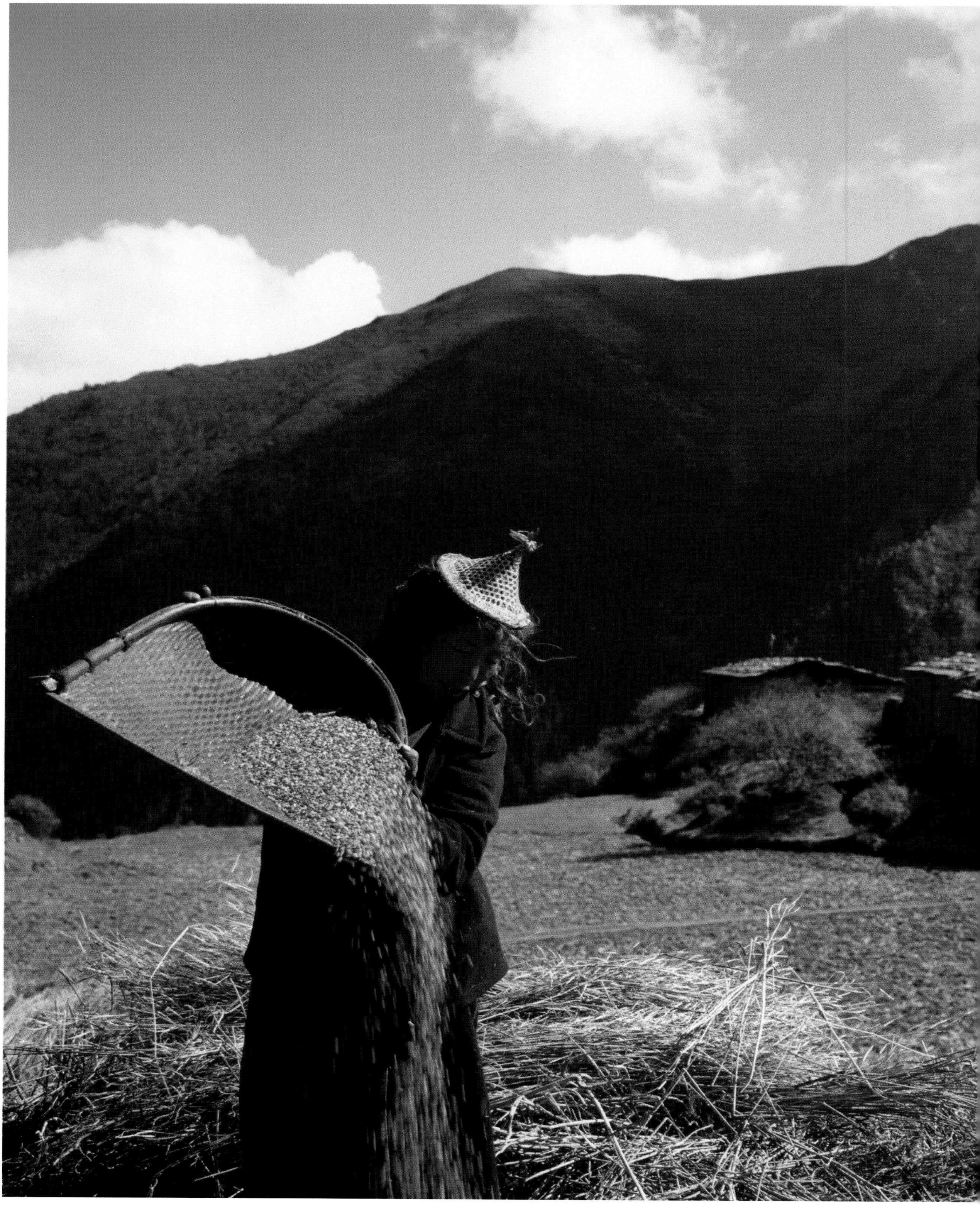

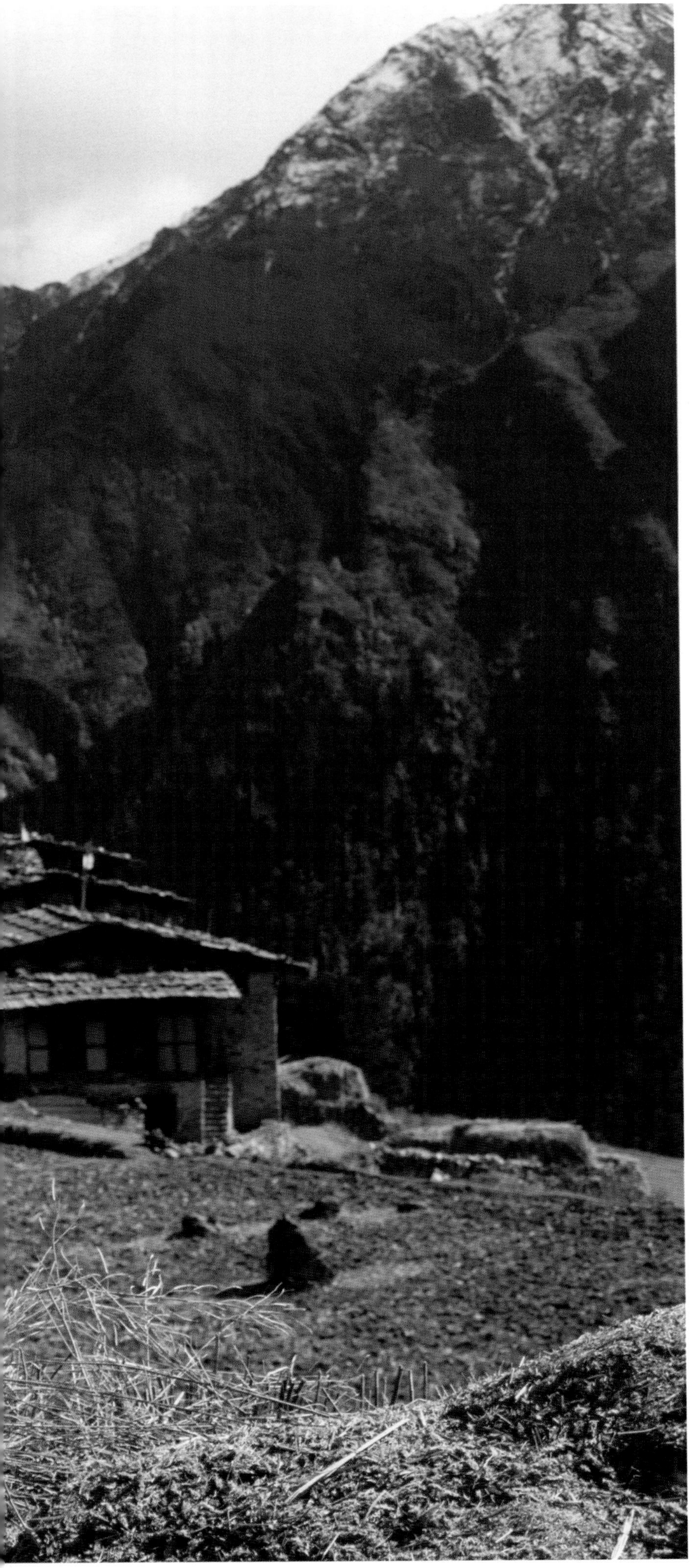

A woman from Laya slowly winnows barley from the husk with a bamboo scoop known as a *becham*. Because the village is so small, nearly all Layaps know each other and often help with communal farm work.

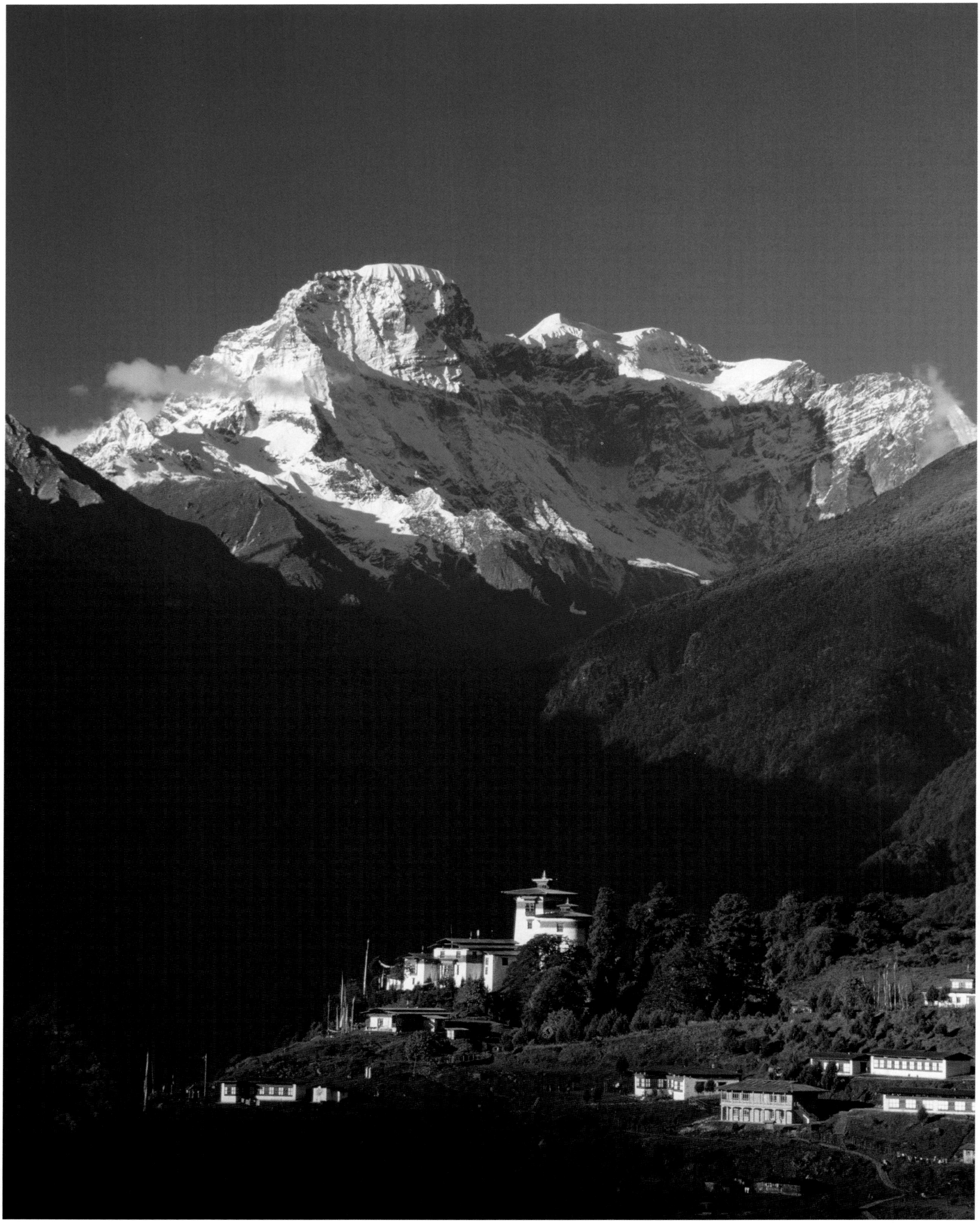

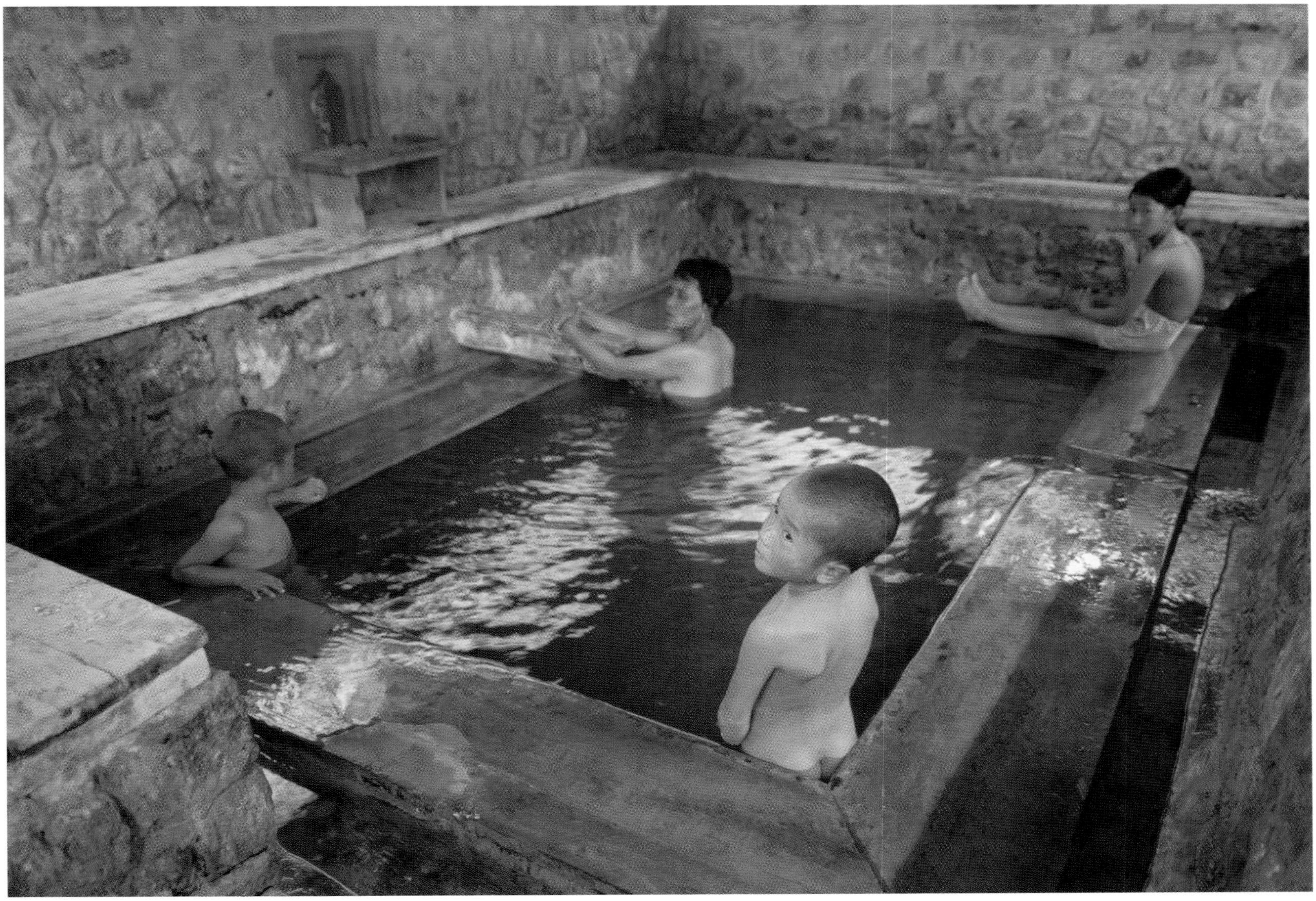

A mother and her three young children enjoy a soak in the natural hot spring located below Gasa village.

Left: The fantastically situated 21,300-foot peak of Khangbum Mountain rises gracefully behind Gasa Dzong, built in 1646. An old legend relates that Gomo, a protective serpent, rose from a small pond near the dzong to defeat an army of invading Tibetans.

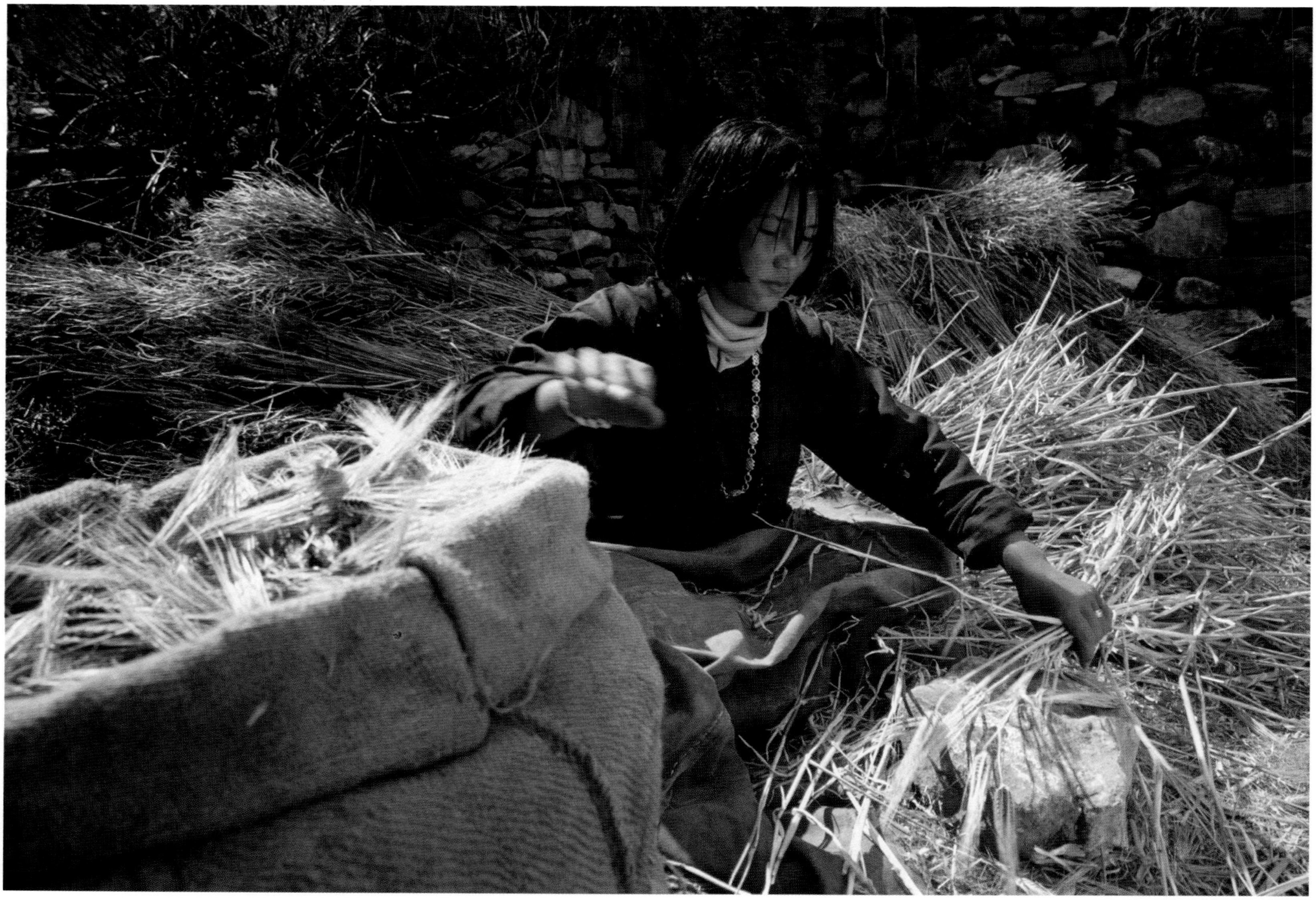

In the small hamlet of Chebisa, Lhababuti, 21, uses a sharp blade tucked between her knees to sever the tops of wheat stalks from the unwanted shafts.

Right: A short distance above Chebisa is a waterfall that freezes completely in winter.

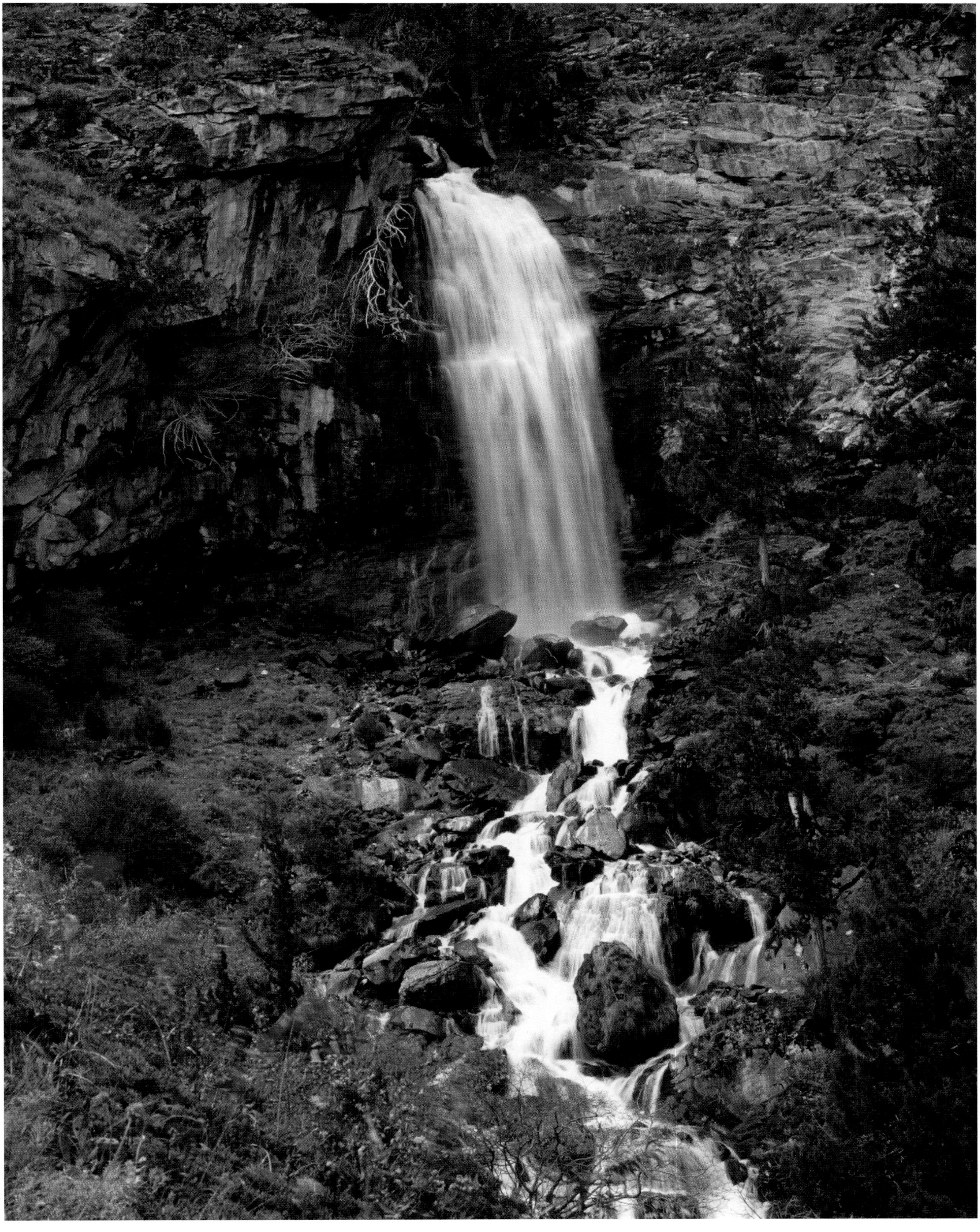

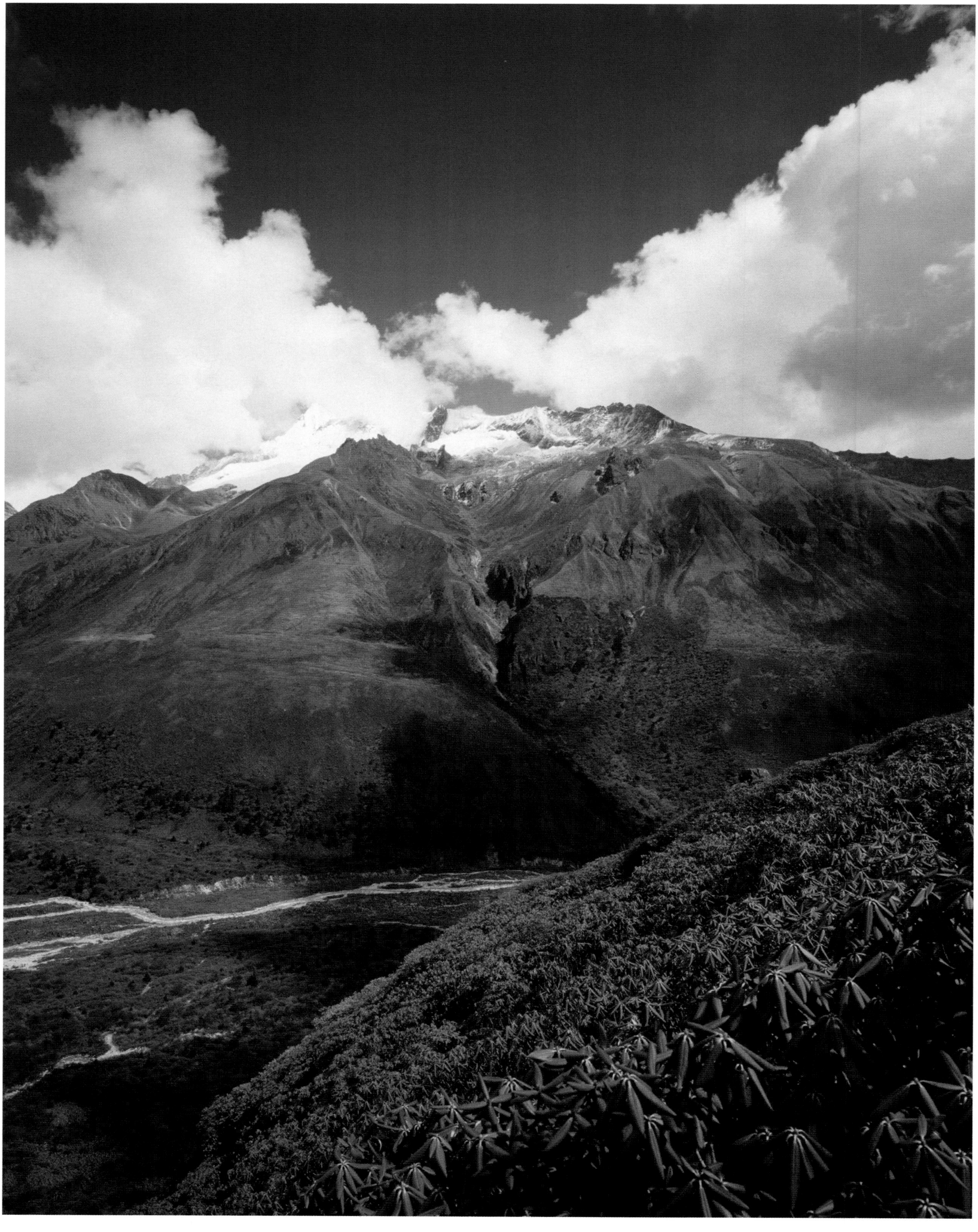

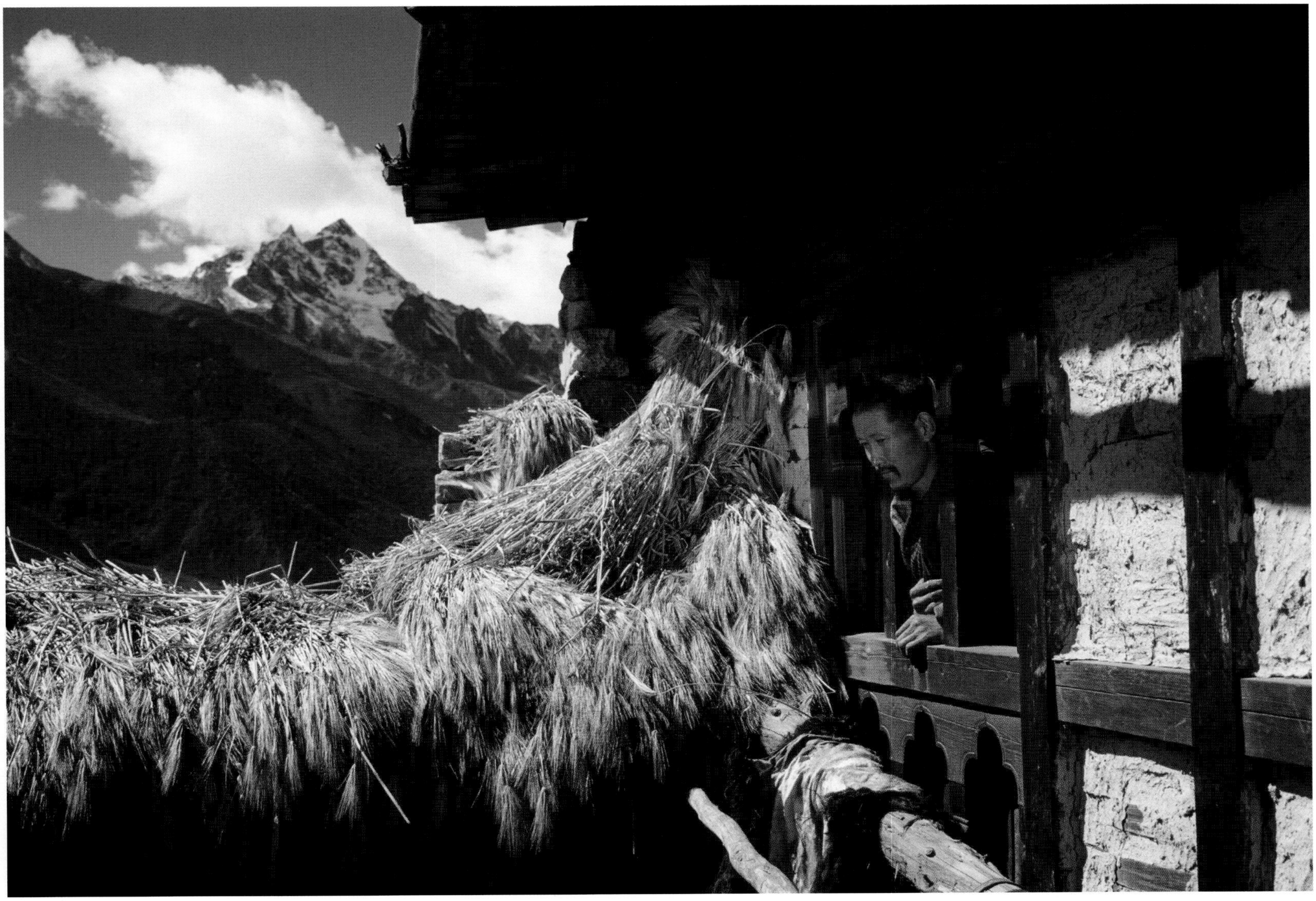

Villagers in Lunana often stack grain alongside their houses to prevent wild animals from eating their harvest.

Left: The trail to Lunana, which passes over the 16,793-foot Karchung Pass, is dotted with rhododendron plants.

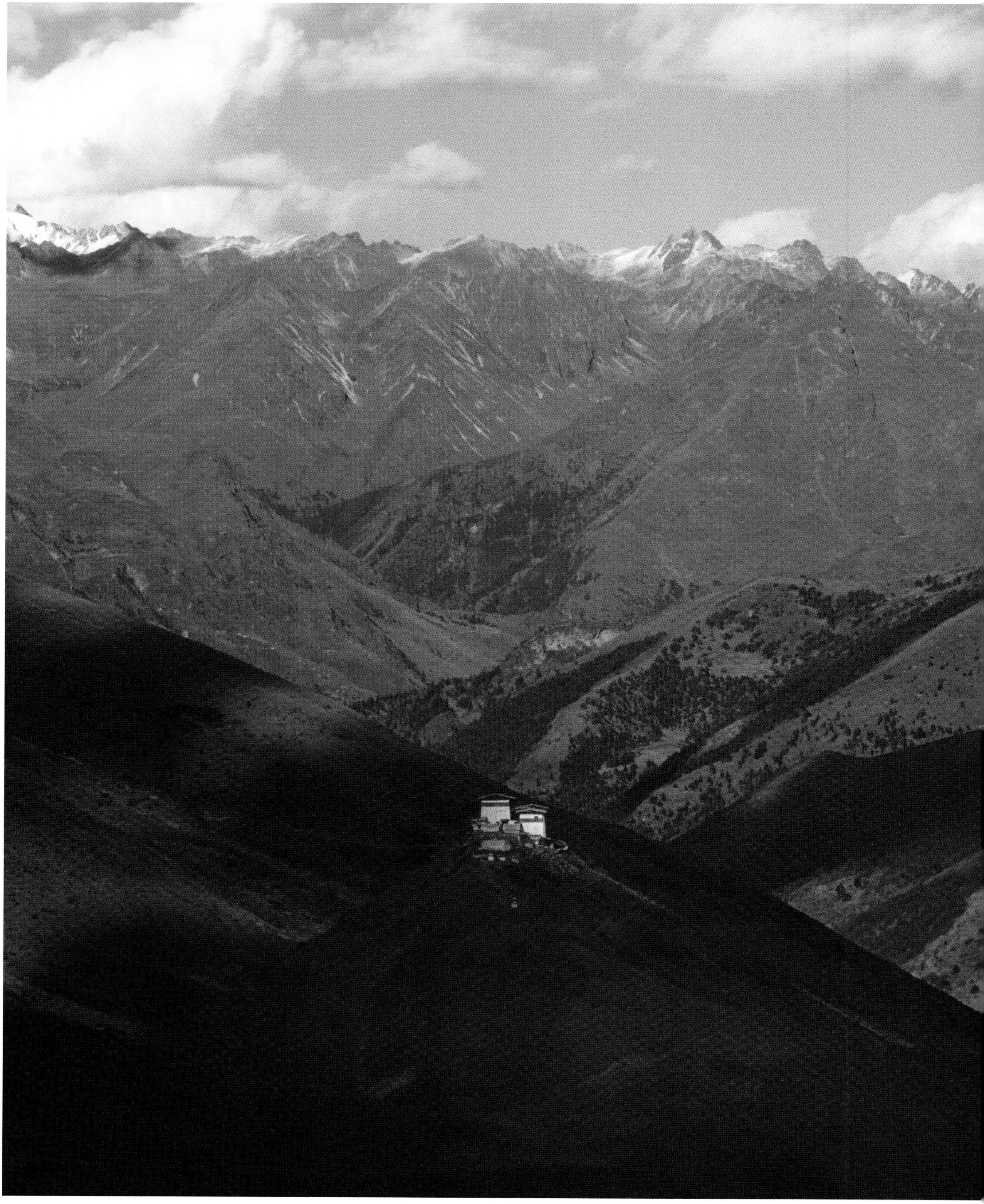

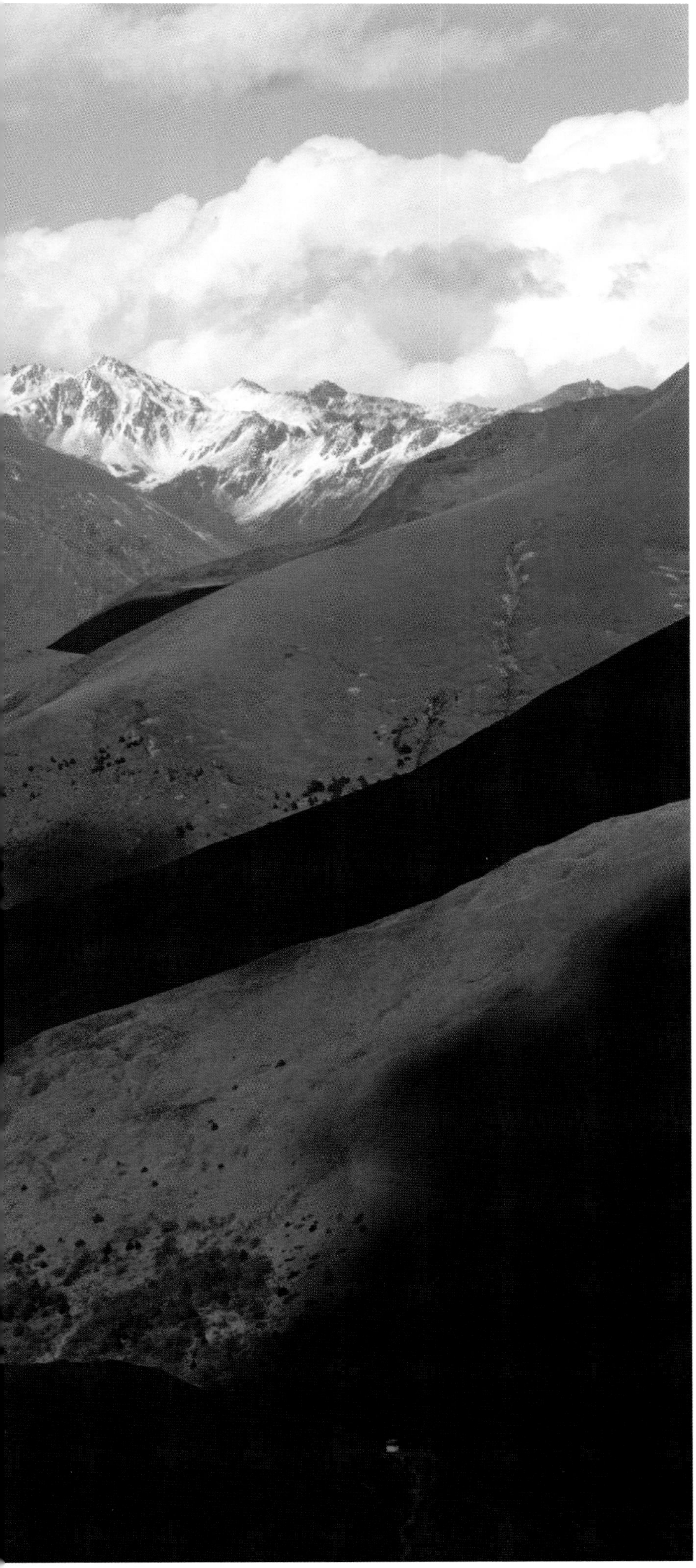

Built in the seventeenth century, Lingshi Dzong (13,841 feet) is the administrative headquarters of the surrounding area. Before the border was closed in the 1950s, the dzong also served to control the flow of trade between Bhutan and Tibet.

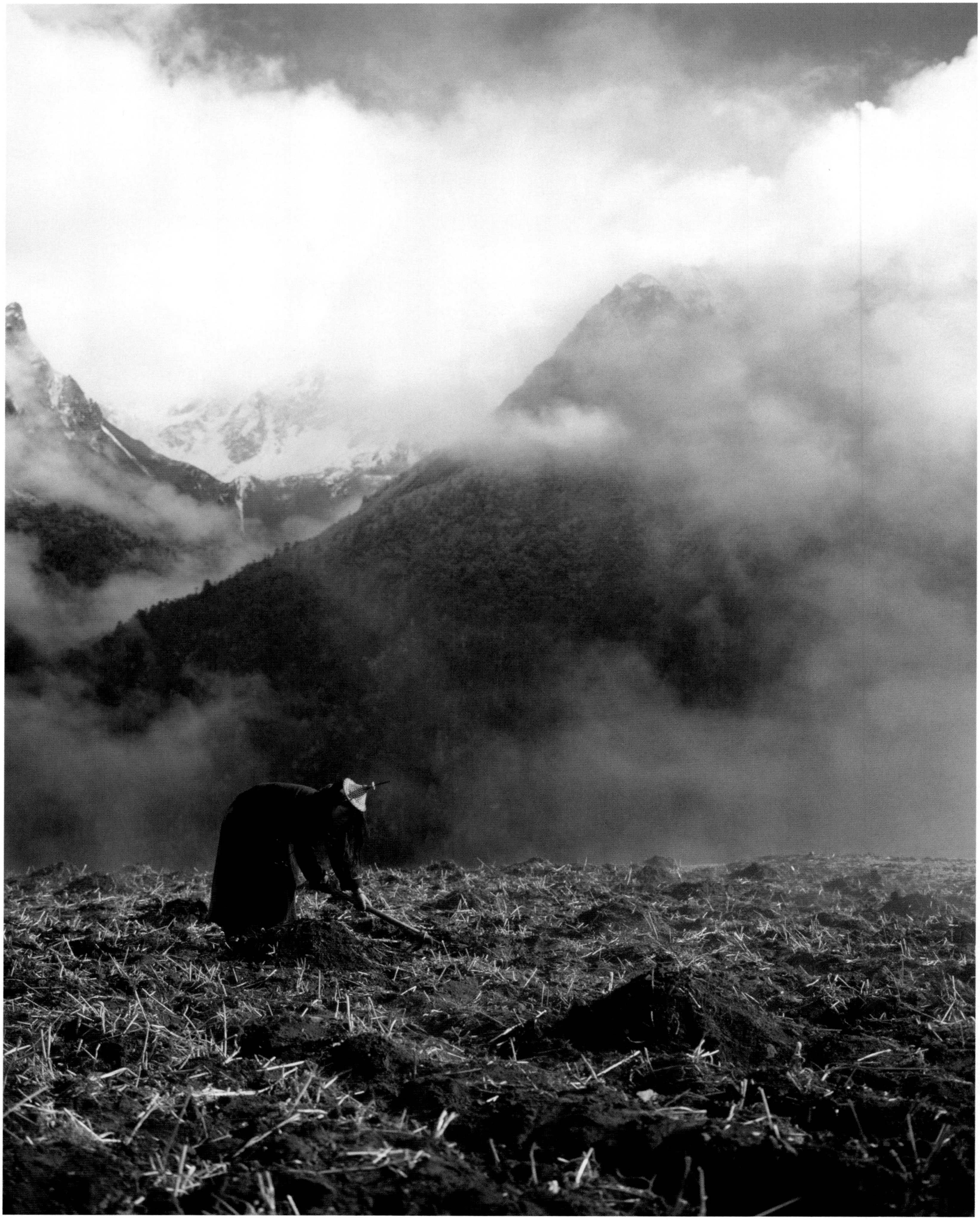

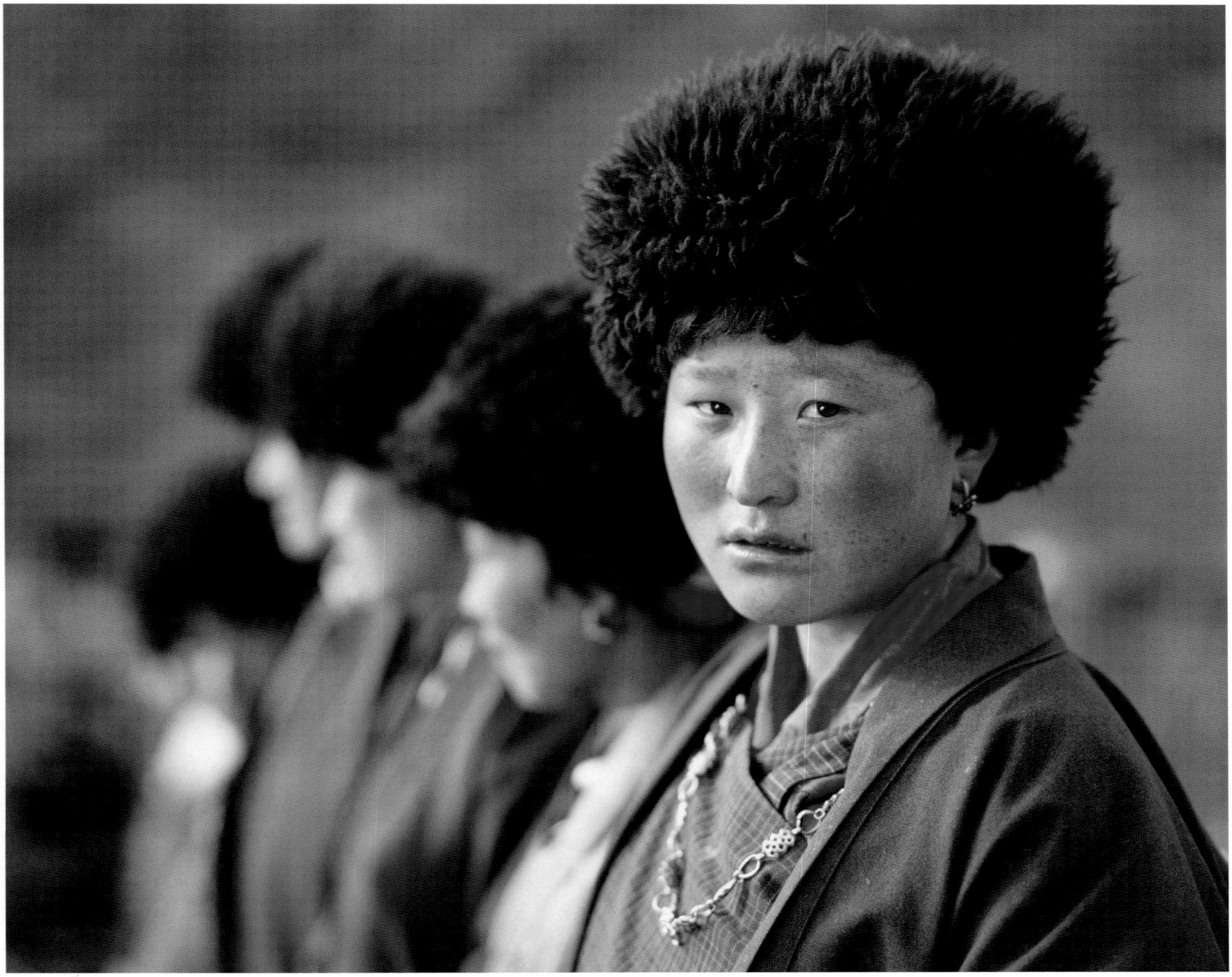

Women from Thanza often wear handmade wool hats to ward off the cold Himalayan chill.

Left: Against a backdrop of misty mountains, a Layap villager digs for turnips early in the morning. Bhutanese villagers in the northern frontier are able to grow only a limited selection of vegetables due to the extreme altitude and short summer.

Following spread: Pema Khandu, 63, gazes across her recently harvested field of barley to the 23,288-foot flat peaks of the aptly named Zhongphu Gang, or "Table," Mountain.

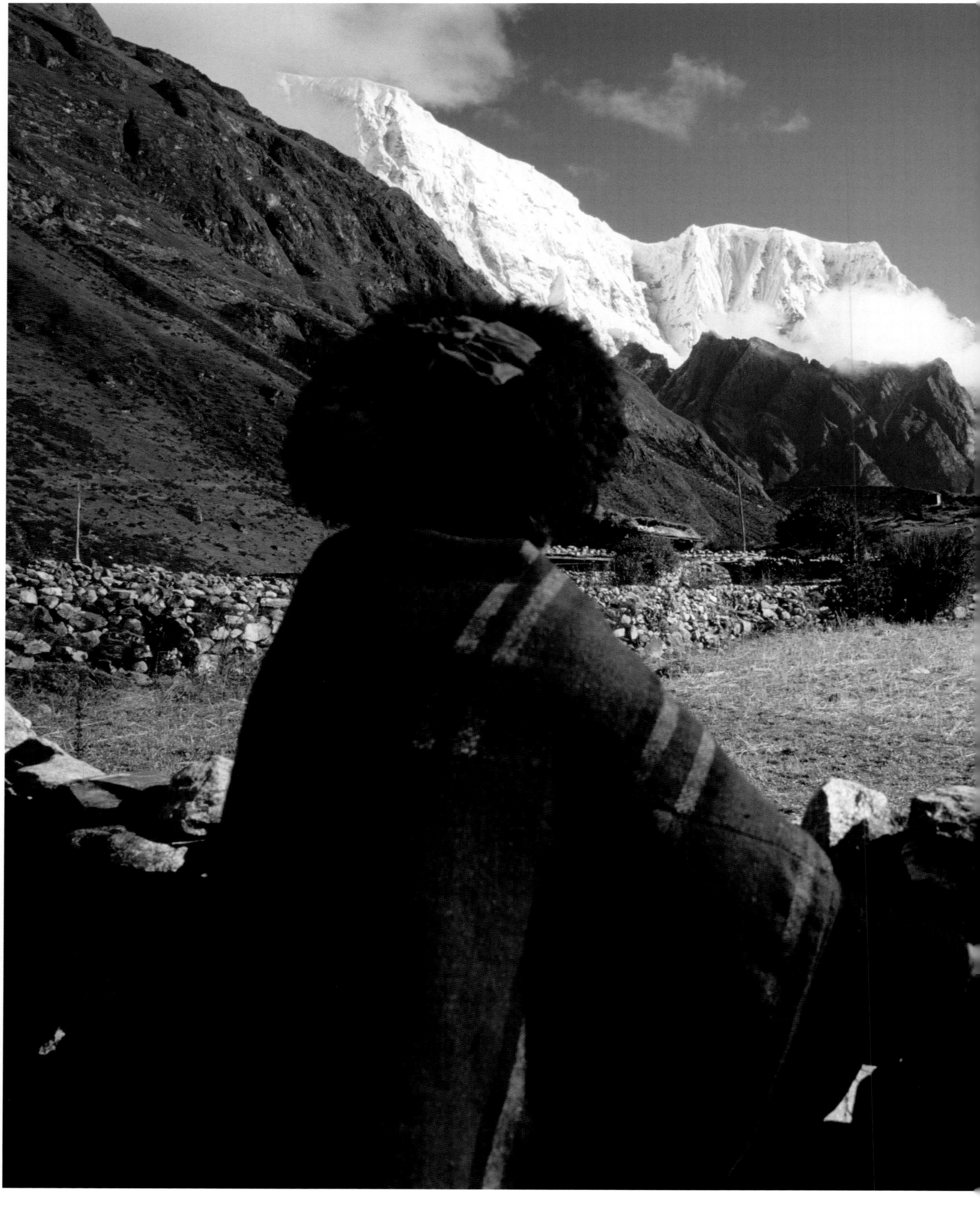

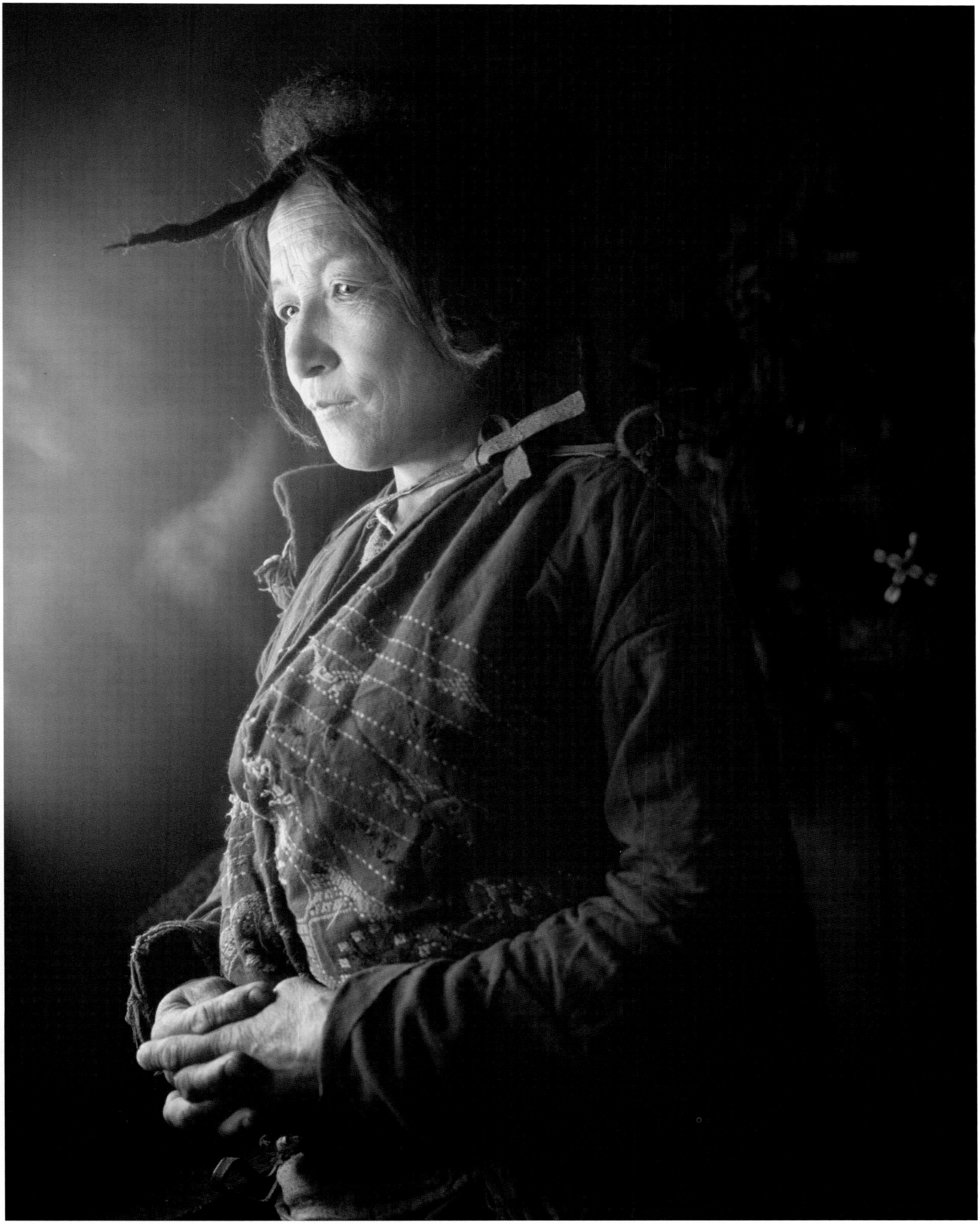

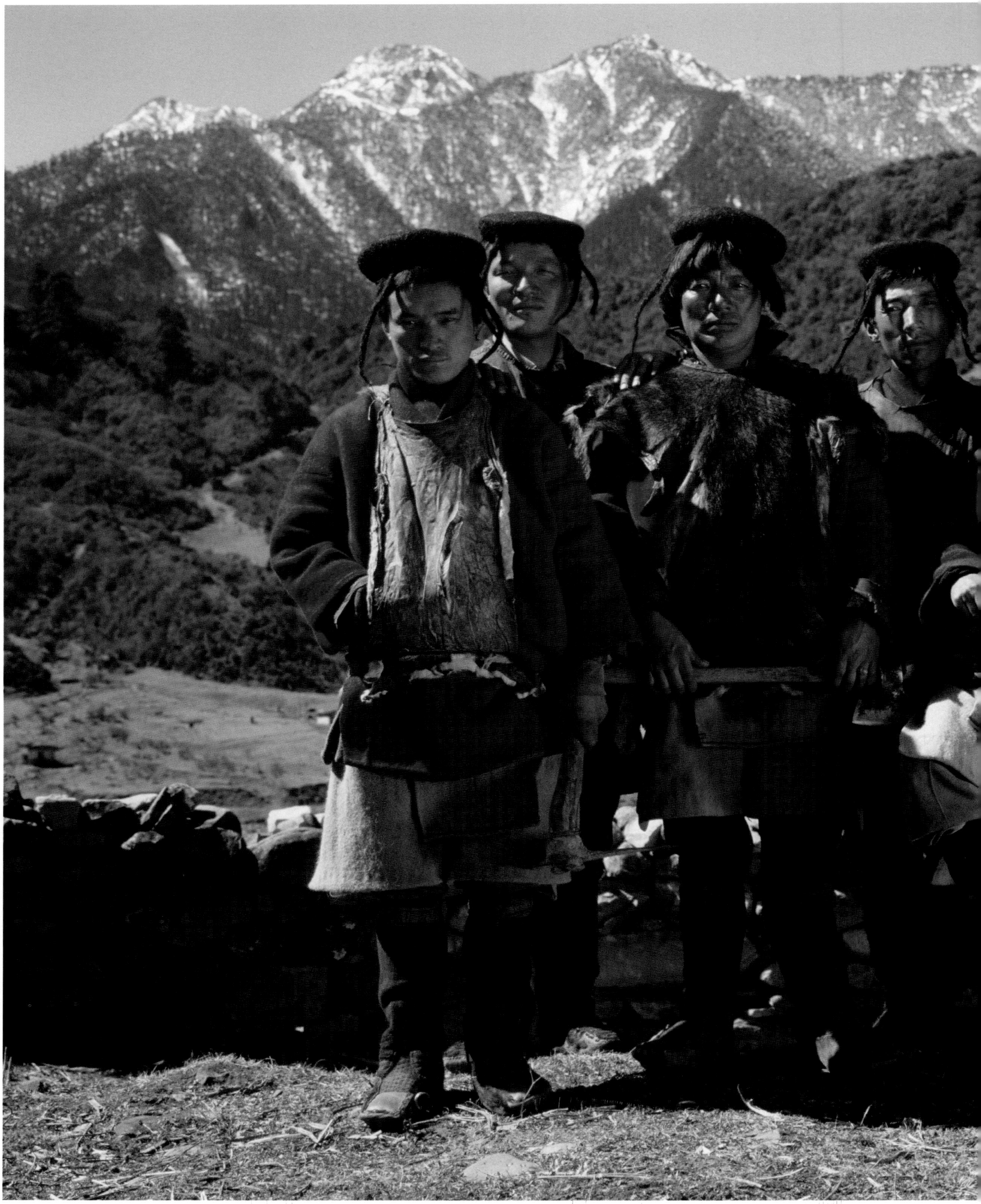

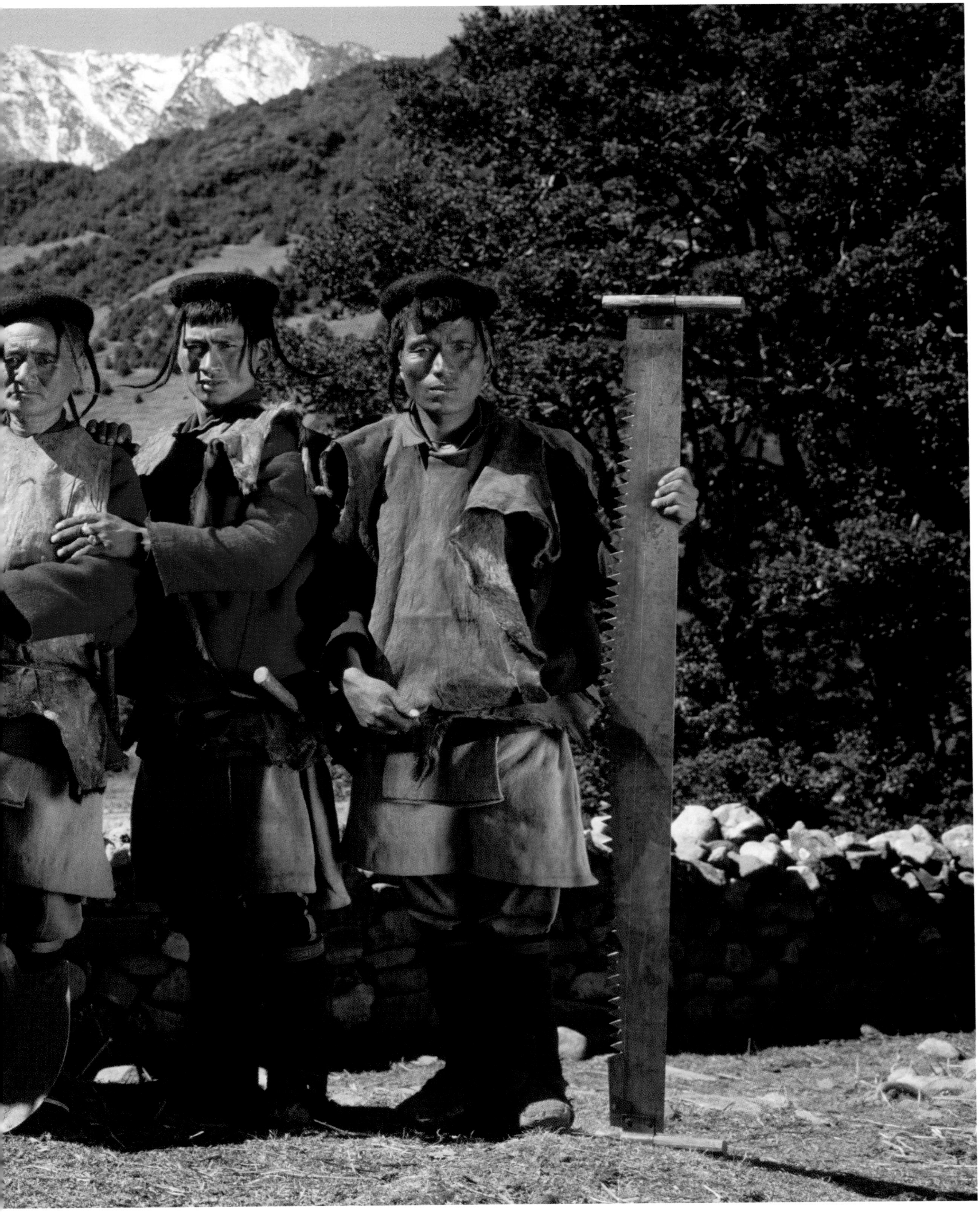

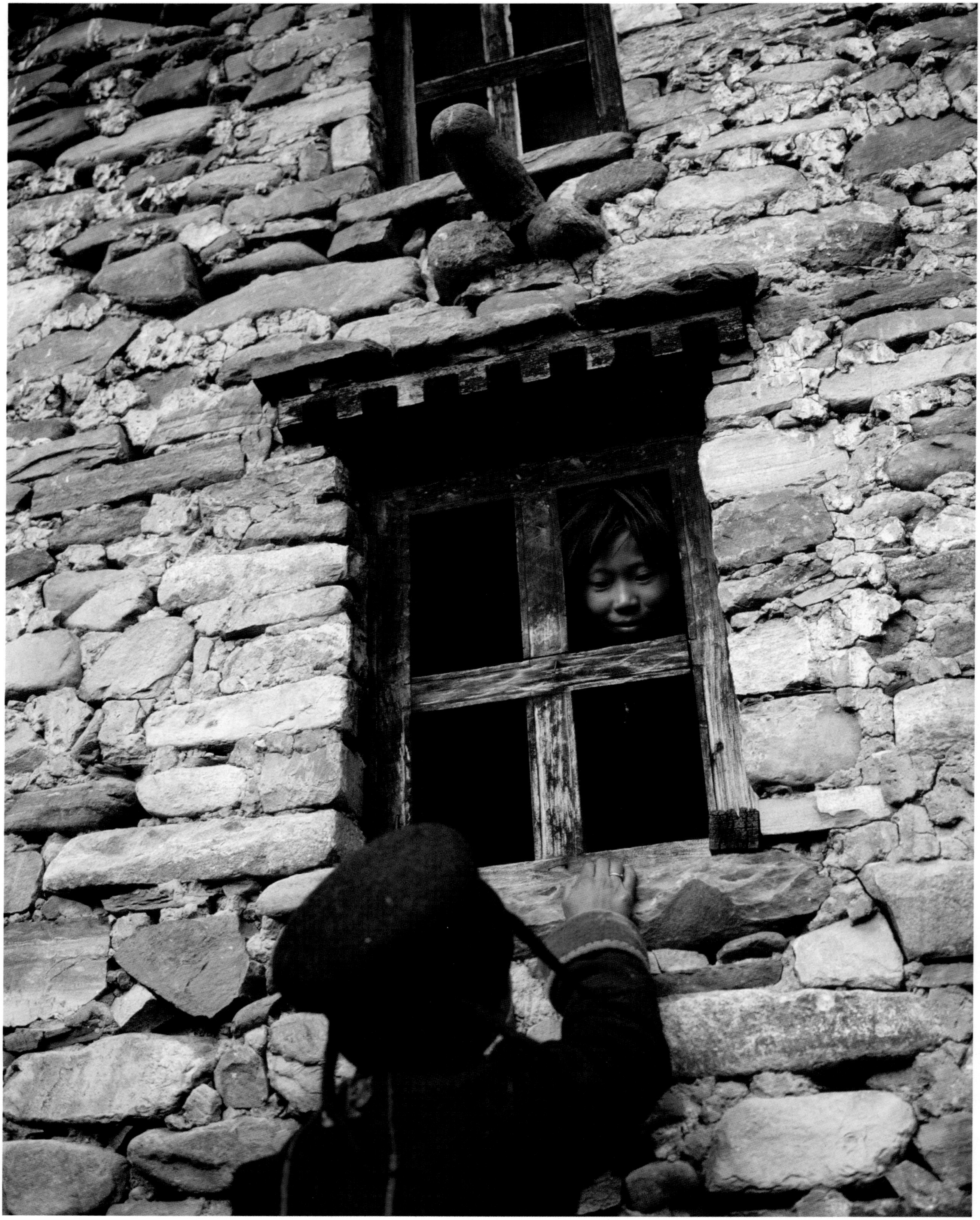

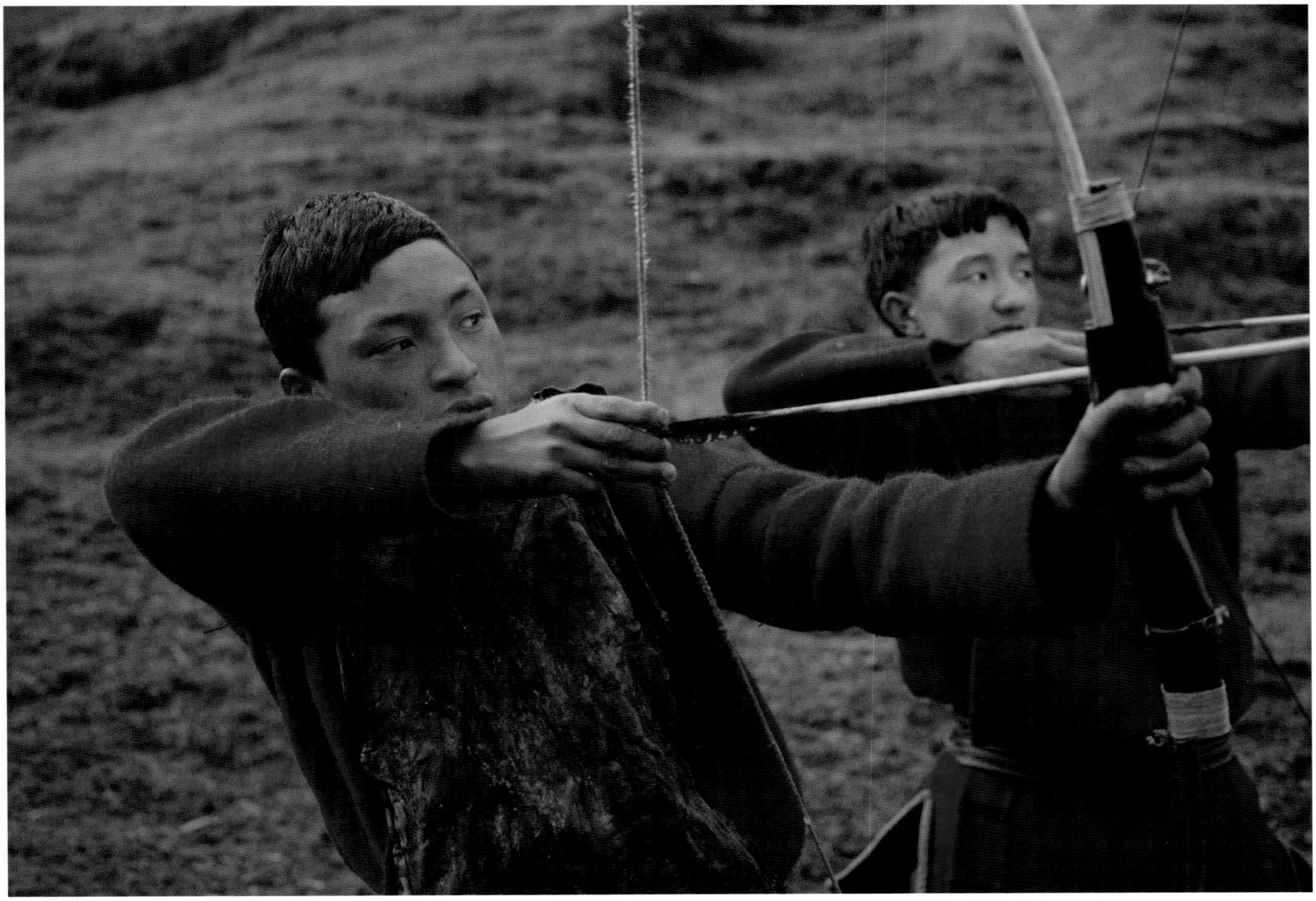

Archery is the national sport of Bhutan. In Sakteng many youngsters continue to use traditional bows and arrows, which are made from bamboo collected at lower elevations.

Left: Leki, 13, chats with her friend Tenzin, 14. The window of Leki's farmhouse is decorated with a stone phallus used to ward off evil.

Previous spread: A group of men from Sakteng pose with their farm tools. Wool jackets and skirts, cow-skin vests, knee-high boots, yak-hair hats, and a long knife held at the waist are commonly seen on Brokpa men.

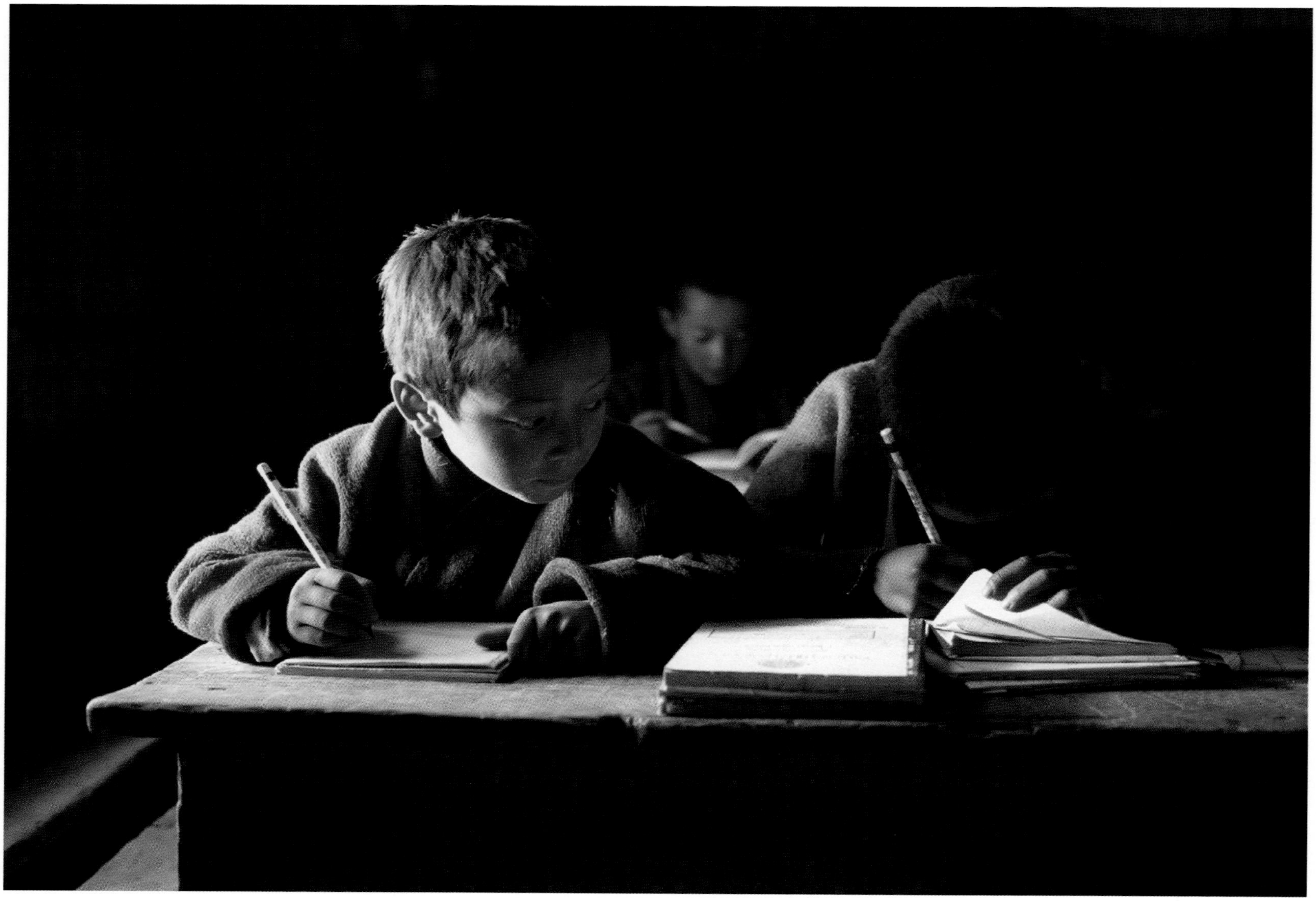

A young student from the Sakteng elementary school struggles to see his neighbor's homework.

Right: During recess, a schoolgirl from Sakteng draws a picture of the legendary ape-like yeti, known in Bhutan as the *migoi*.

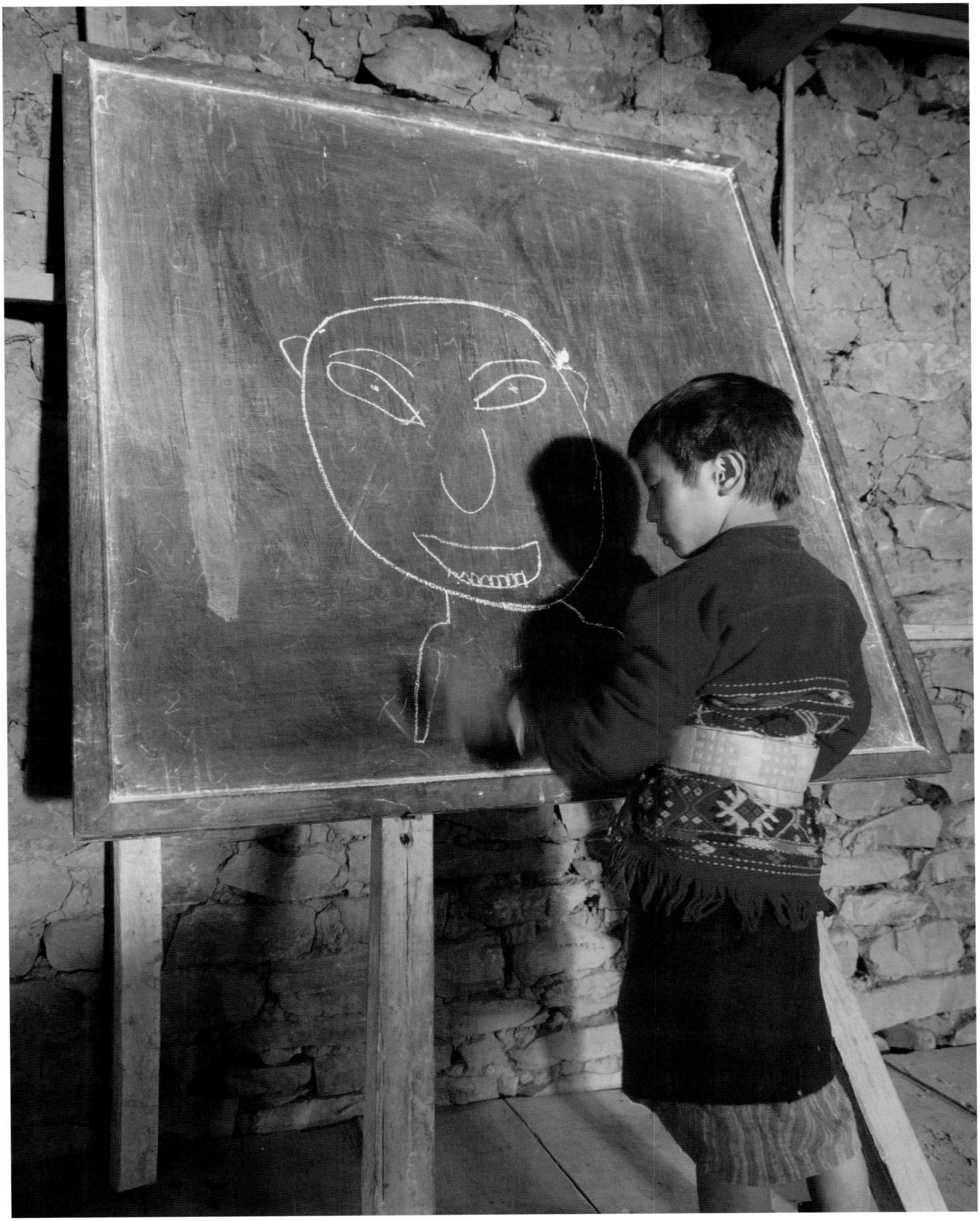

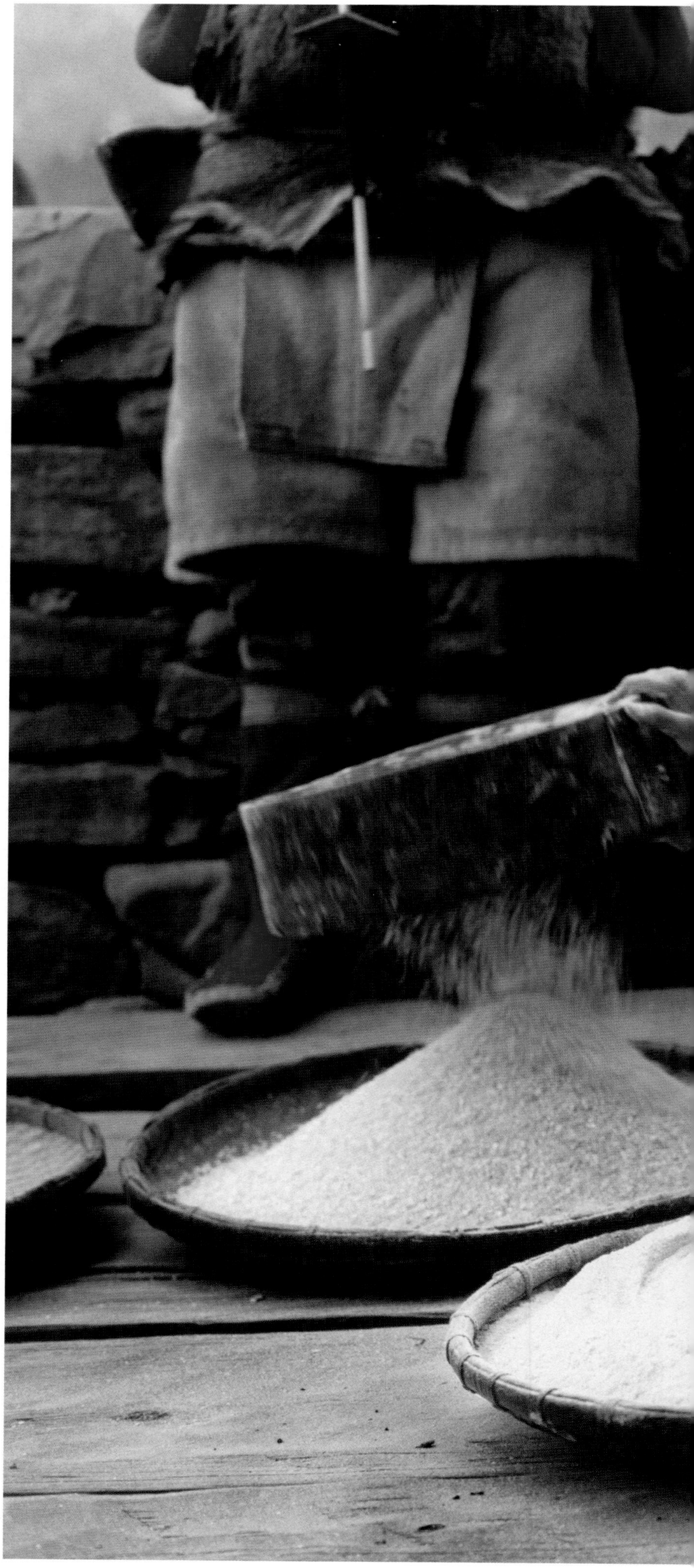

An elderly woman sifts ground corn into different grades of size and quality. The finely ground corn is used to feed sheep and make pancake-like flat bread.

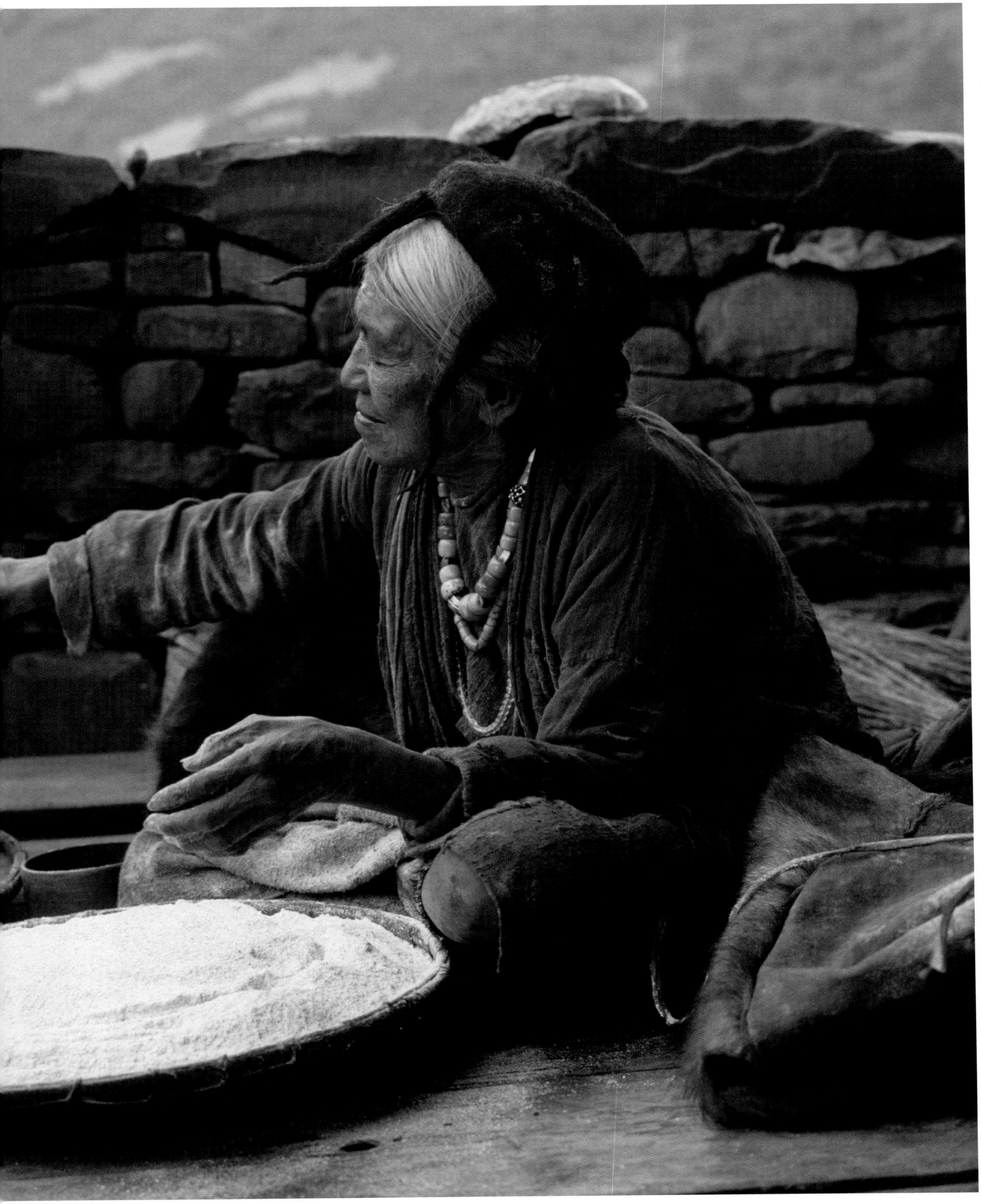

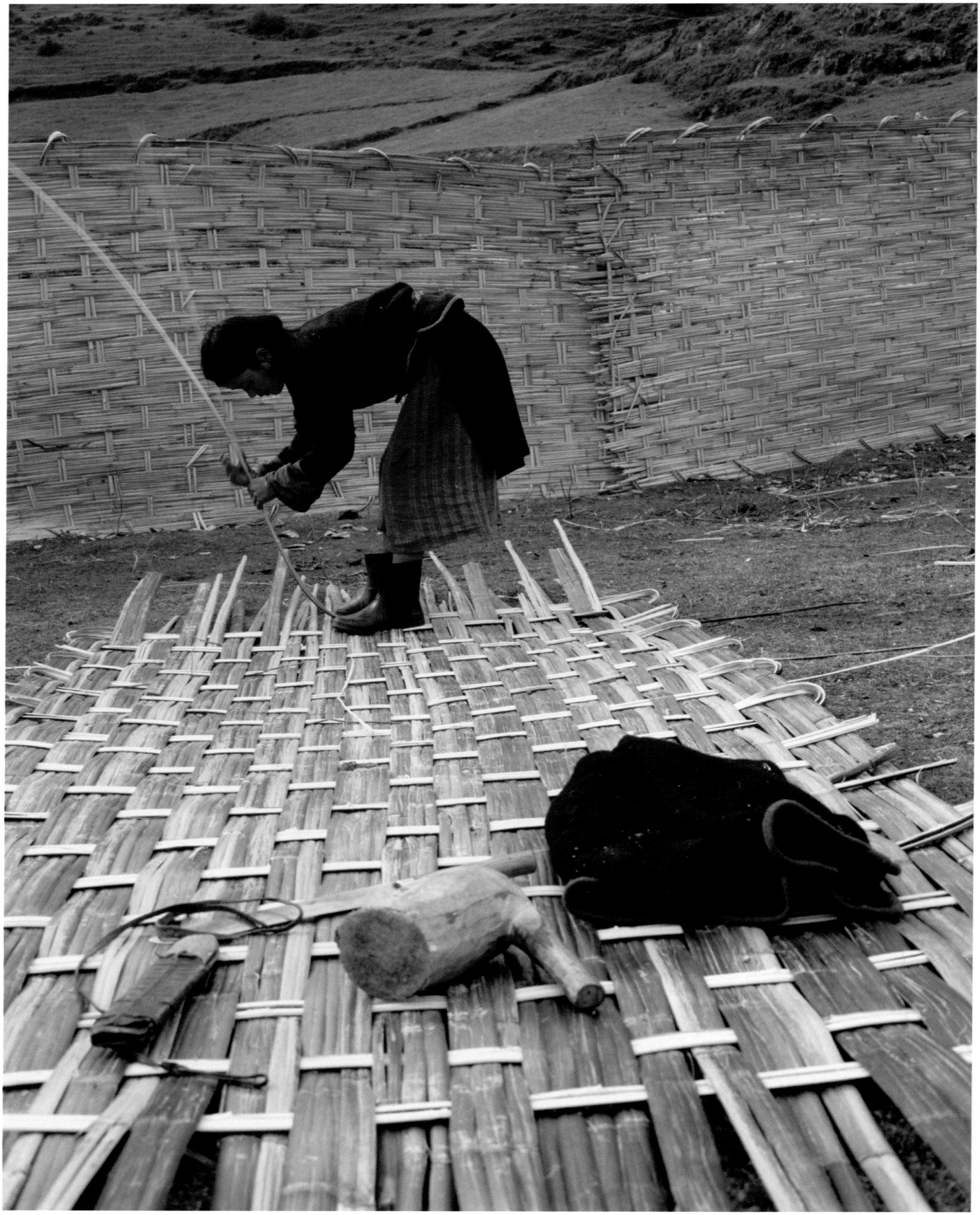

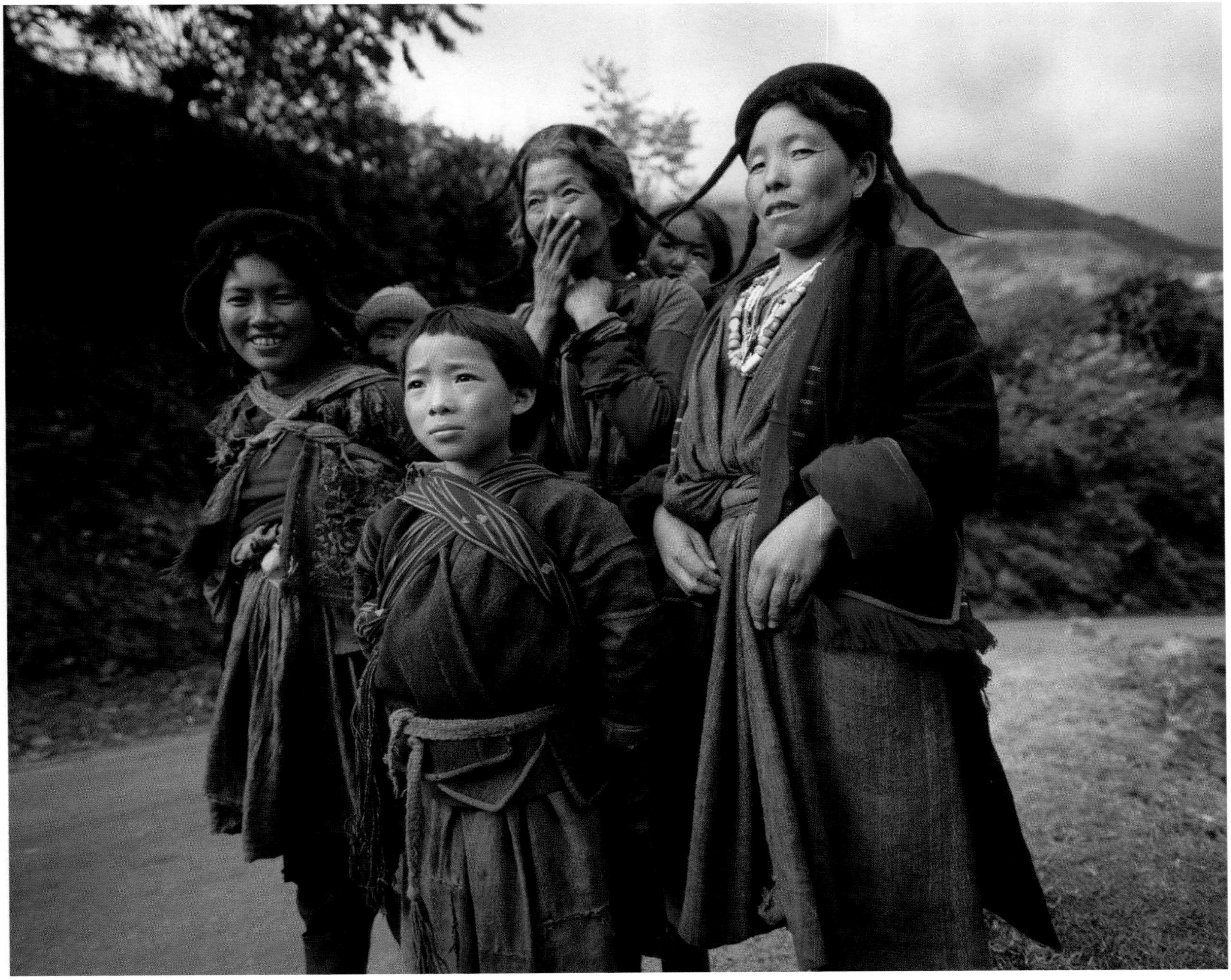

A group of women and children from Merak wait by the side of the road near Wamrong in eastern Bhutan.

Left: A village girl weaves freshly cut bamboo strips into a fence used to corral sheep and yaks. The fences are also brought to the Trashigang area and sold for one dollar each. The large wooden hammer in the foreground is used to smash the bamboo so that it can be cut into thin strips.

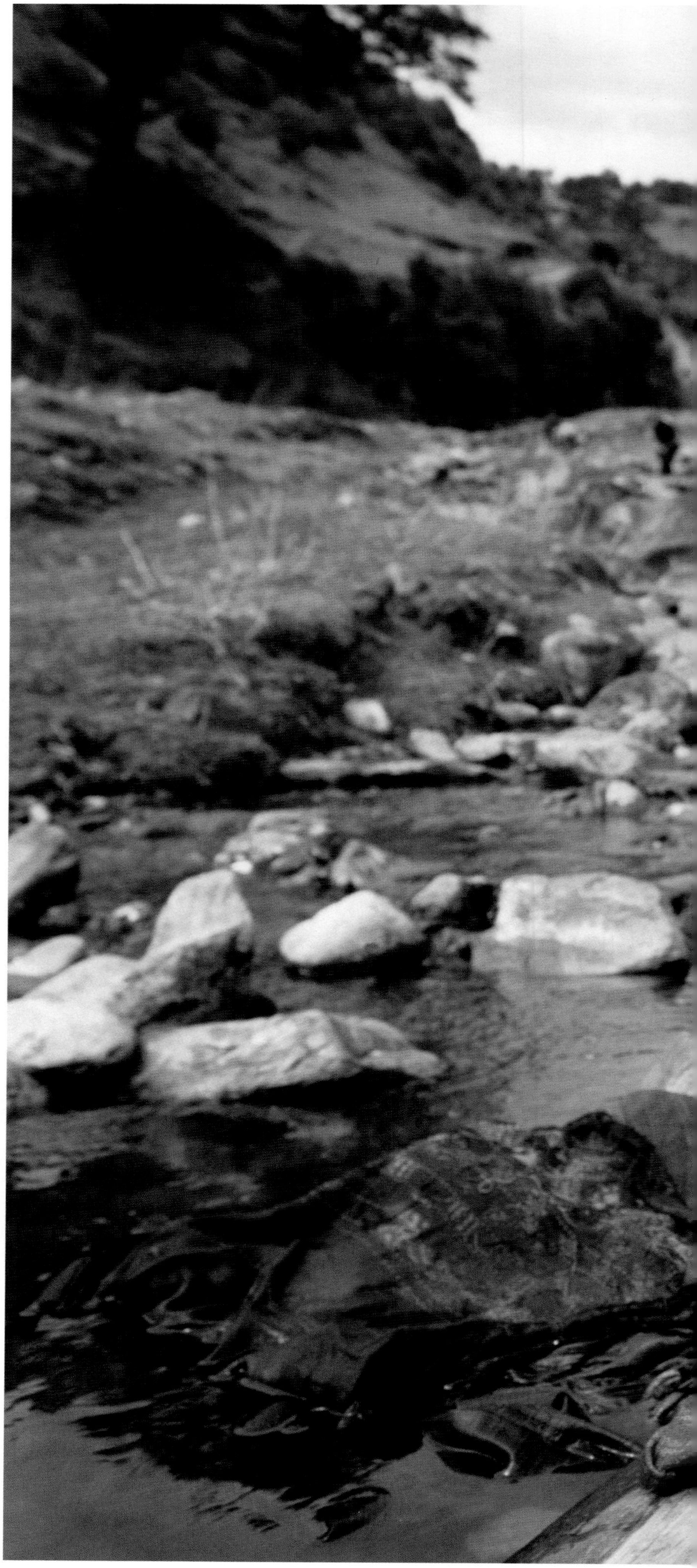

Kinley, 32, briefly pauses while washing her clothes to check on a nearby commotion. The unusual hats Brokpas wear are made from yak hair and function to keep the owner dry in a rainstorm by funneling water down the thin strands along the outer edge of the hat.

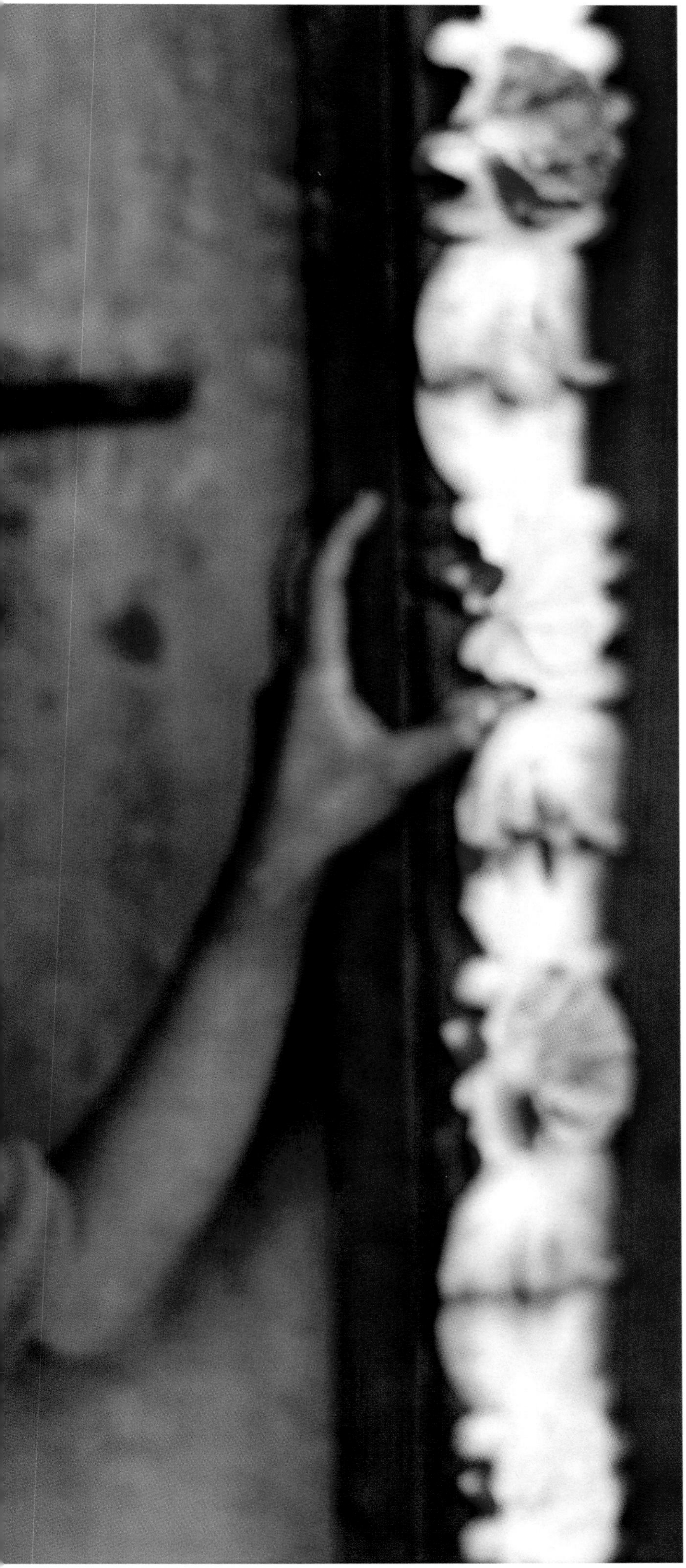

Santamon, 12, looks out from the doorway of his family's house. Many Lhotshampas use backpack-like baskets for farm work that feature a strap worn across the forehead for extra balance and support.

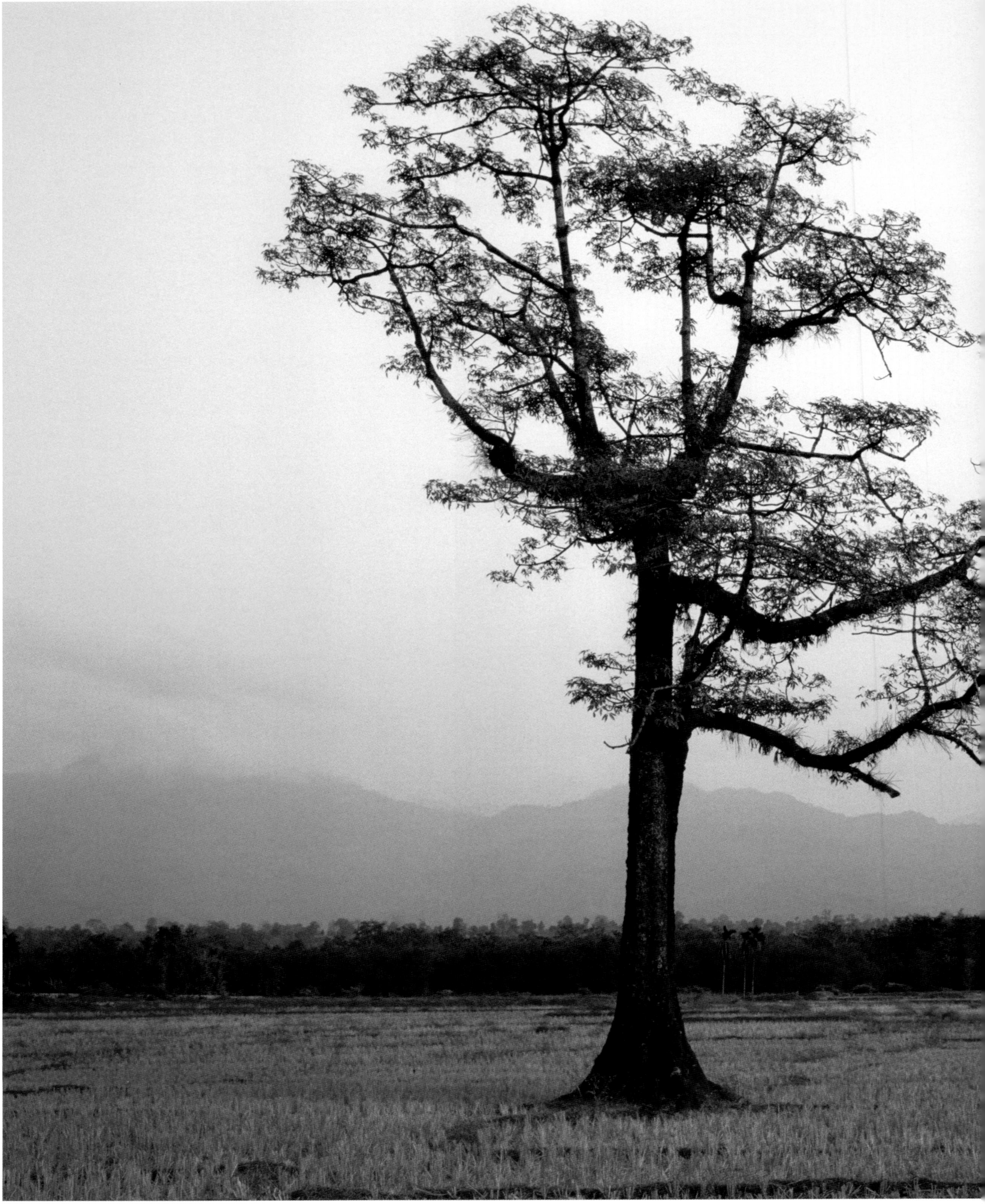

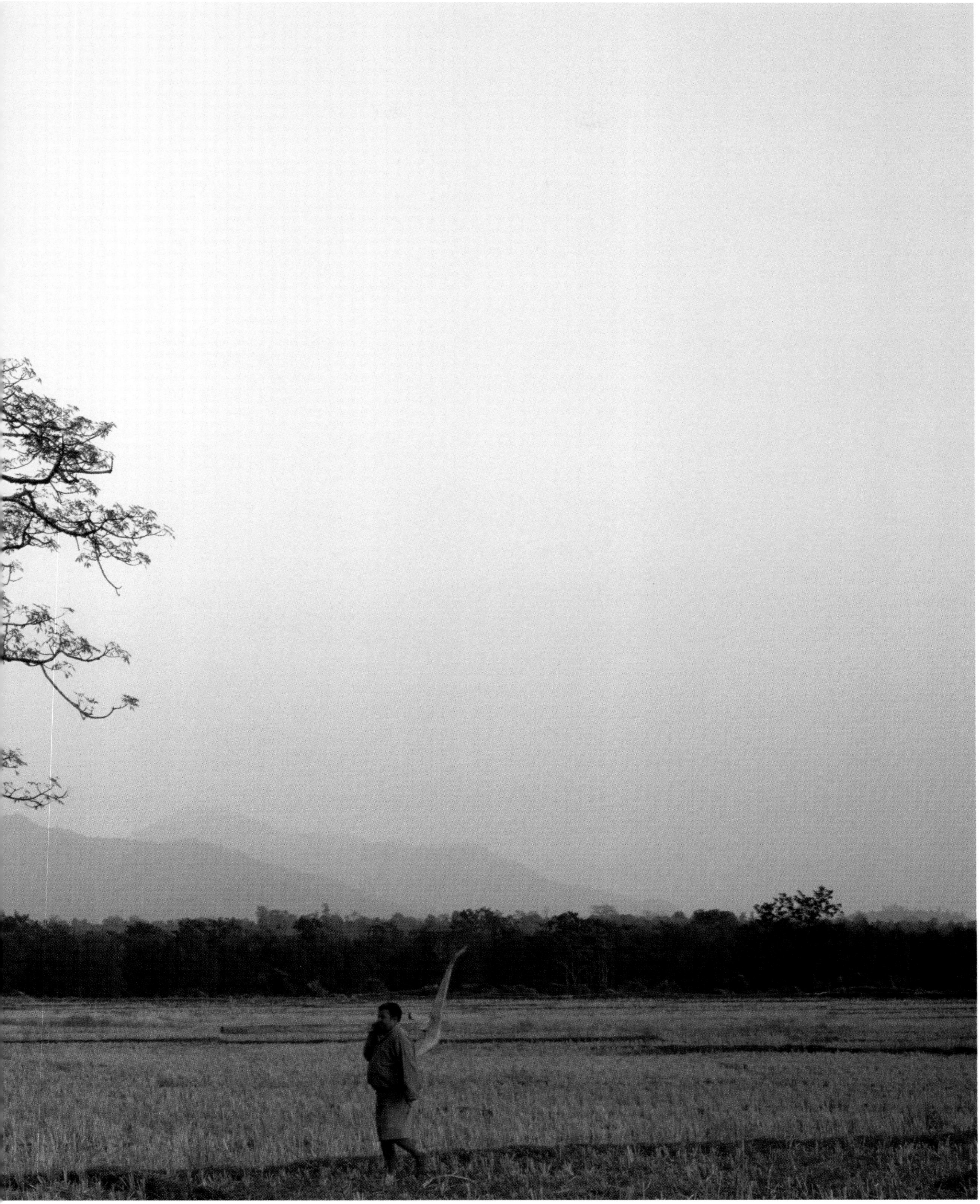

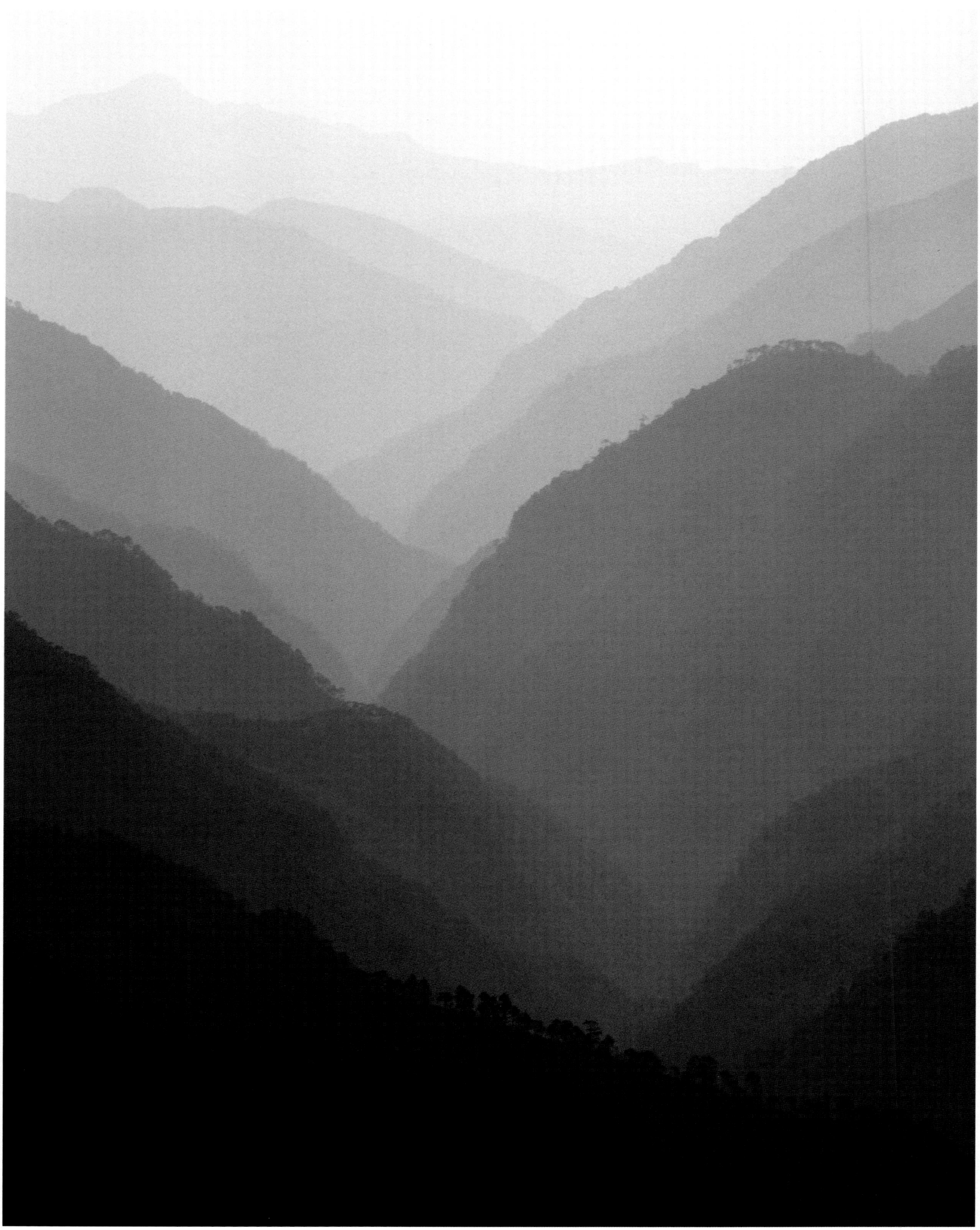

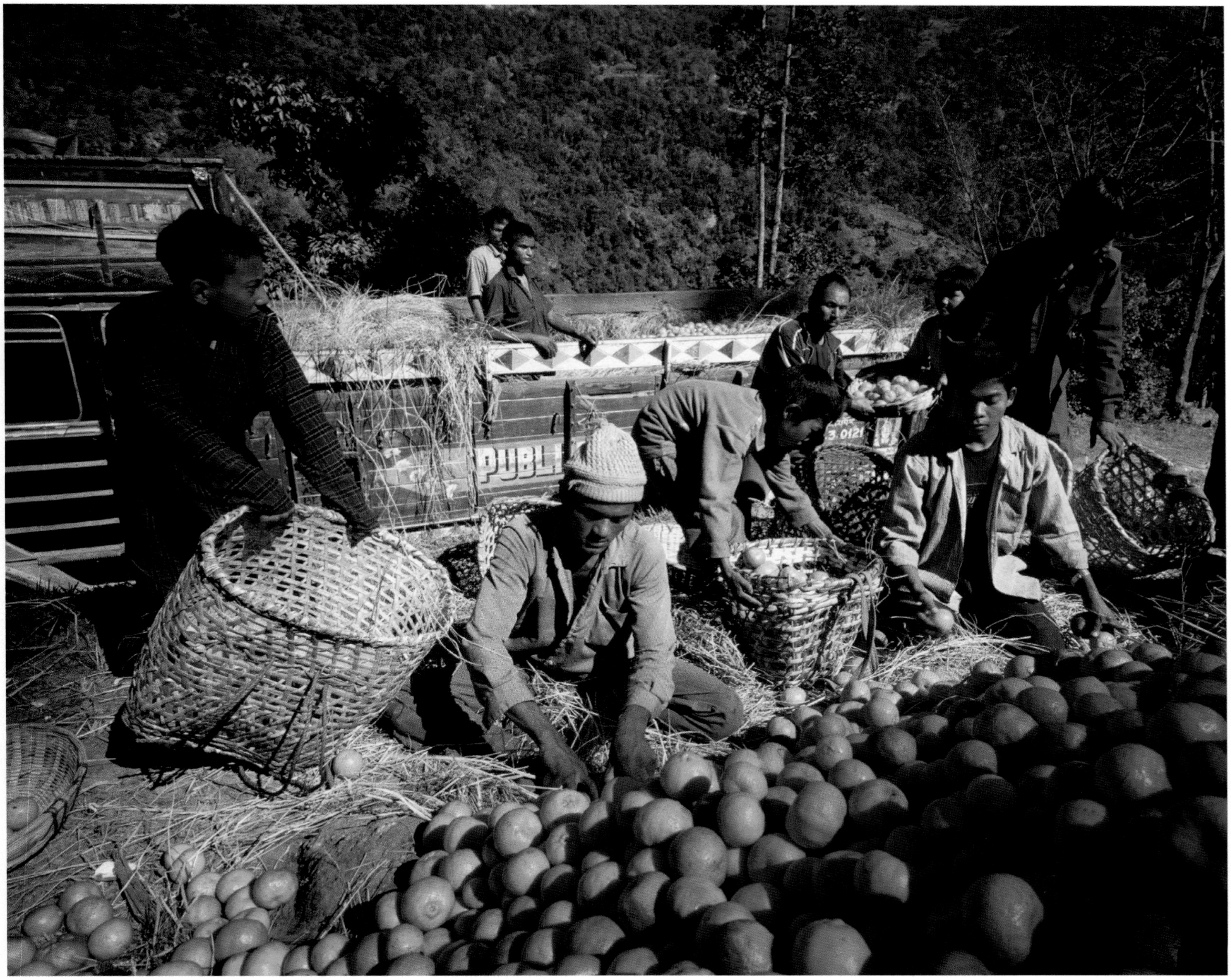

A group of villagers sort oranges according to quality and size.

Left: A view of the countryside between Zhemgang and Gelephu reveals an undulating stretch of land that is prone to landslides in the rainy summer months.

Previous spread: A villager from Gelephu heads home in the evening carrying a wooden plow. A small portion of the country around Gelephu is totally flat, a contrast to the rest of Bhutan.

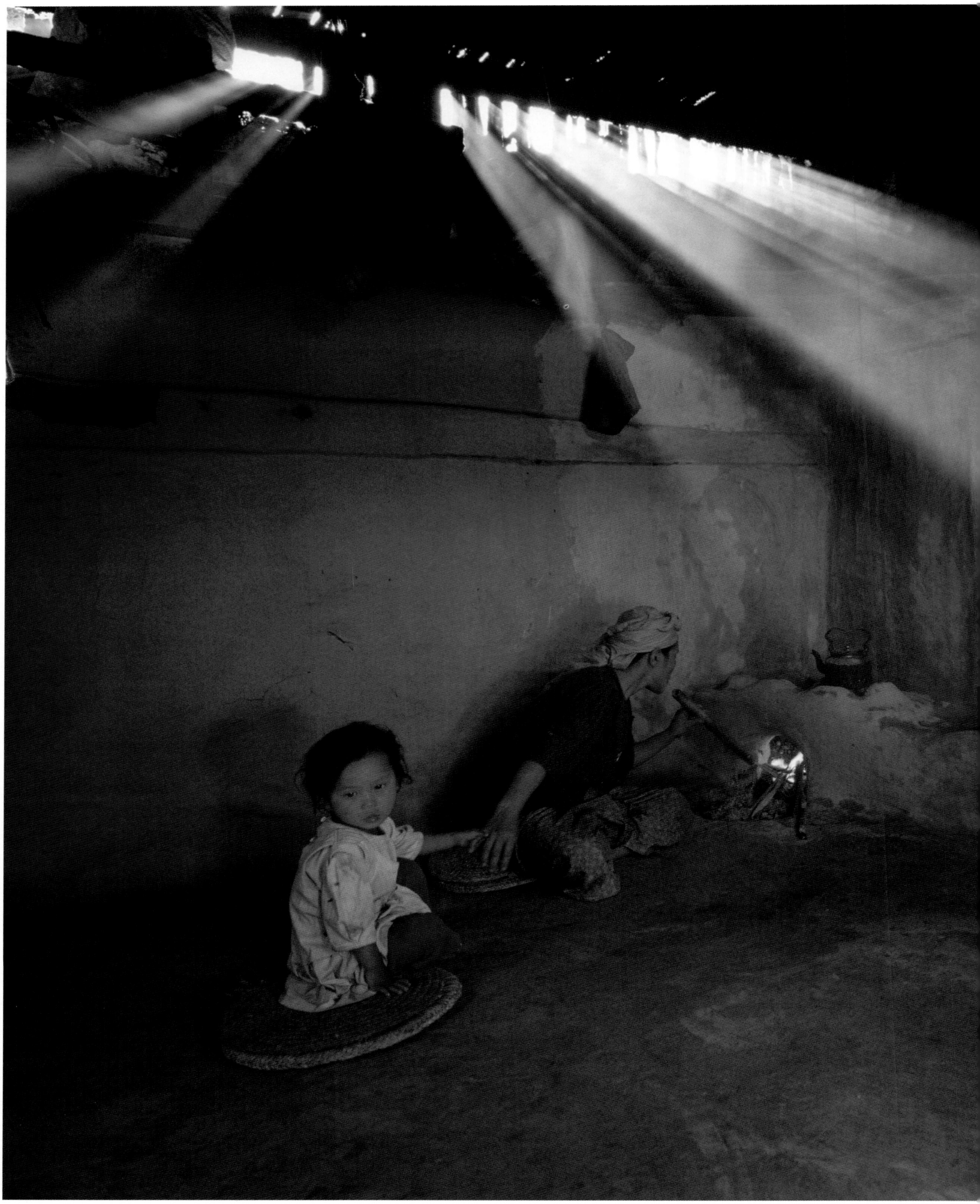

A mother blows on her kitchen fireplace with a bamboo tube while stretching out to comfort her young child. The kitchens of most Lhotshampa homes are separate from the living quarters to minimize the risk from fires.

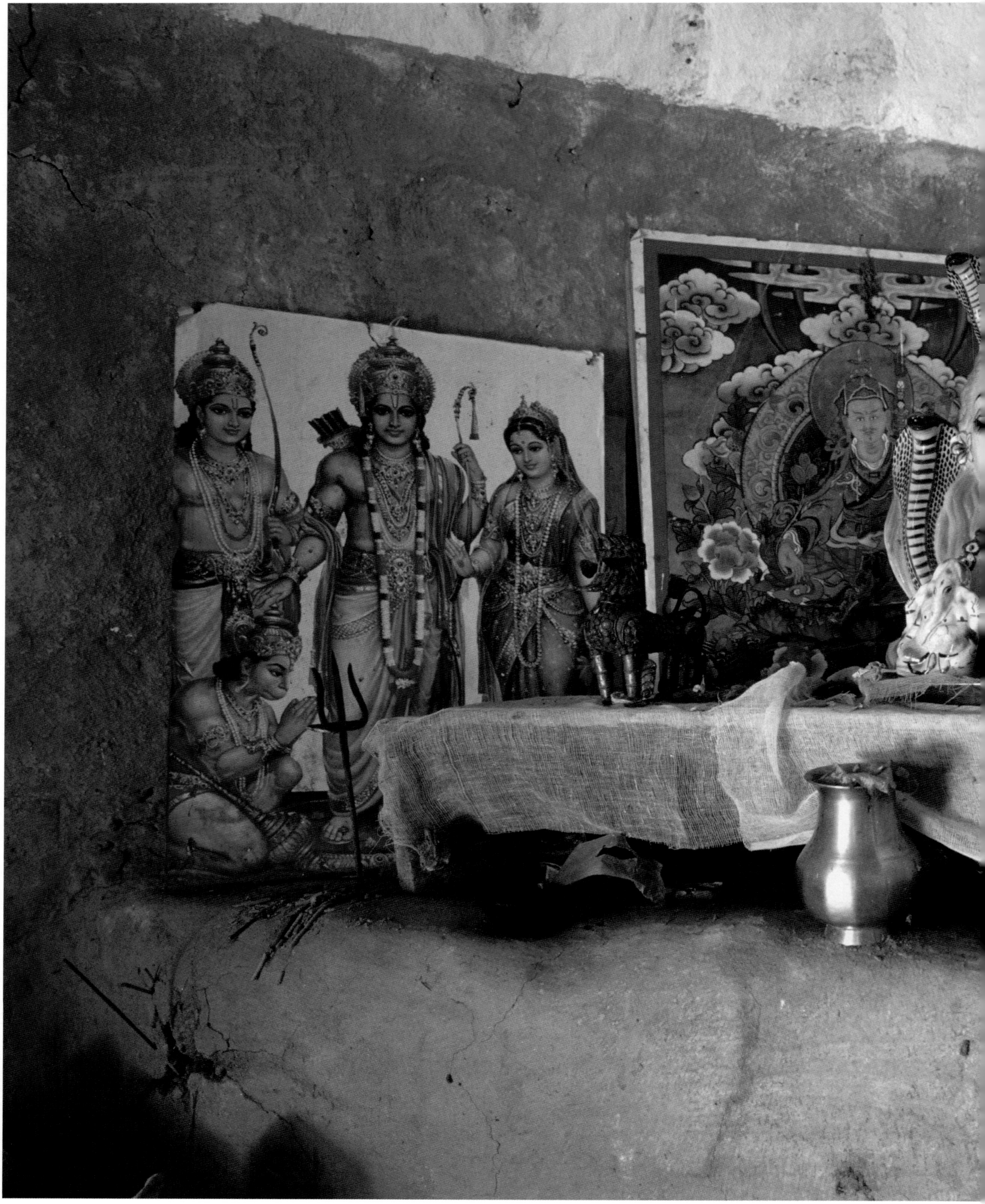

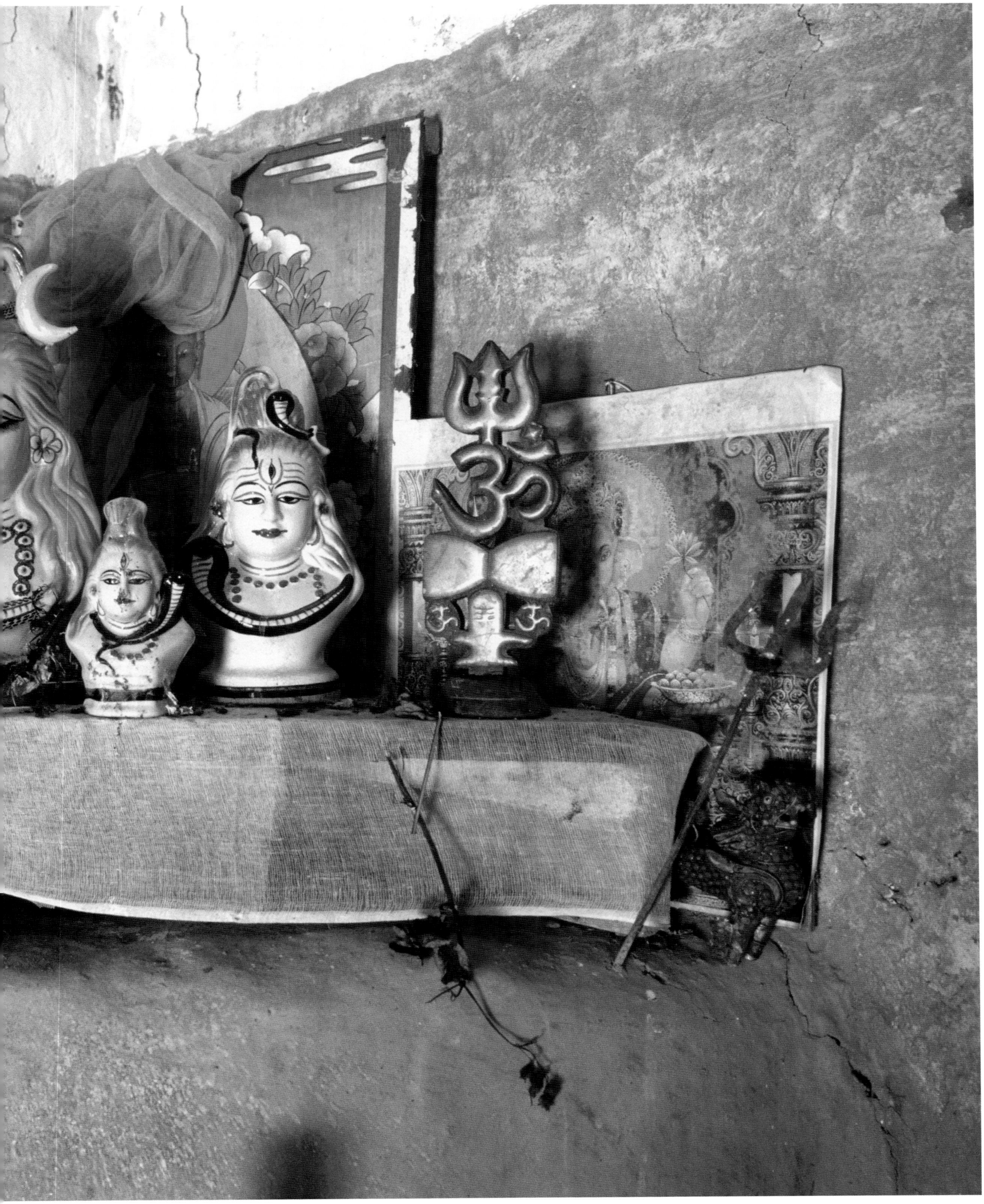

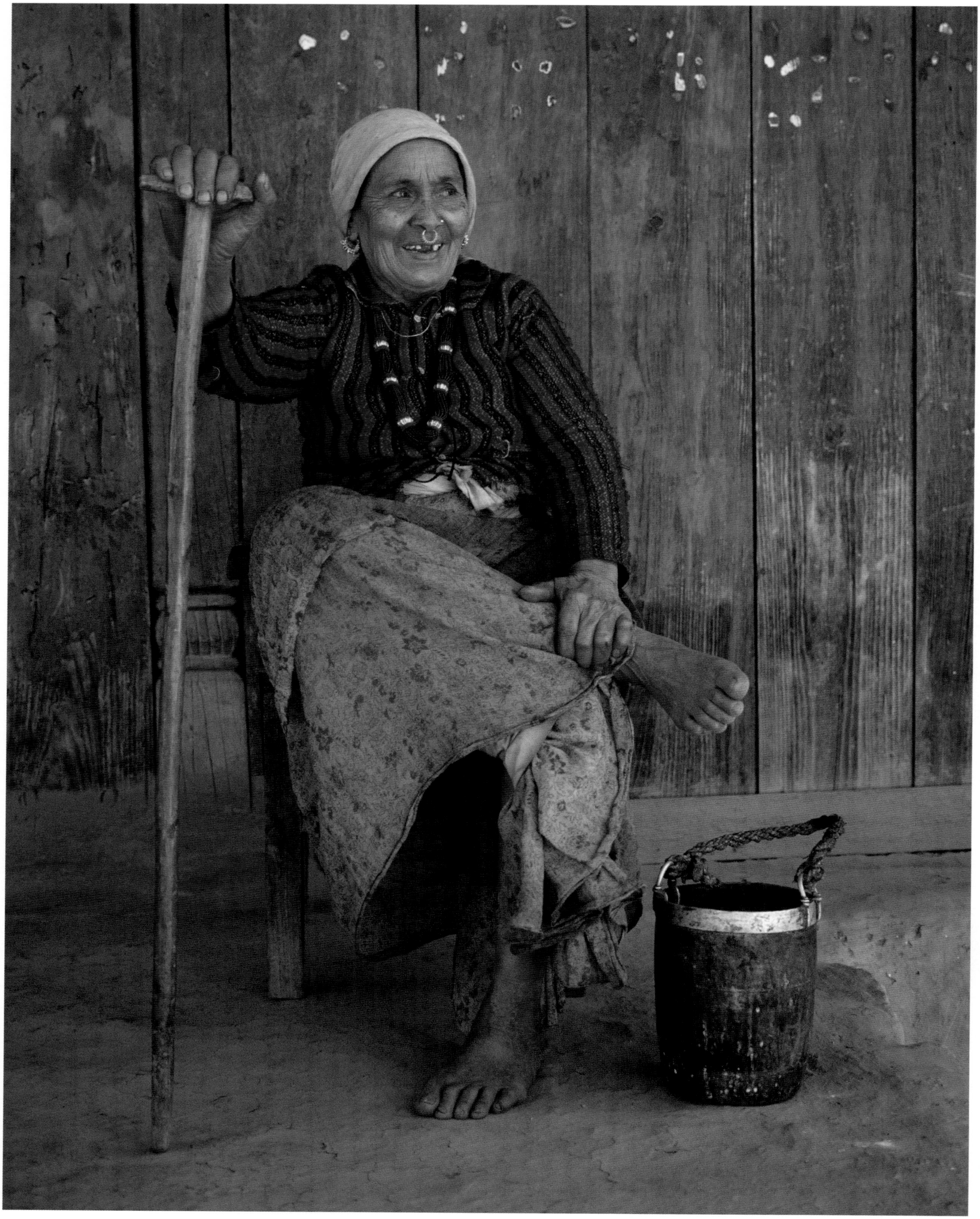

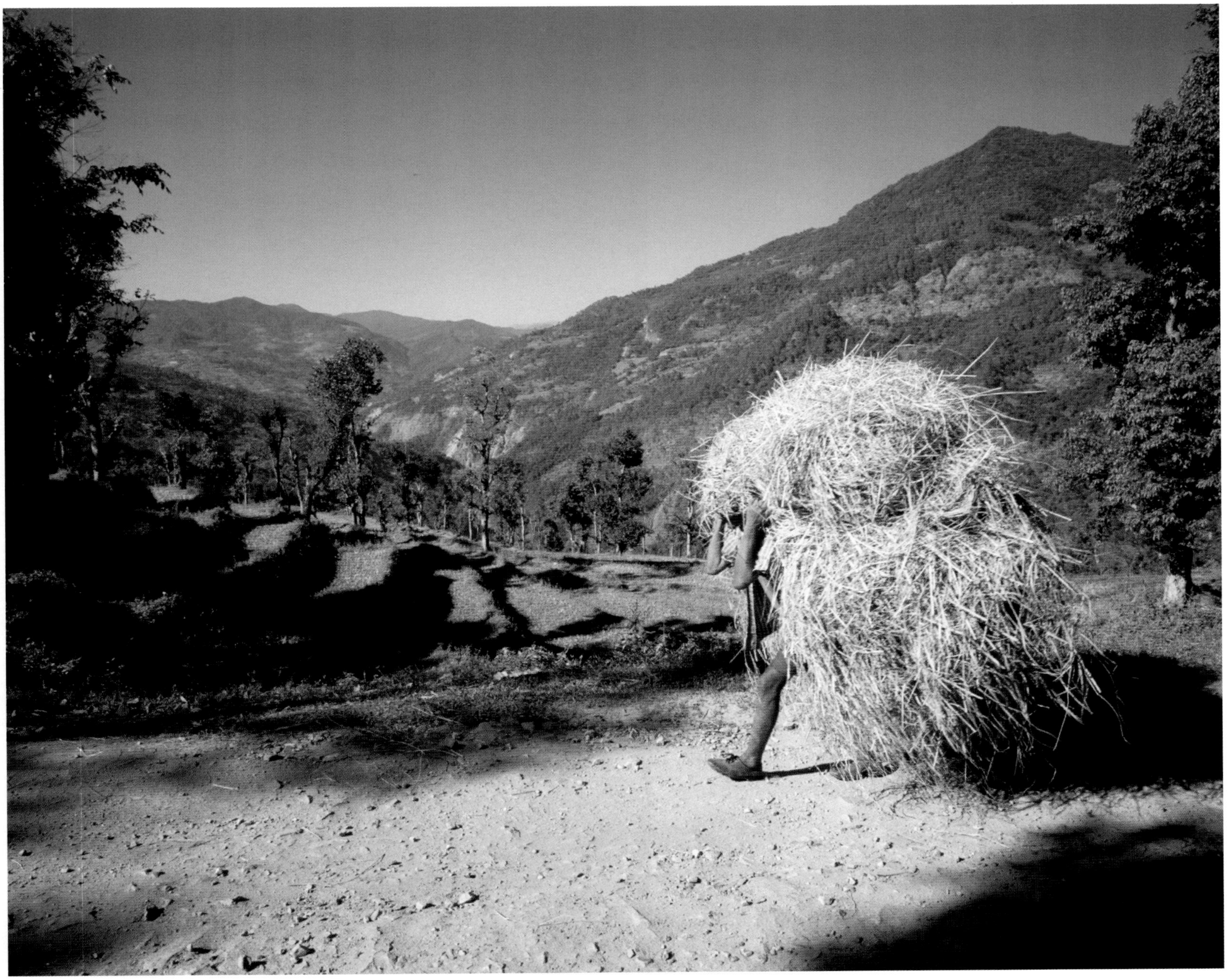

A Lhotshampa villager carries a load of hay on his back along the road leading up from Dagapela to Dagana.

Left: Monmaya, 77, enjoys a laugh sitting on the packed-earth deck adjacent to her house.

Previous spread: A Lhotshampa Hindu altar is home to images of Hanuman, Ganesh, and Shiva.

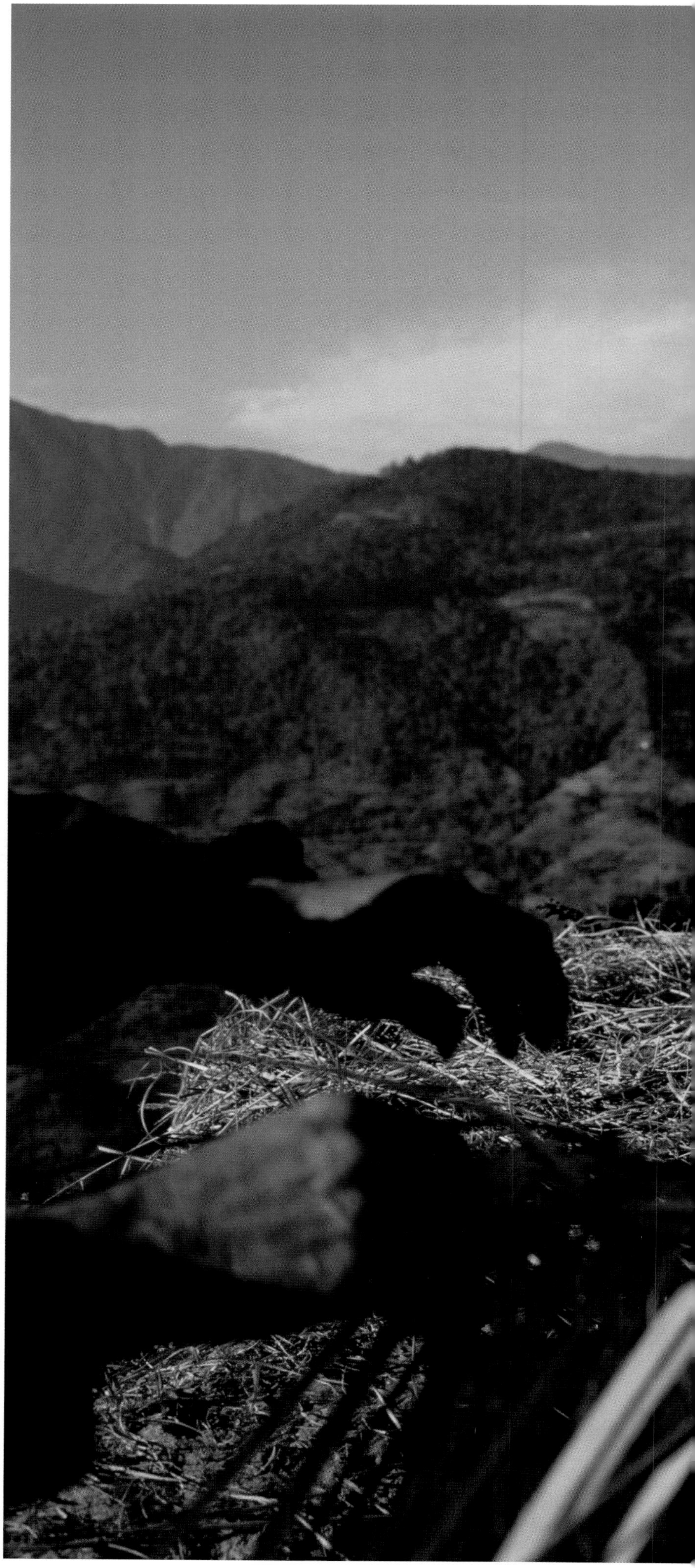

Laxmimaya, 43, rests on bales of hay after a long day of farm work as her husband weaves a new basket.

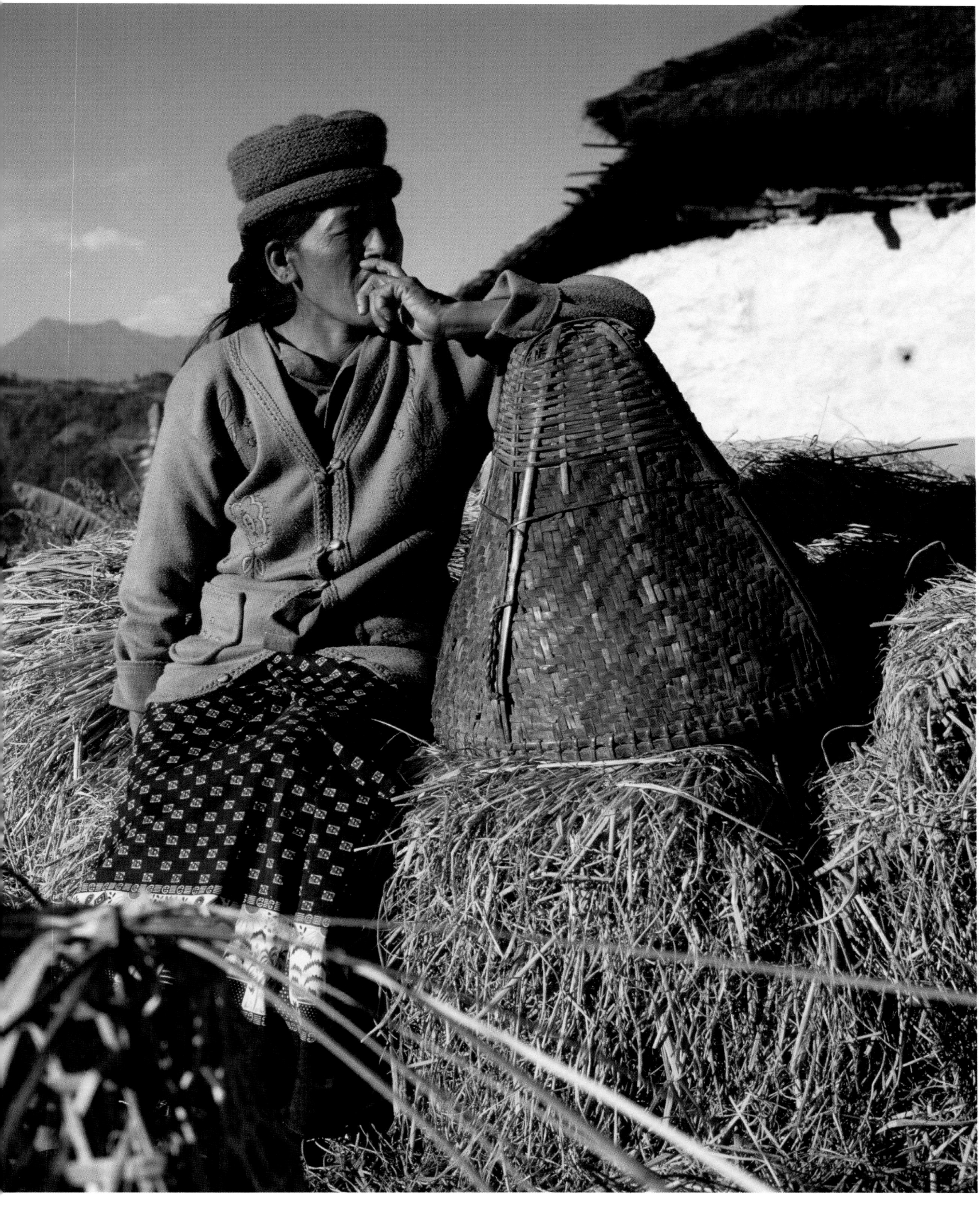

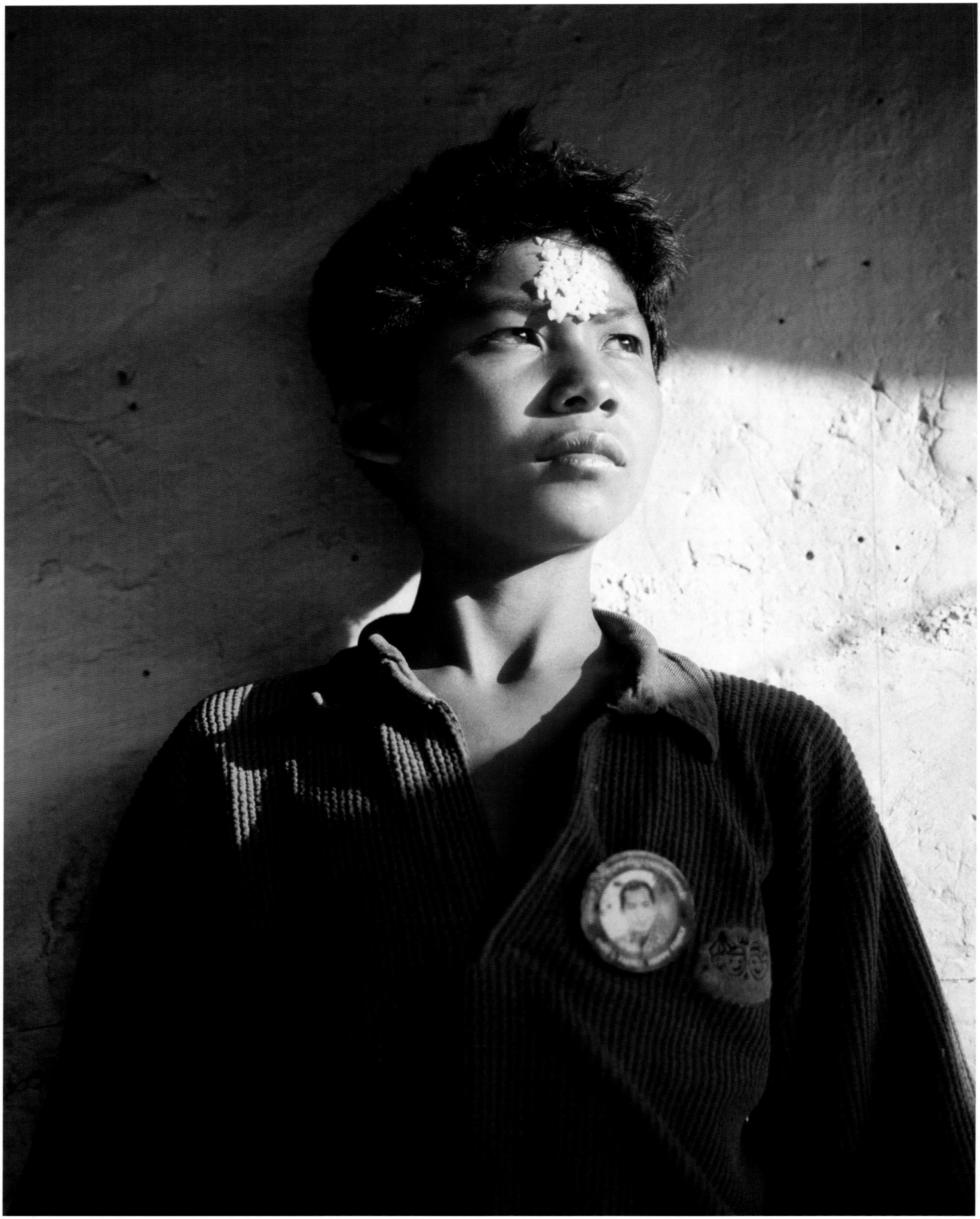

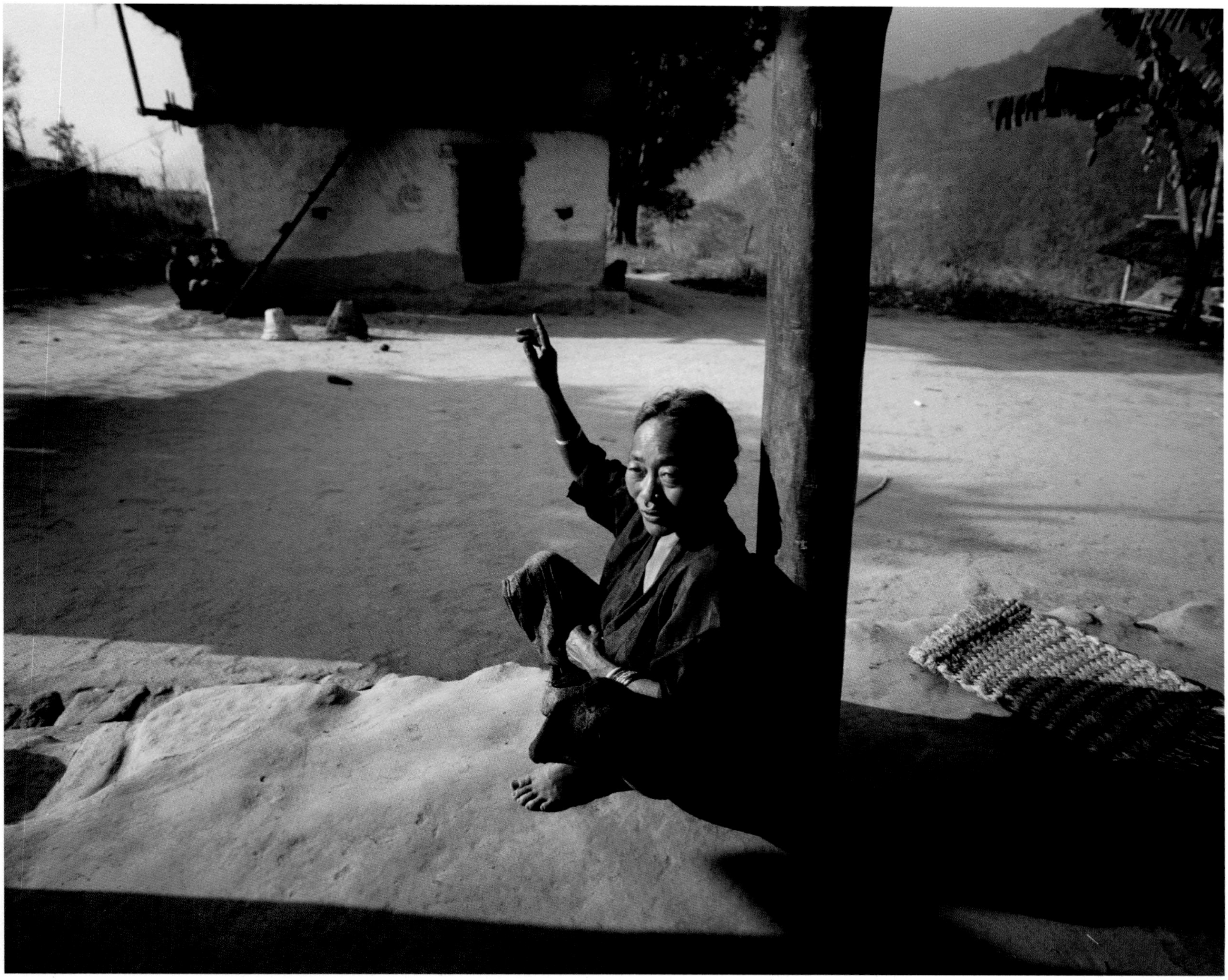

Monmaya, 72, points the way to Dagana Dzong located a few miles north of her house. The villages around Dagana feature a mix of both Lhotshampa homes and traditional Bhutanese homes.

Left: Santamon, 13, wears wet rice on his forehead after receiving a traditional Hindu Dasai blessing.

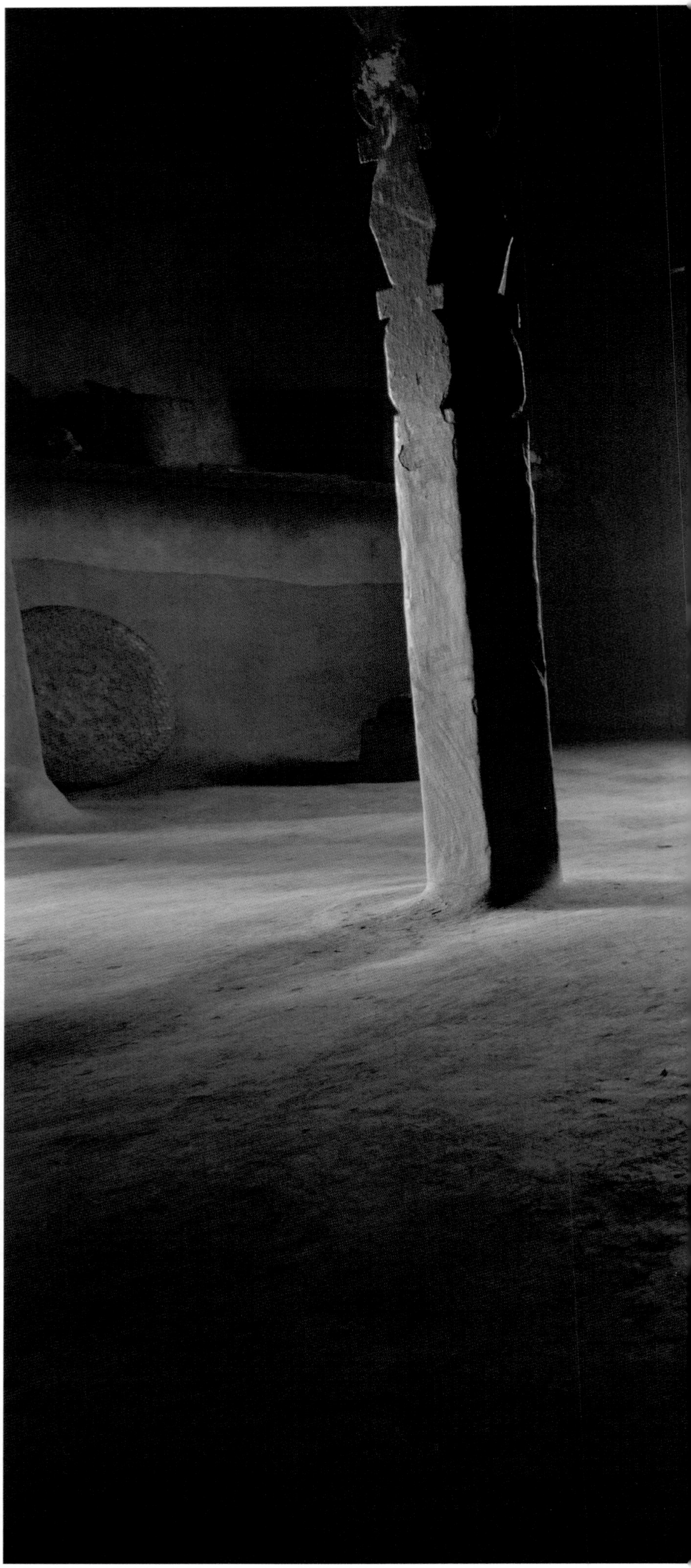

A house cat keeps watch as a kettle boils inside a Lhotshampa kitchen. Cats are often kept as pets throughout Bhutan to keep vermin at bay.

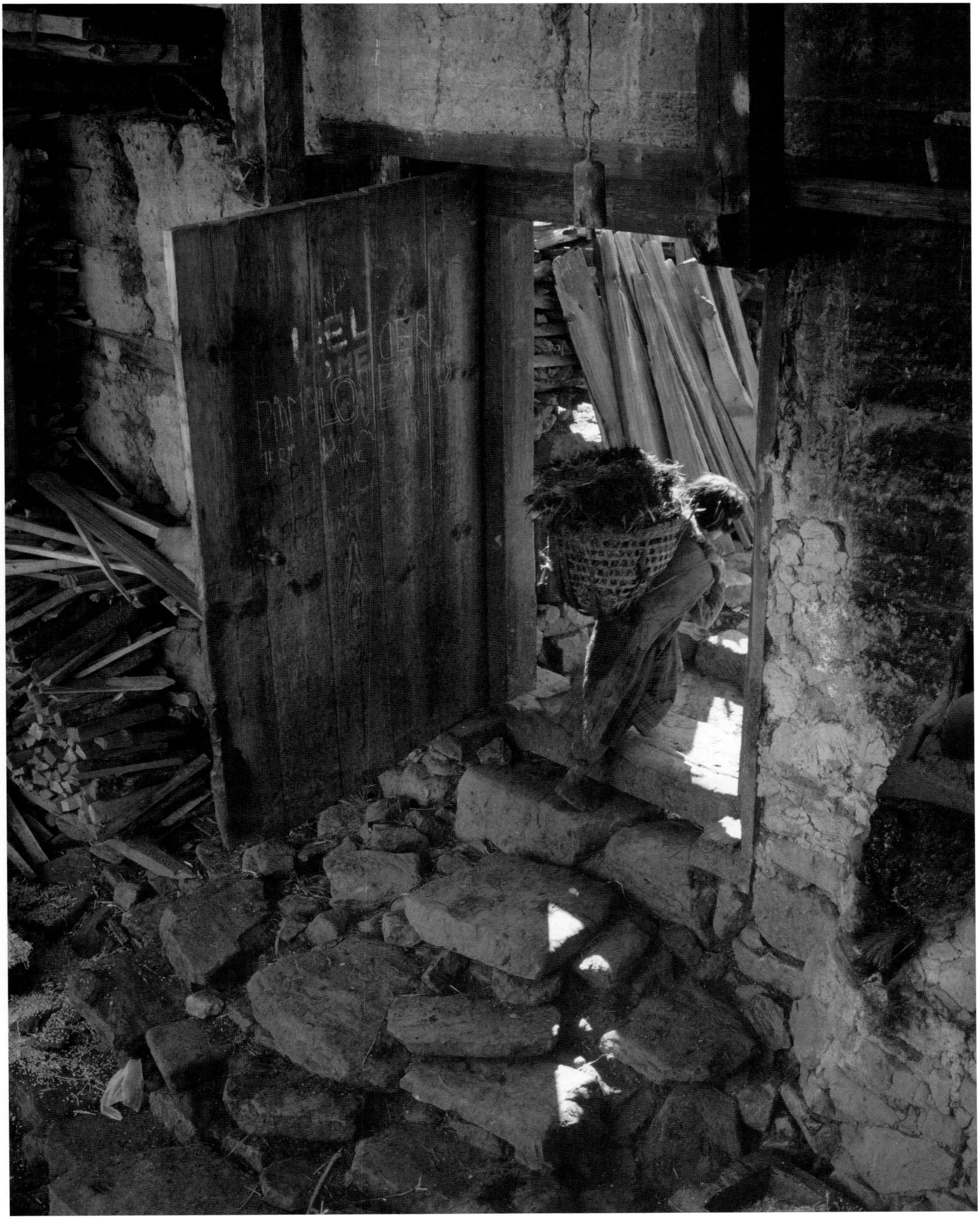

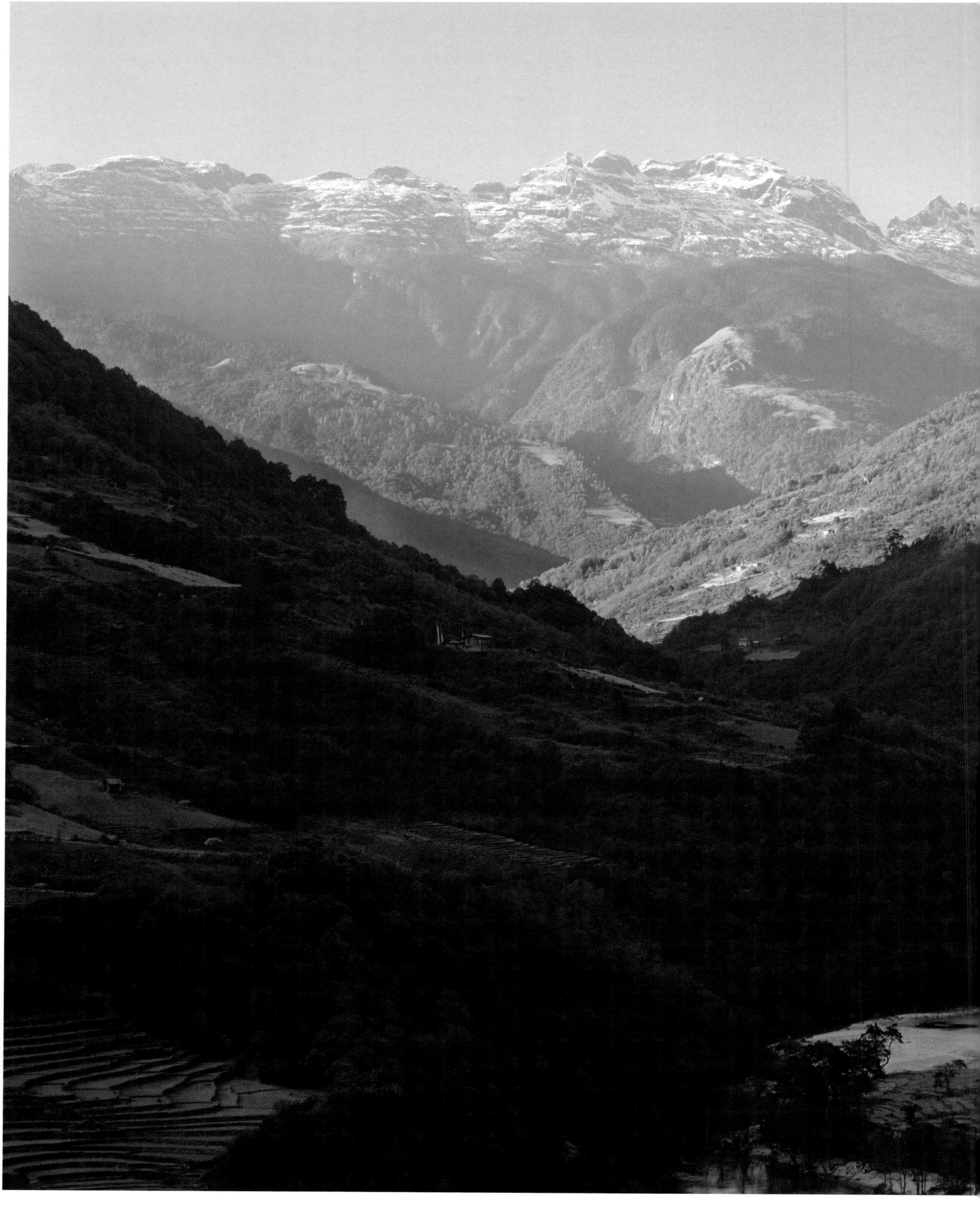

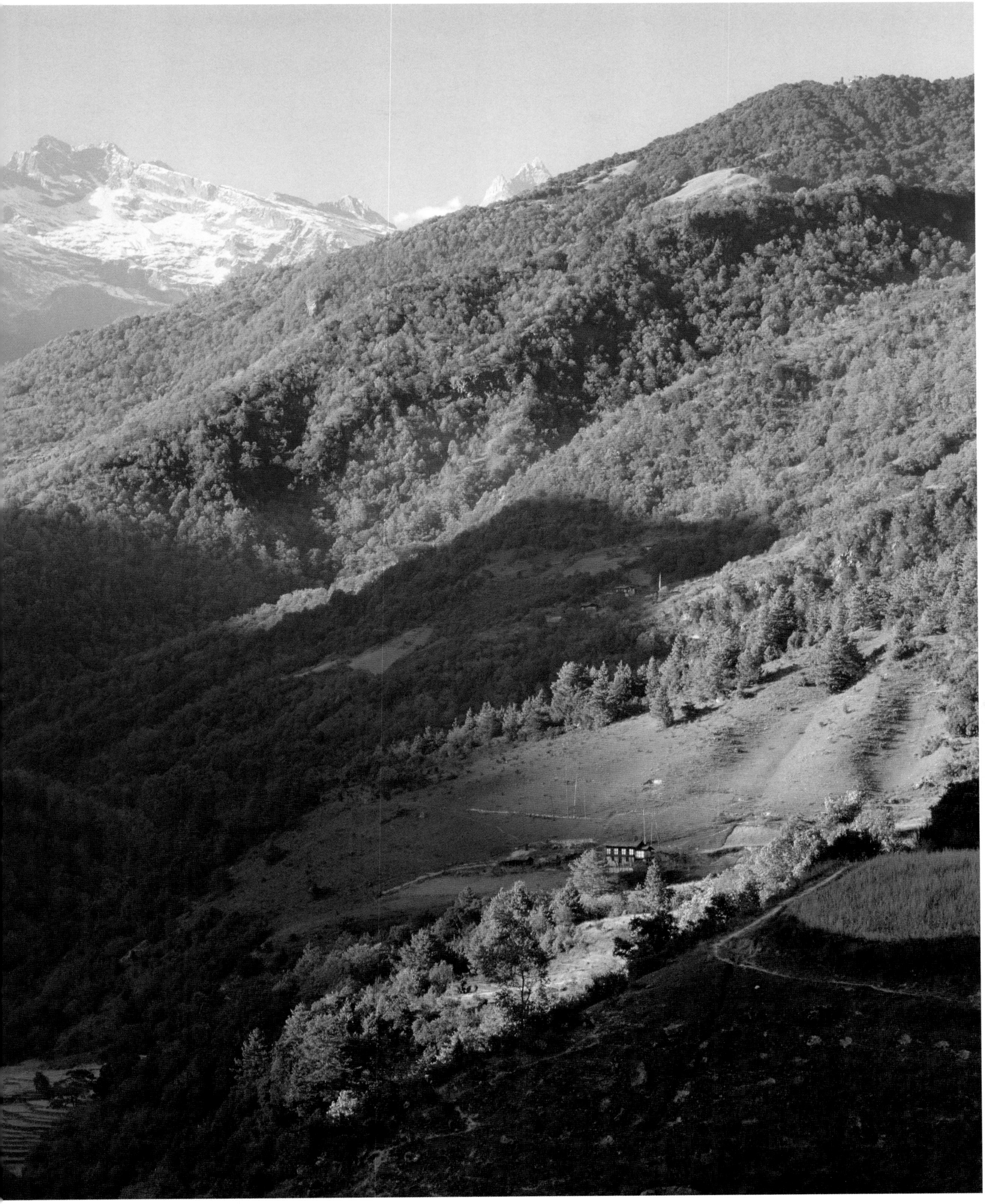

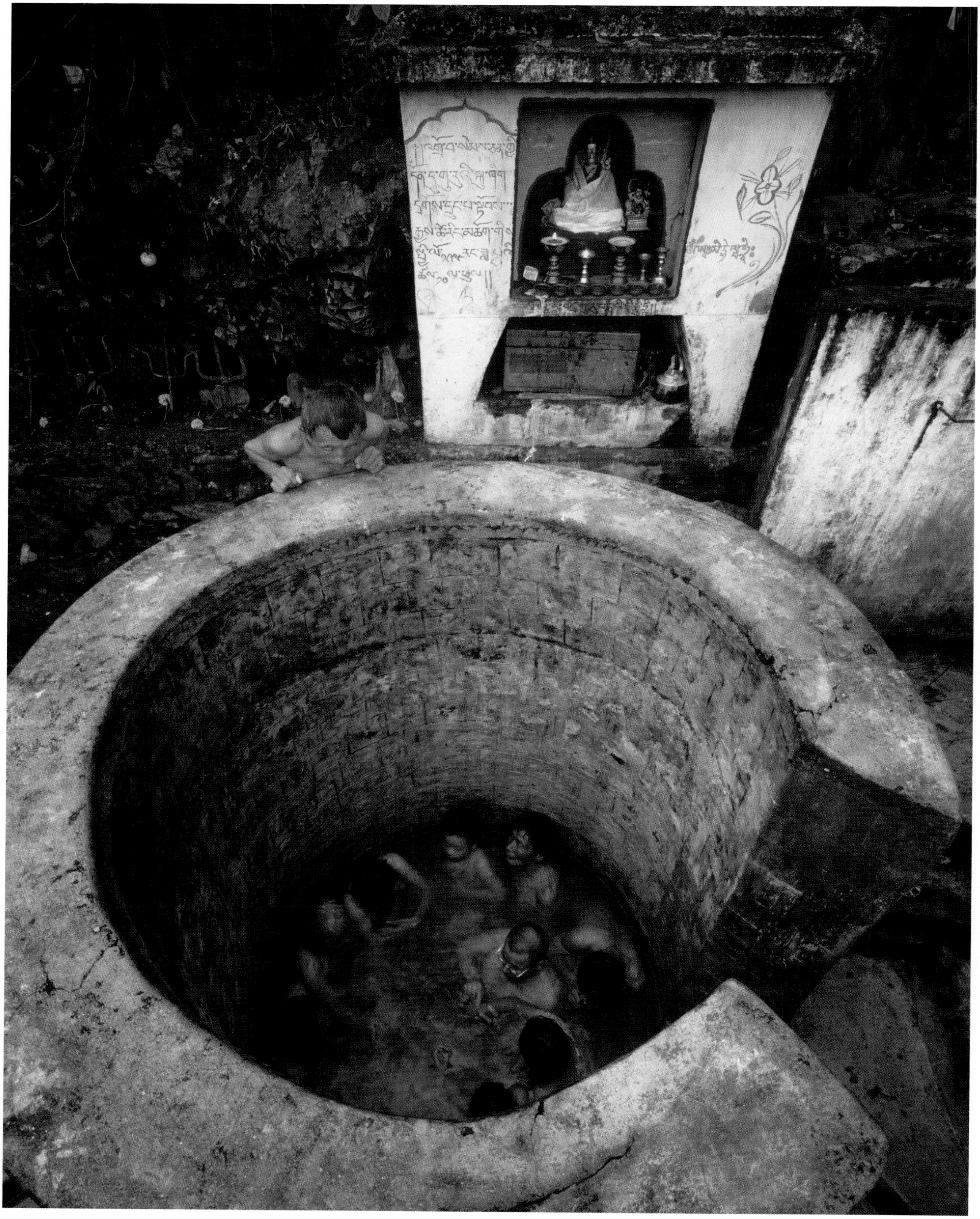

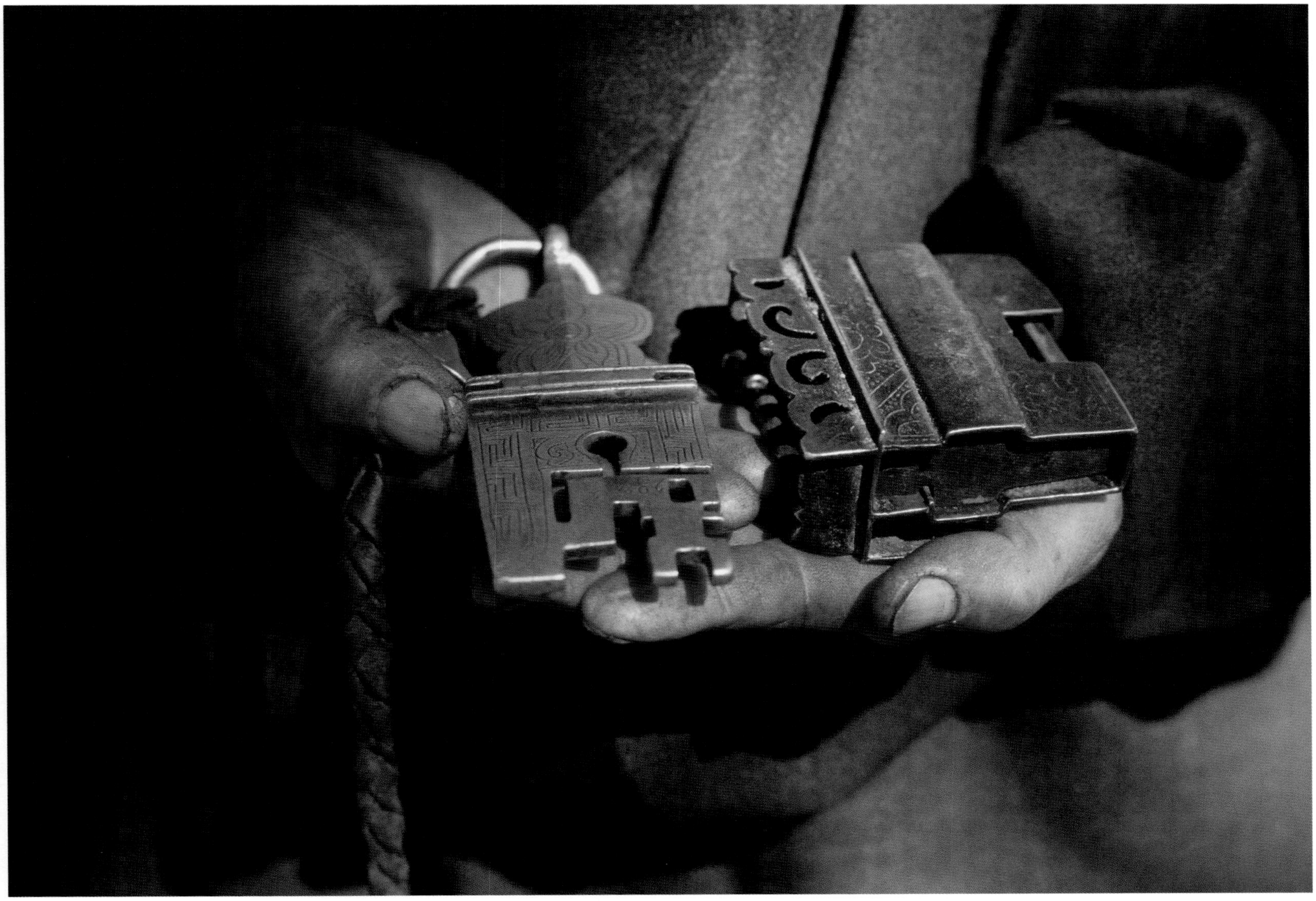

The caretaker for the temple in Nangsayperi holds the large lock and key used to secure the central prayer room.

Left: Bathers enjoy a soak in the Gelephu hot spring next to a small shrine dedicated to Padmasambhava.

Previous spread: The view north of Tashi Yangtse reveals the Kulong River and a trace of snow on the 15,000-foot peaks that separate this valley from the Lhuntsi district further to the west.

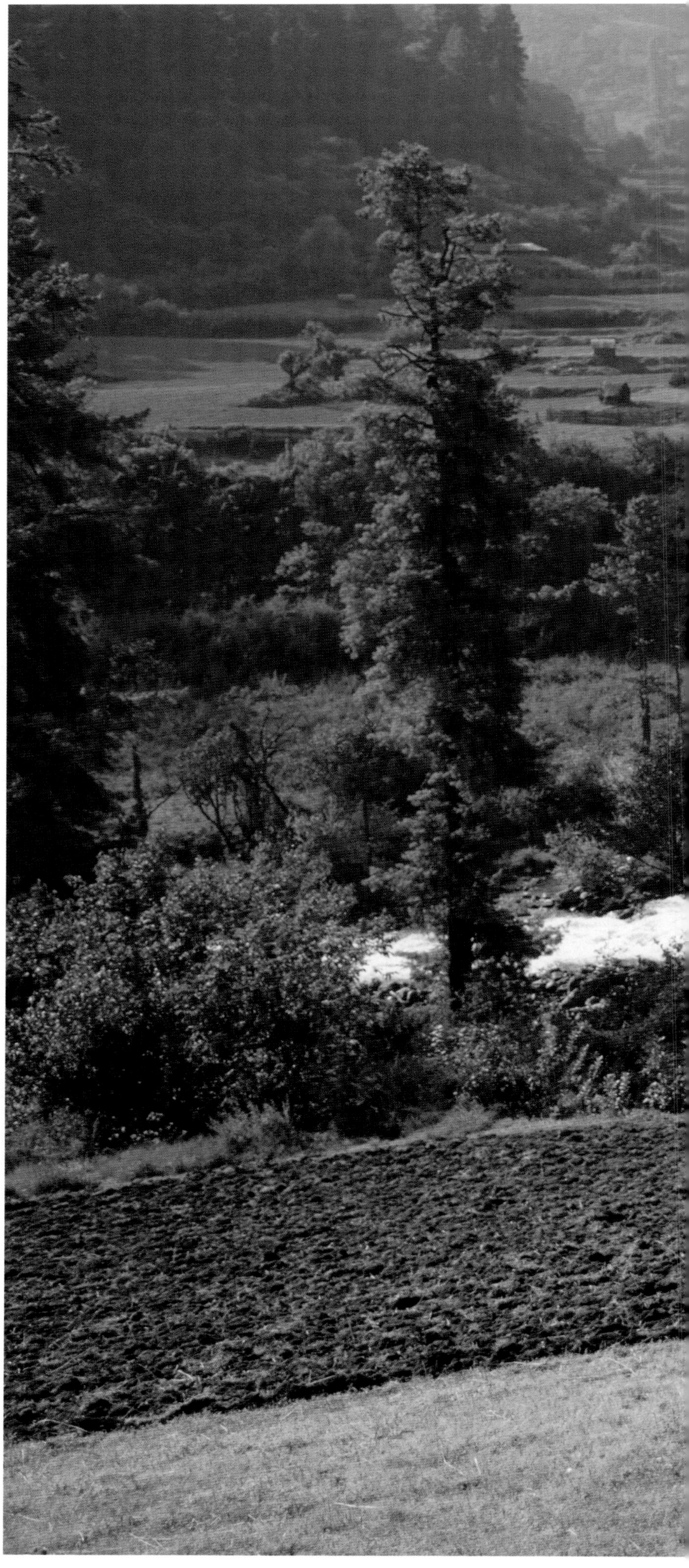

A pair of oxen plows a field near Chendebji.

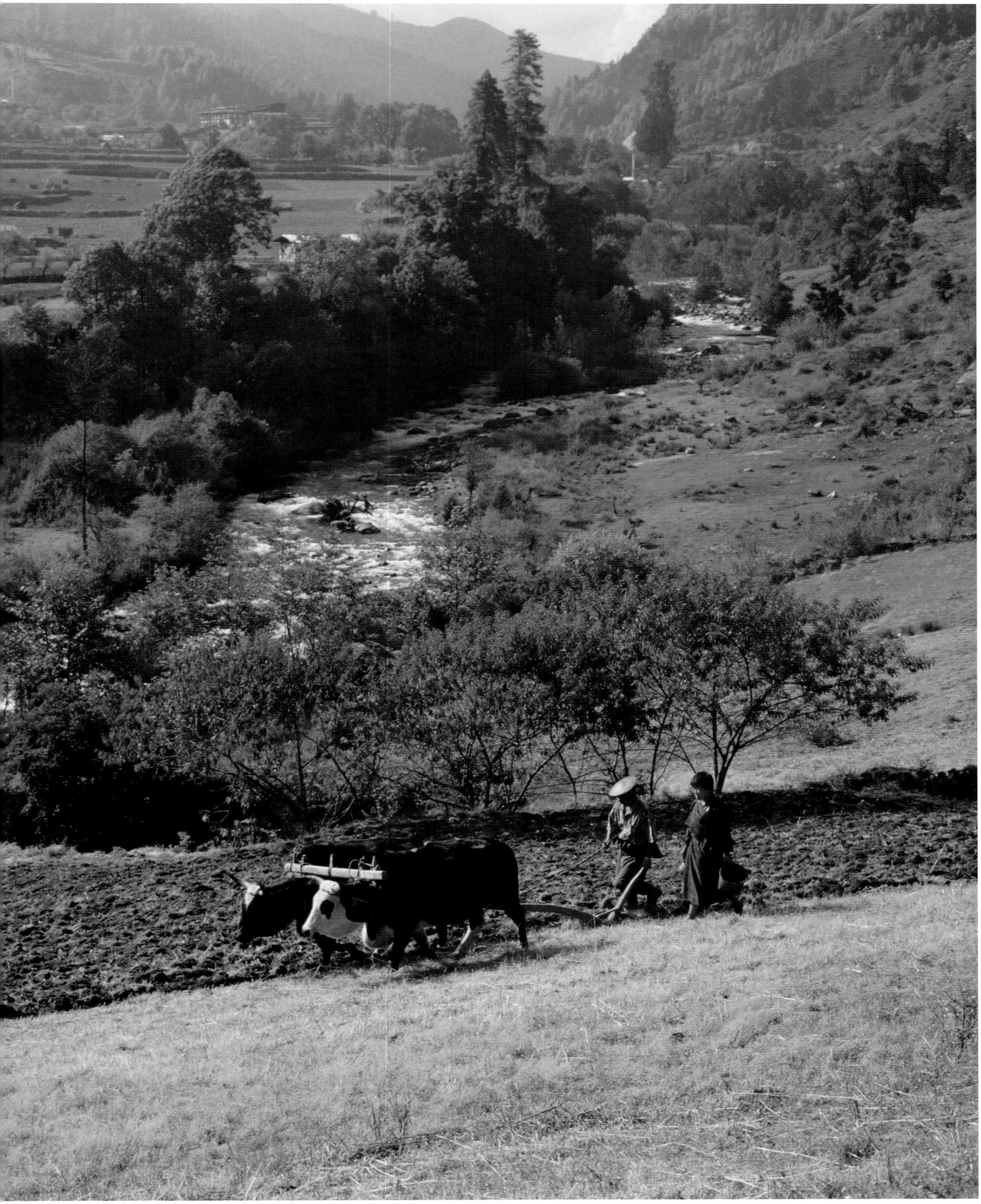

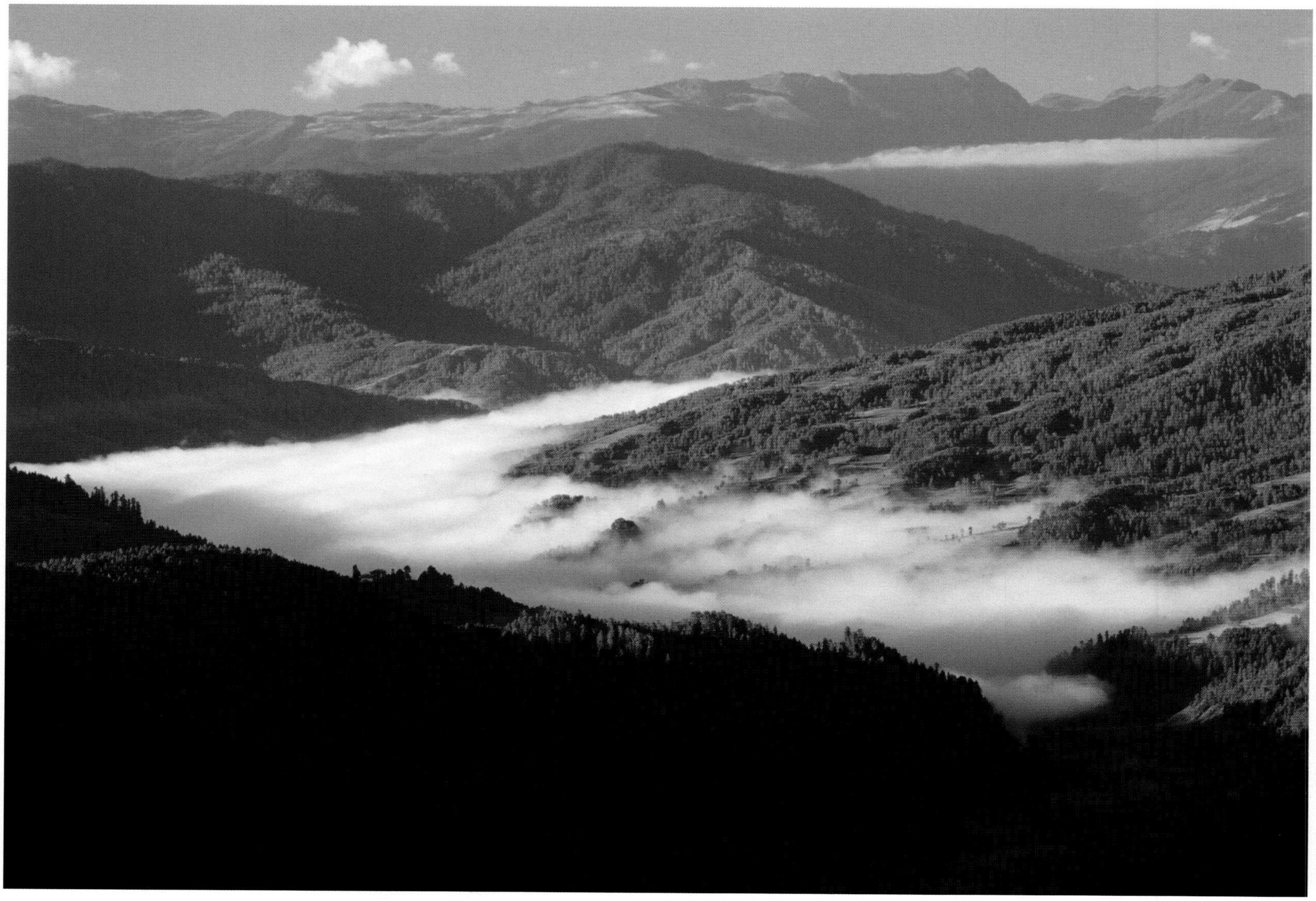

Morning fog obscures the Tang Valley as seen from the cliff-top Towada Monastery.

Right: Tenzin, 43, stands behind an old chain protecting the entrance to Thankabi Lhakhang. When he was younger, Tenzin was injured by a flying splinter of wood that accidentally left him blind in one eye.

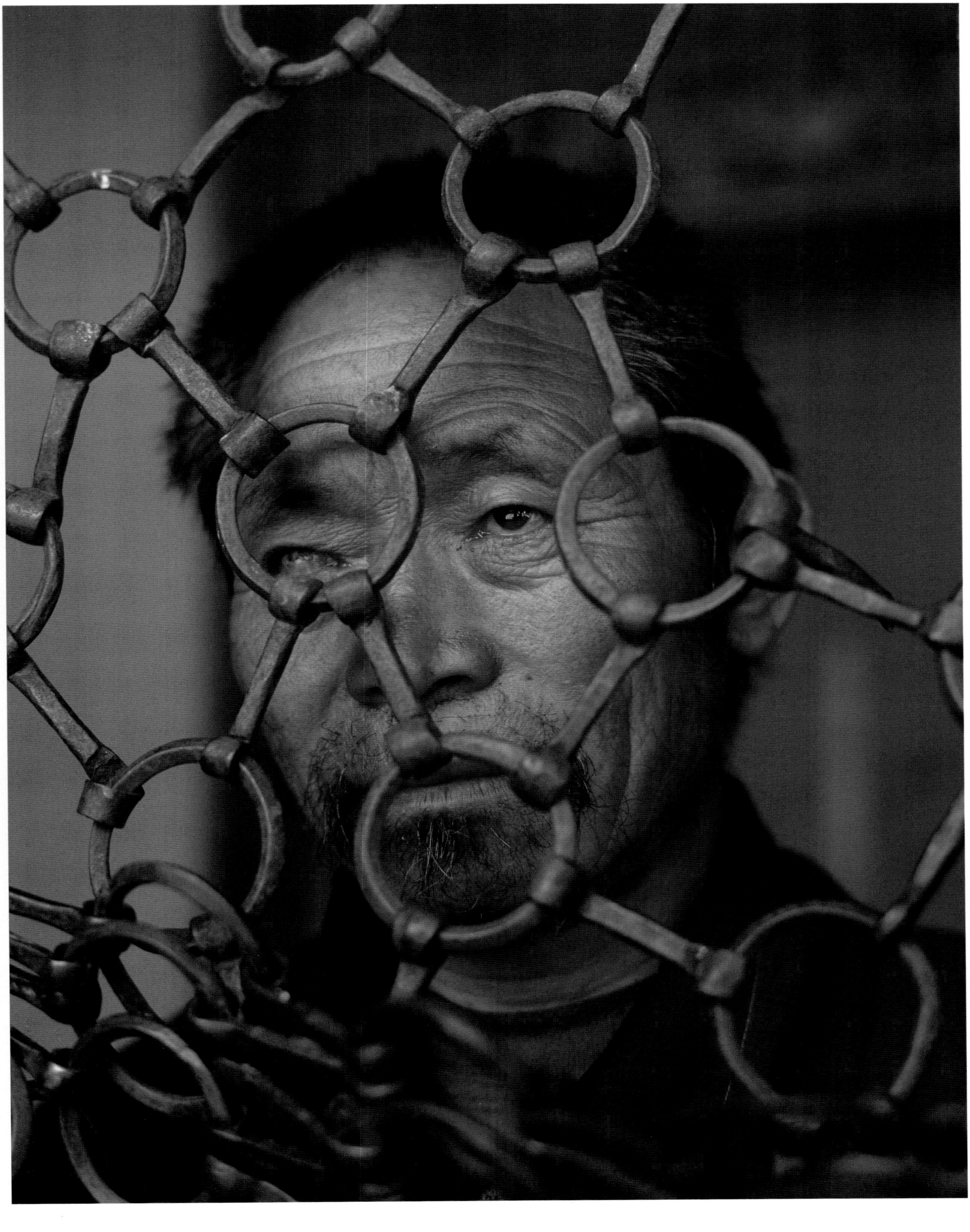

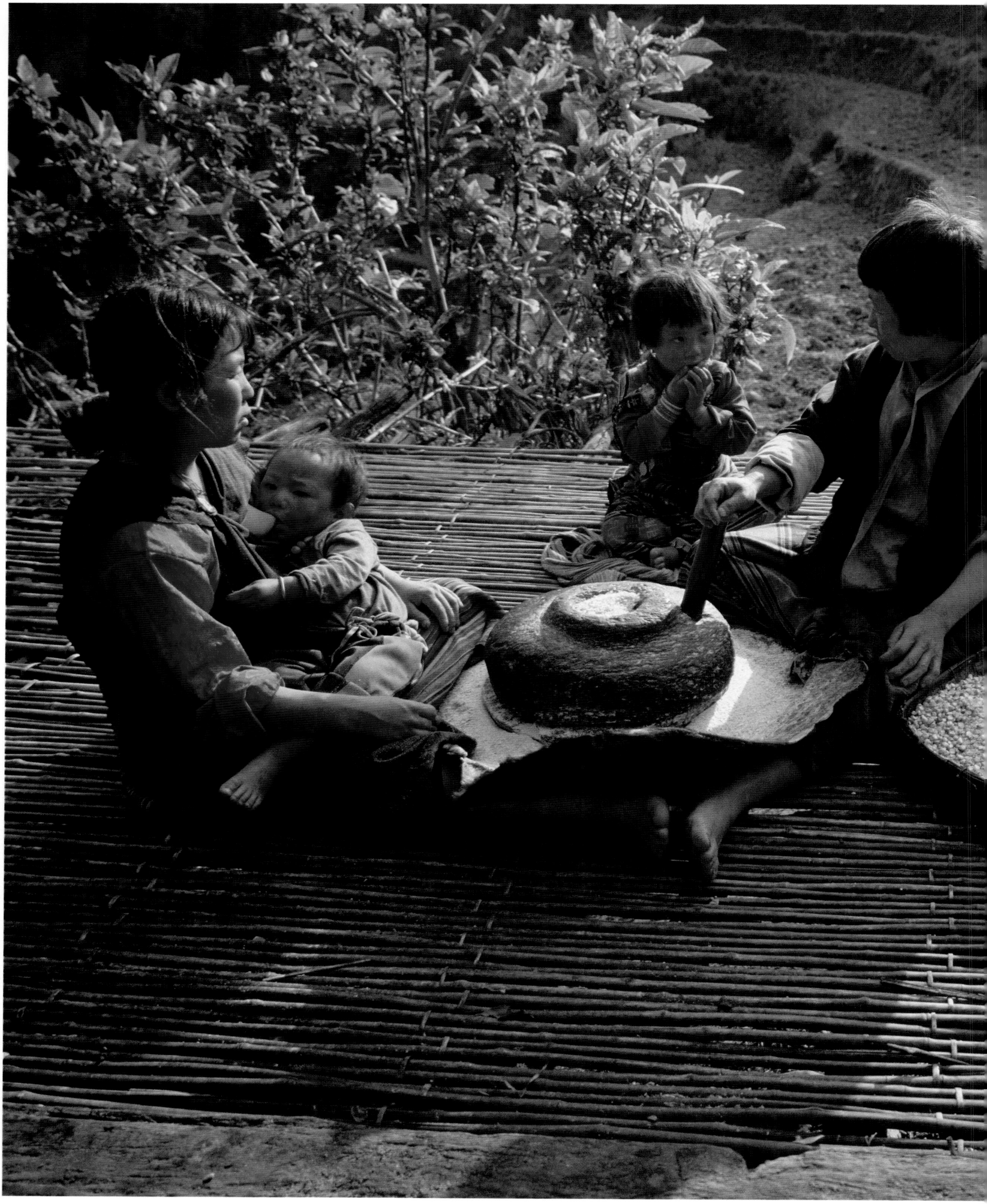

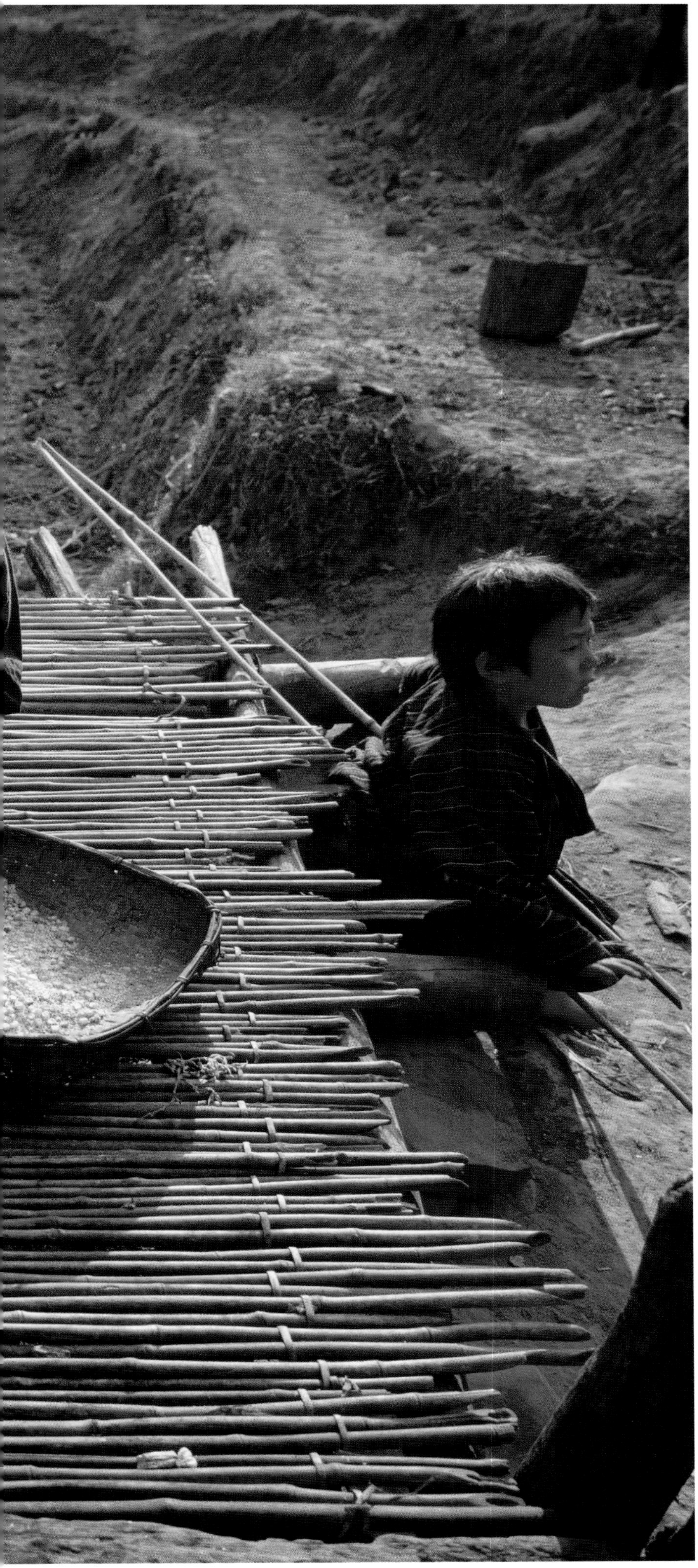

Two mothers and their children take a break from preparing stoneground corn in Phrumzor.

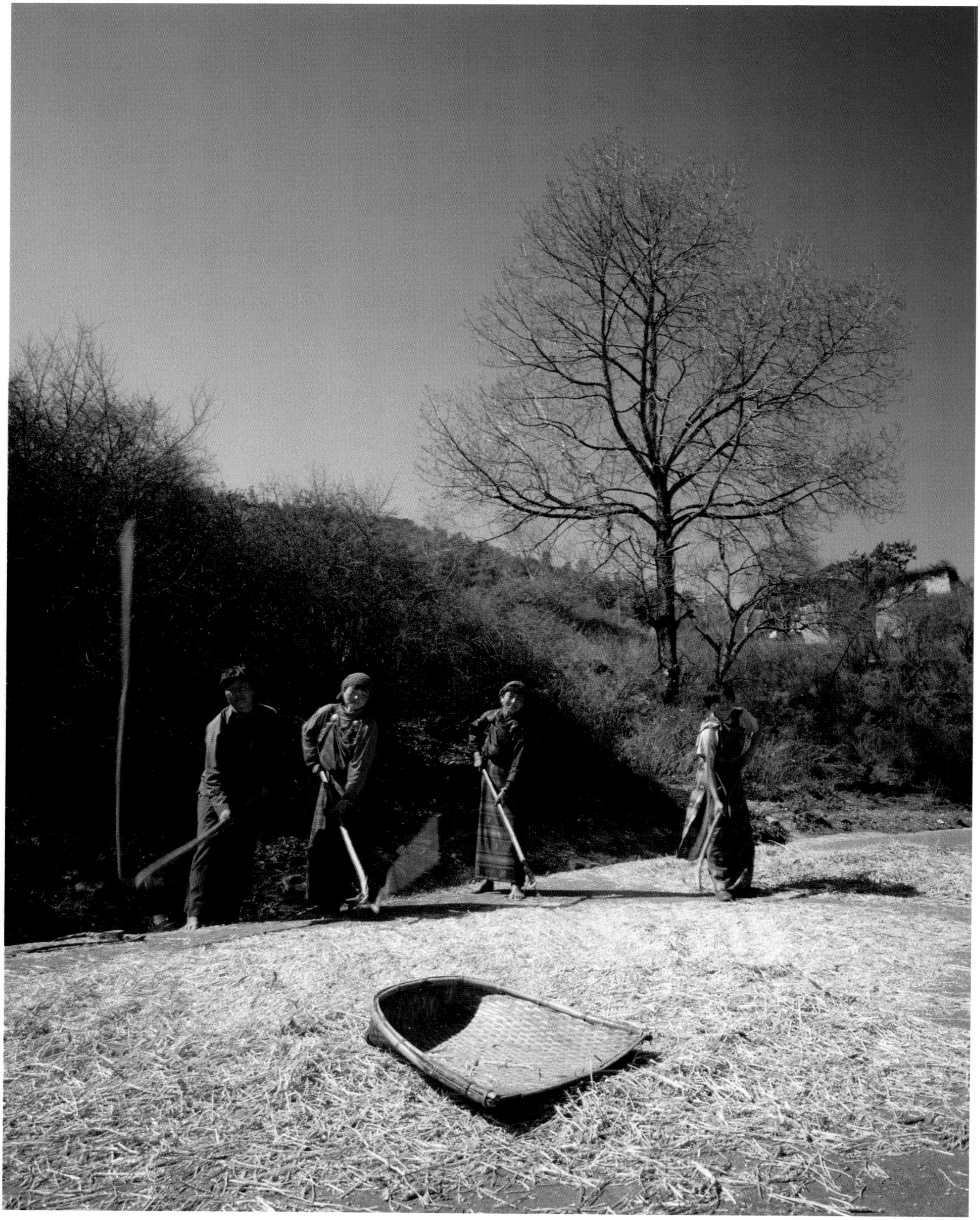

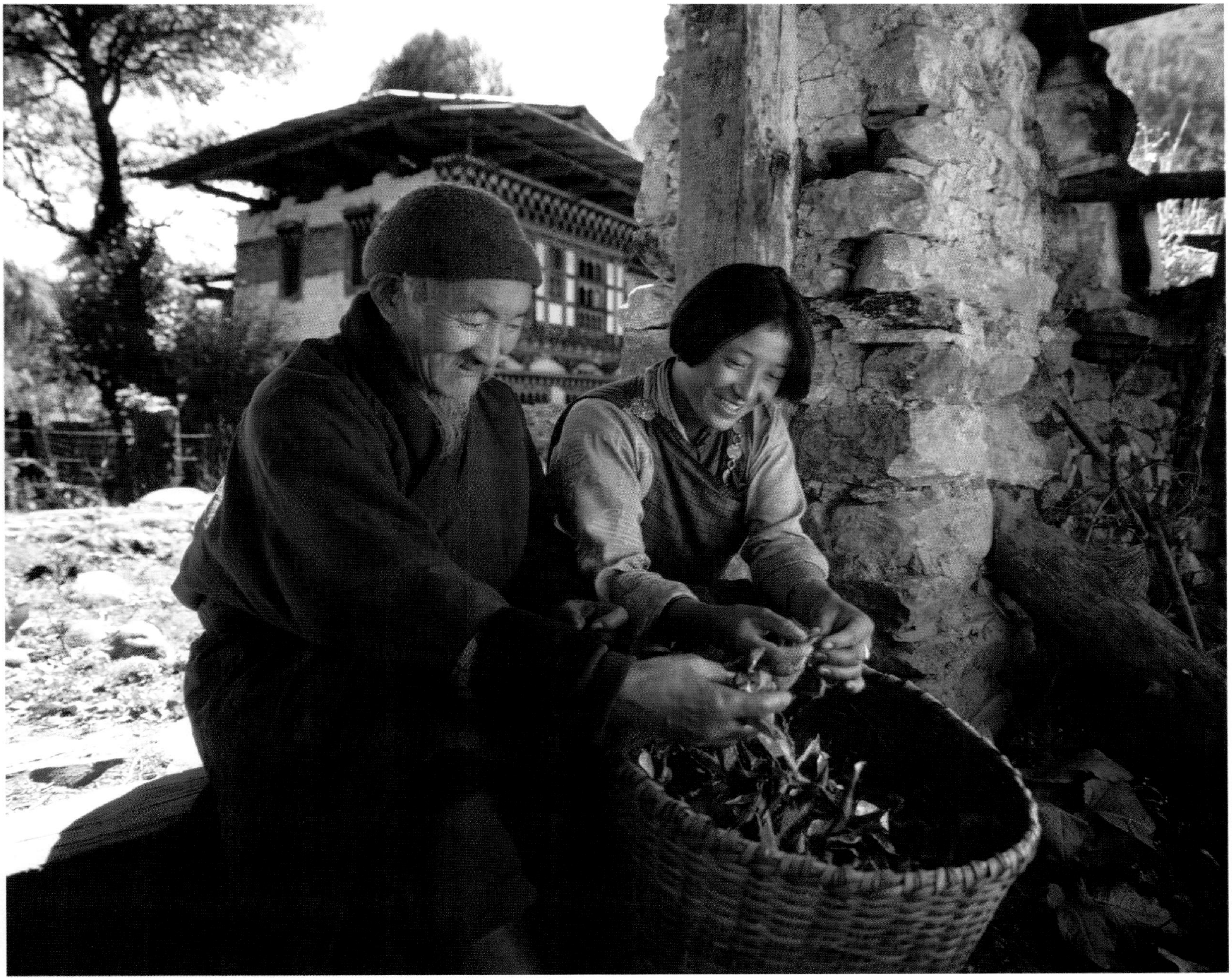

Pema, 80, and his neighbor, Pema, 24, enjoy a moment together while sifting bean pods in a basket. Many Bhutanese names are used by both men and women.

Left: Using long hinged poles, women from Bitekha rhythmically beat piles of wheat to extract the kernels. The occasional vehicle that drives over the harvest further helps the process.

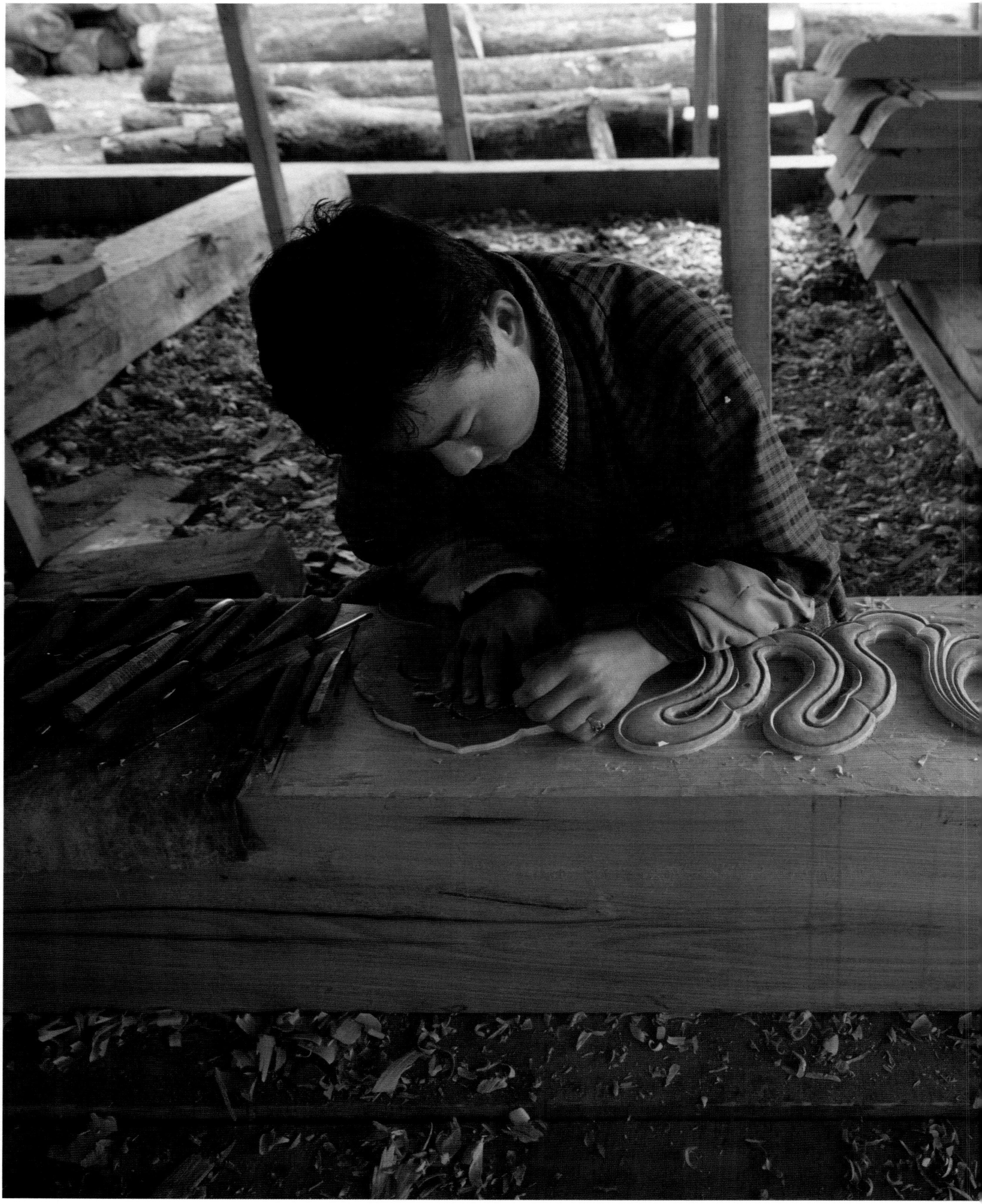

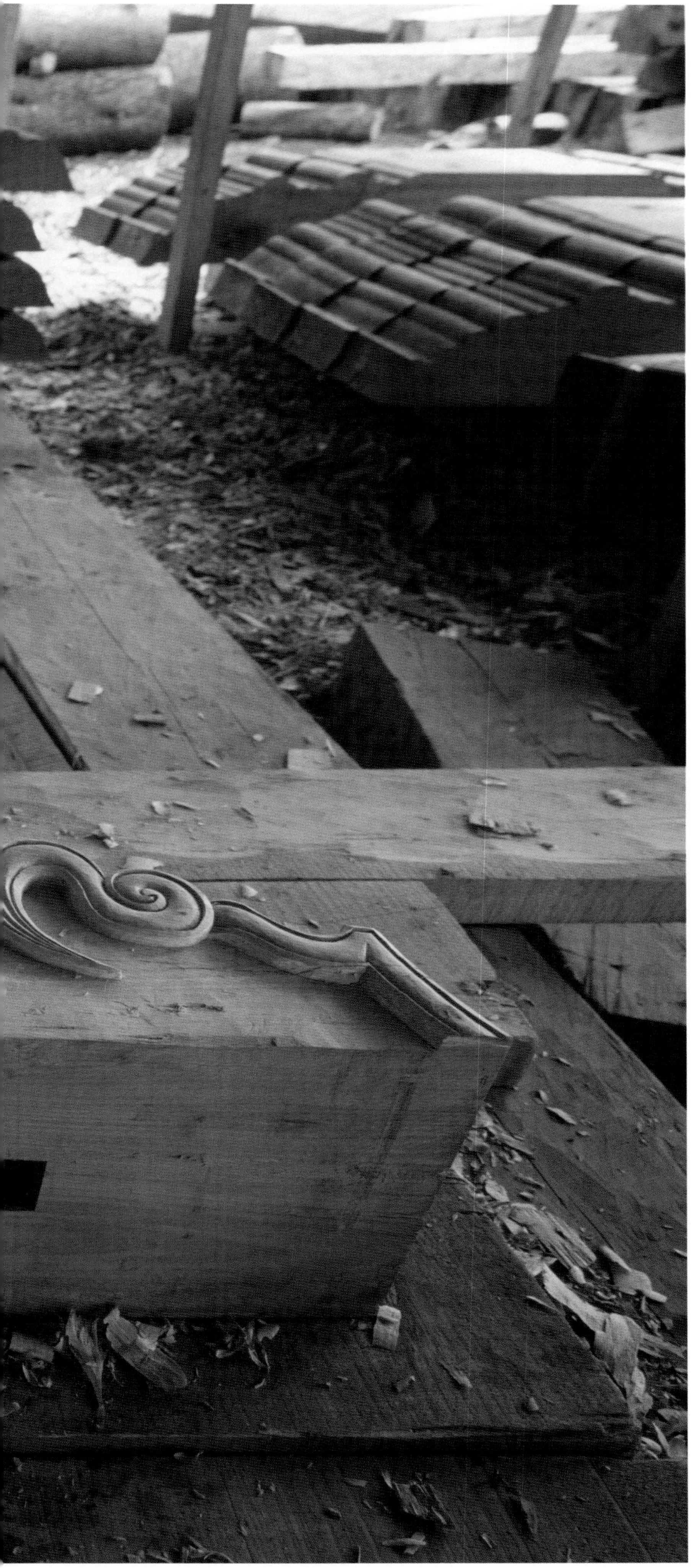

Sonam, 22, slowly carves decorative relief into a log beam to be used at Gangtey Monstery. Each beam requires nearly one hundred hours of work to complete.

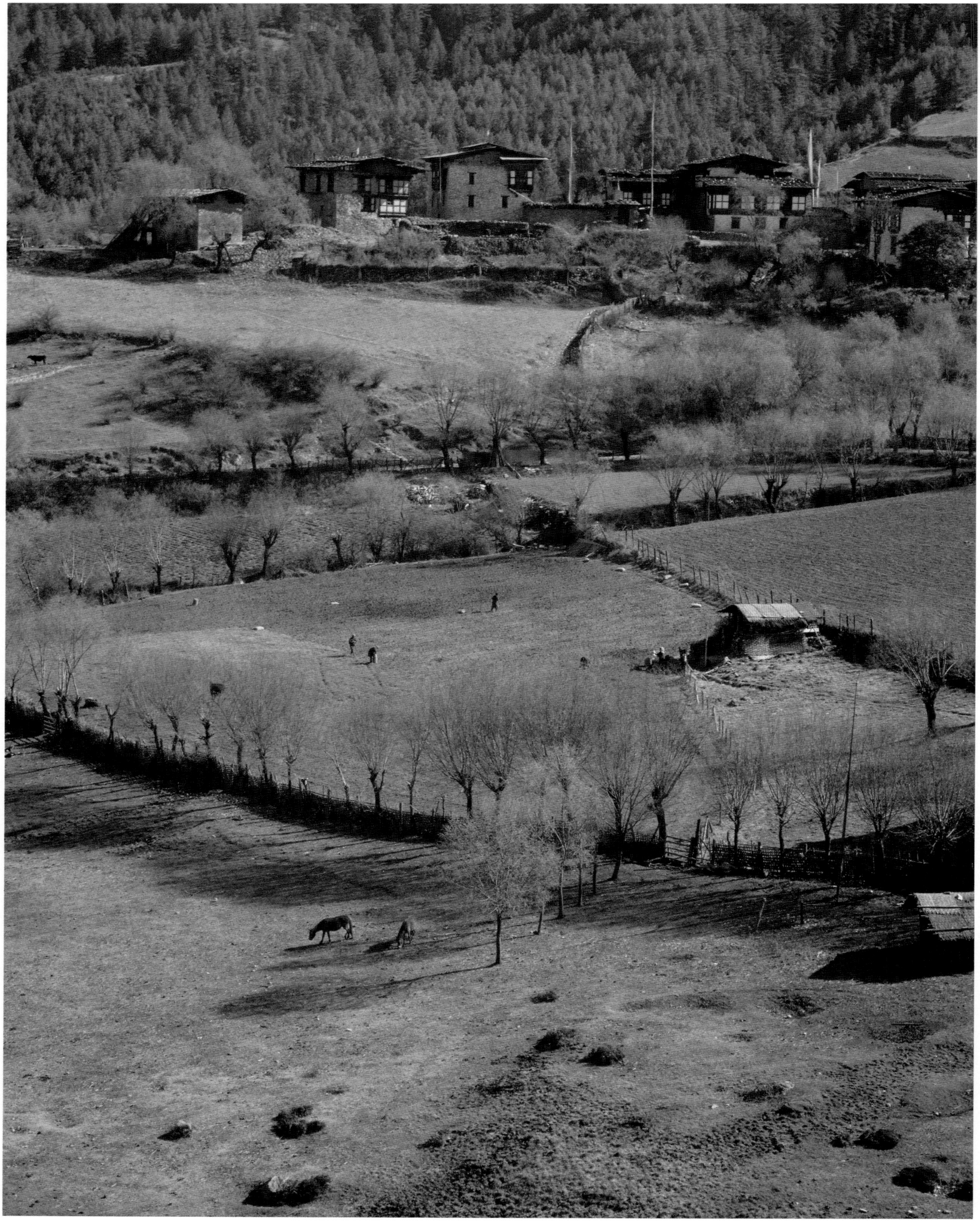

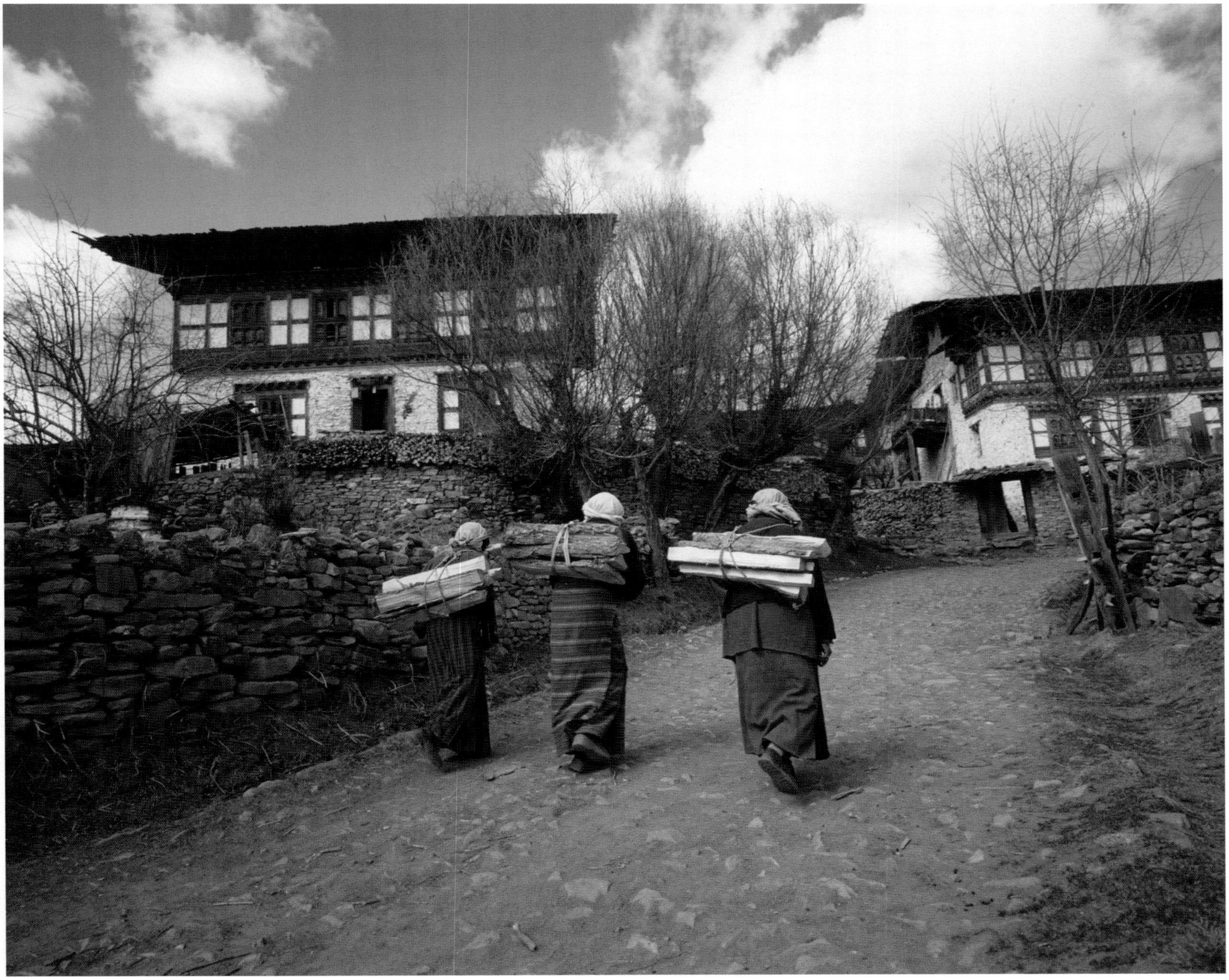

Three women from Ura head home carrying heavy loads of firewood.

Left: A road runs between farmhouses and fields near Ura.

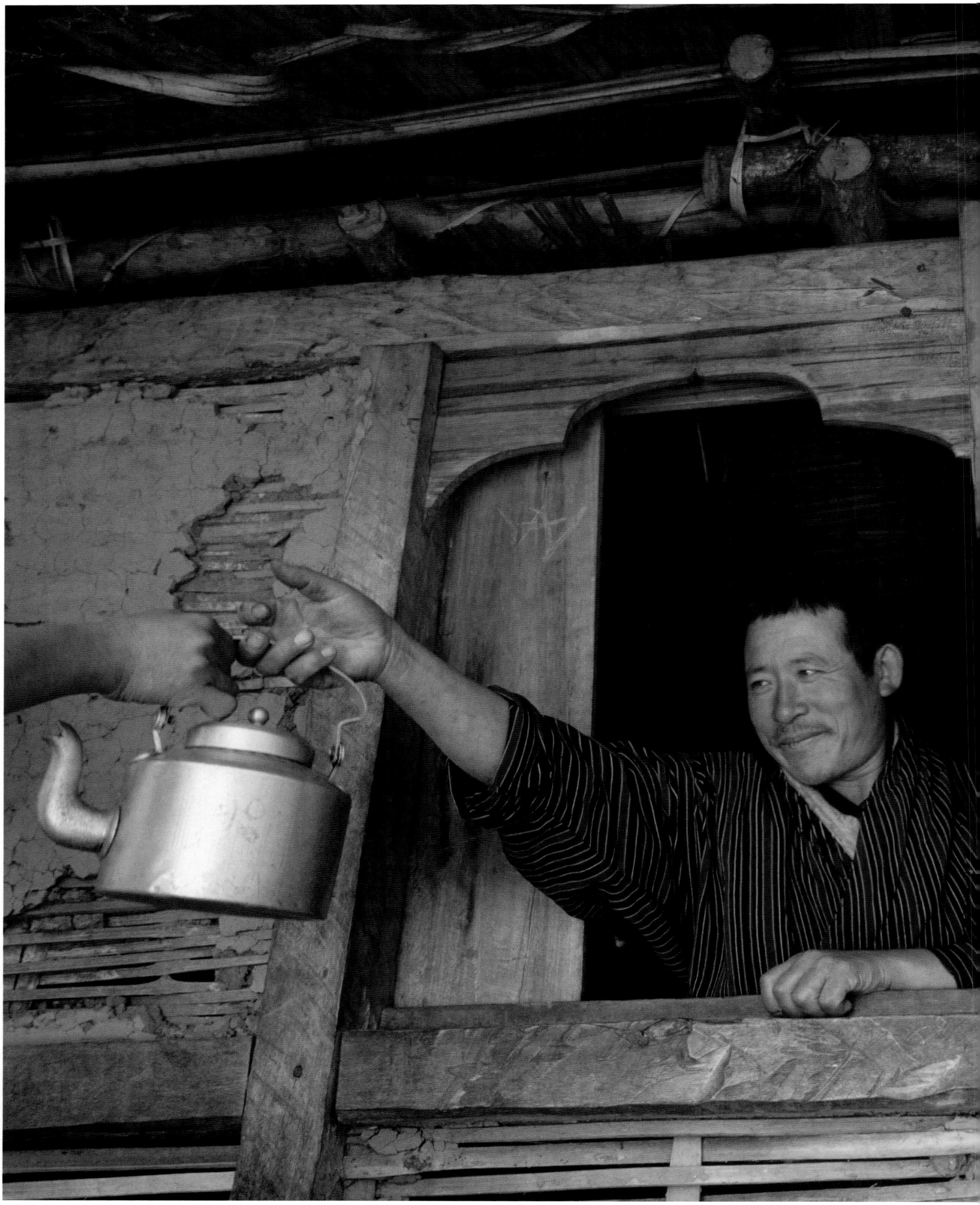

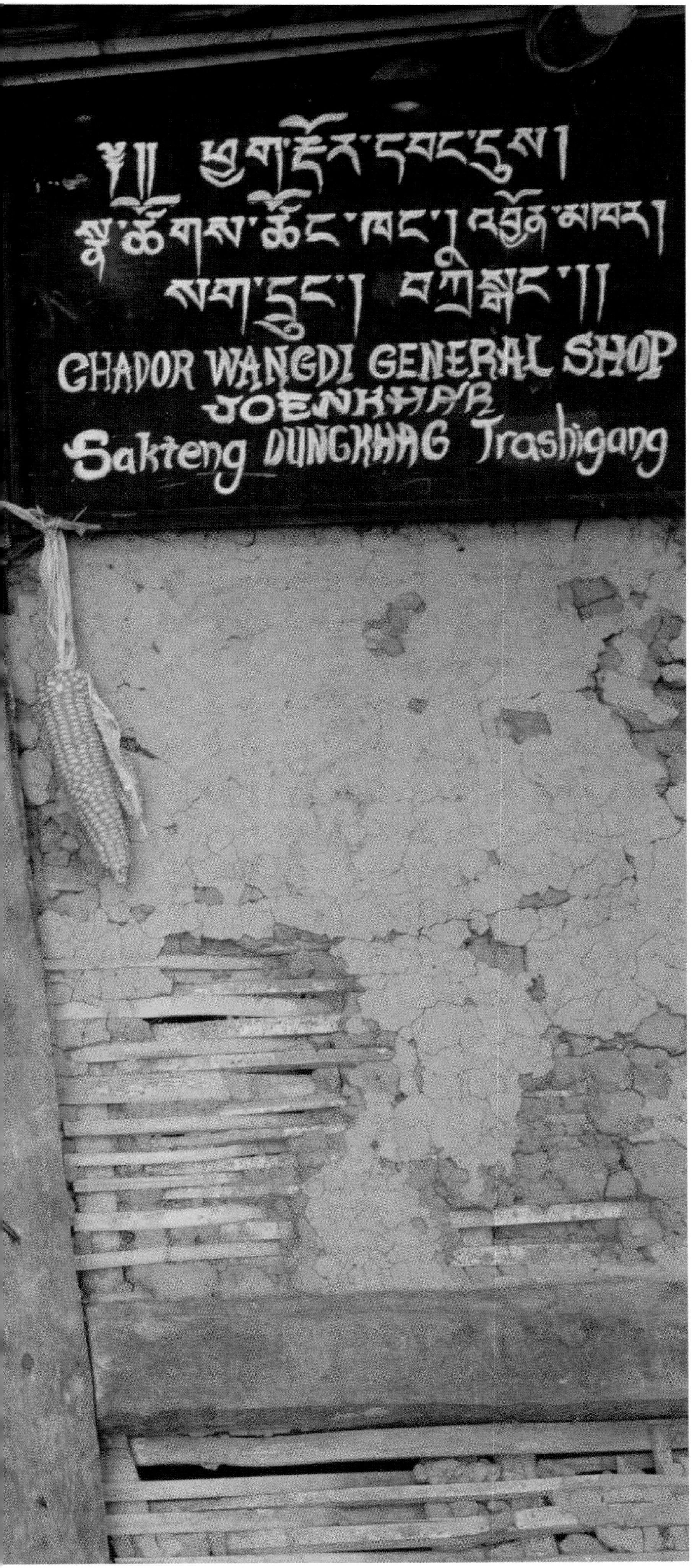

A shopkeeper in Joenkhar passes a kettle from the window of his general store. Nearly all the villages in Bhutan, regardless of size, have a few shops selling basic necessities.

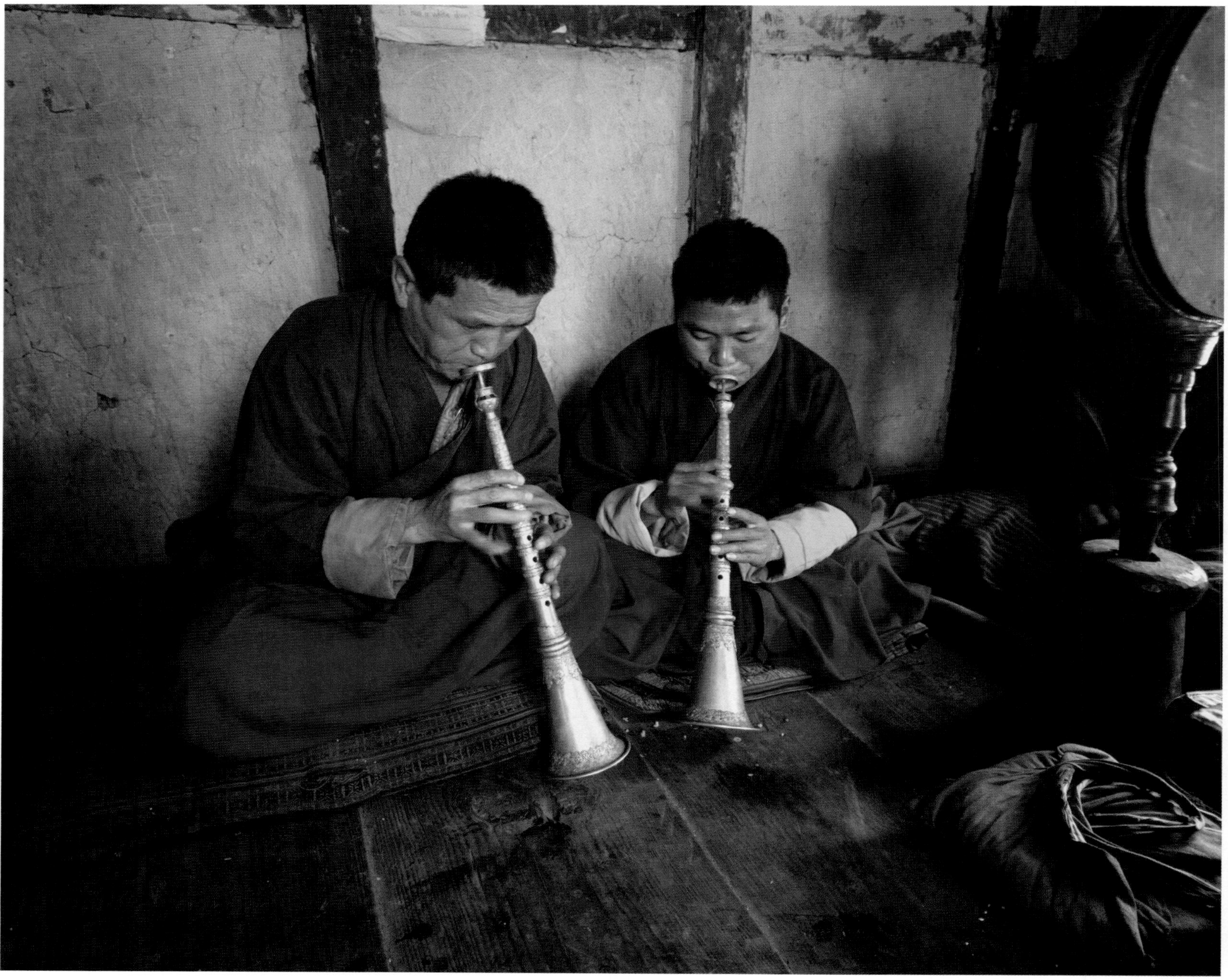

Two gomchens from Wangkha play trumpets during a private religious ceremony. Bhutanese regularly request local monks and gomchens to perform ceremonies in their houses to invoke the protection of particular deities.

Right: Nearly every house in Bhutan has a separate room dedicated as a Buddhist chapel.

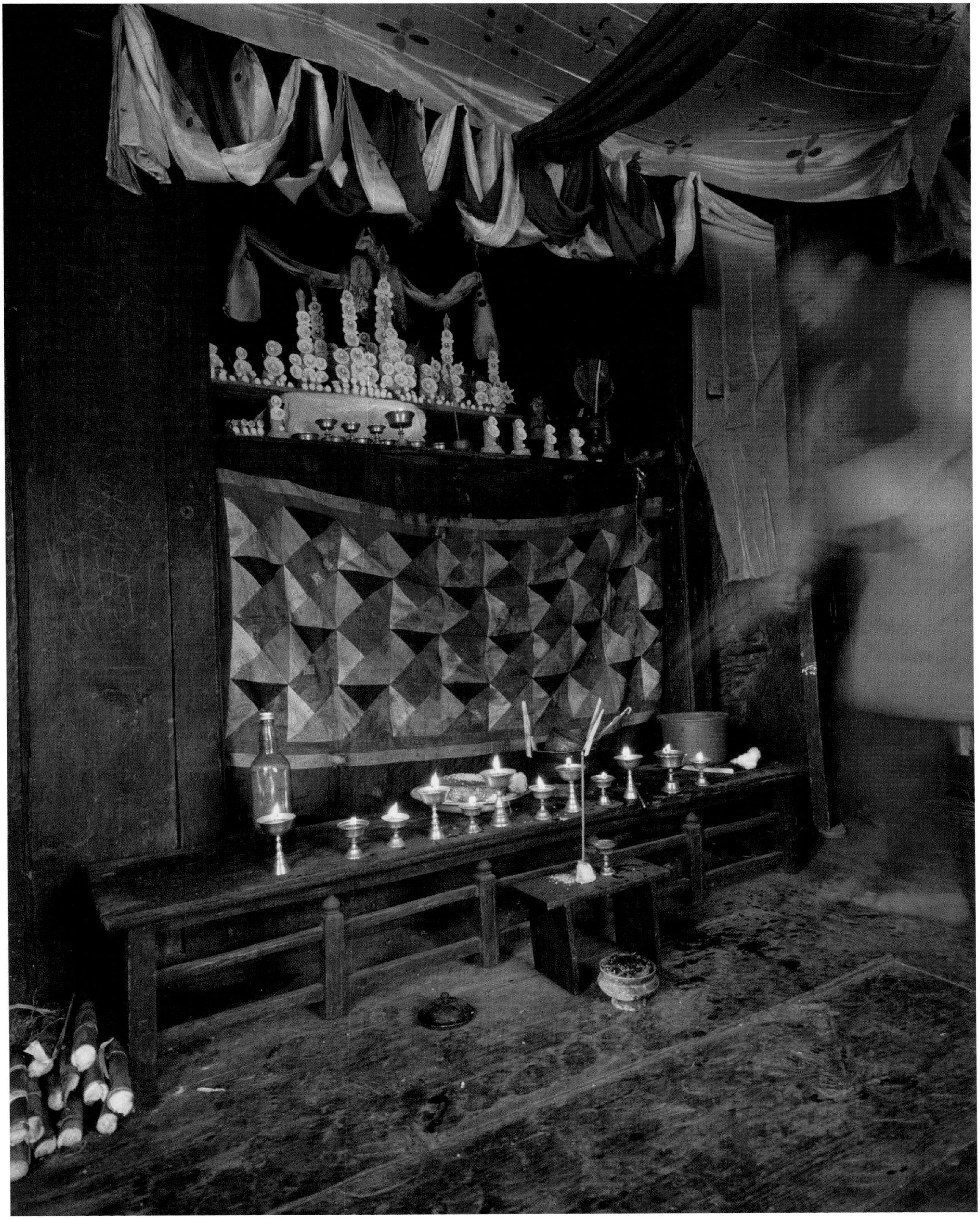

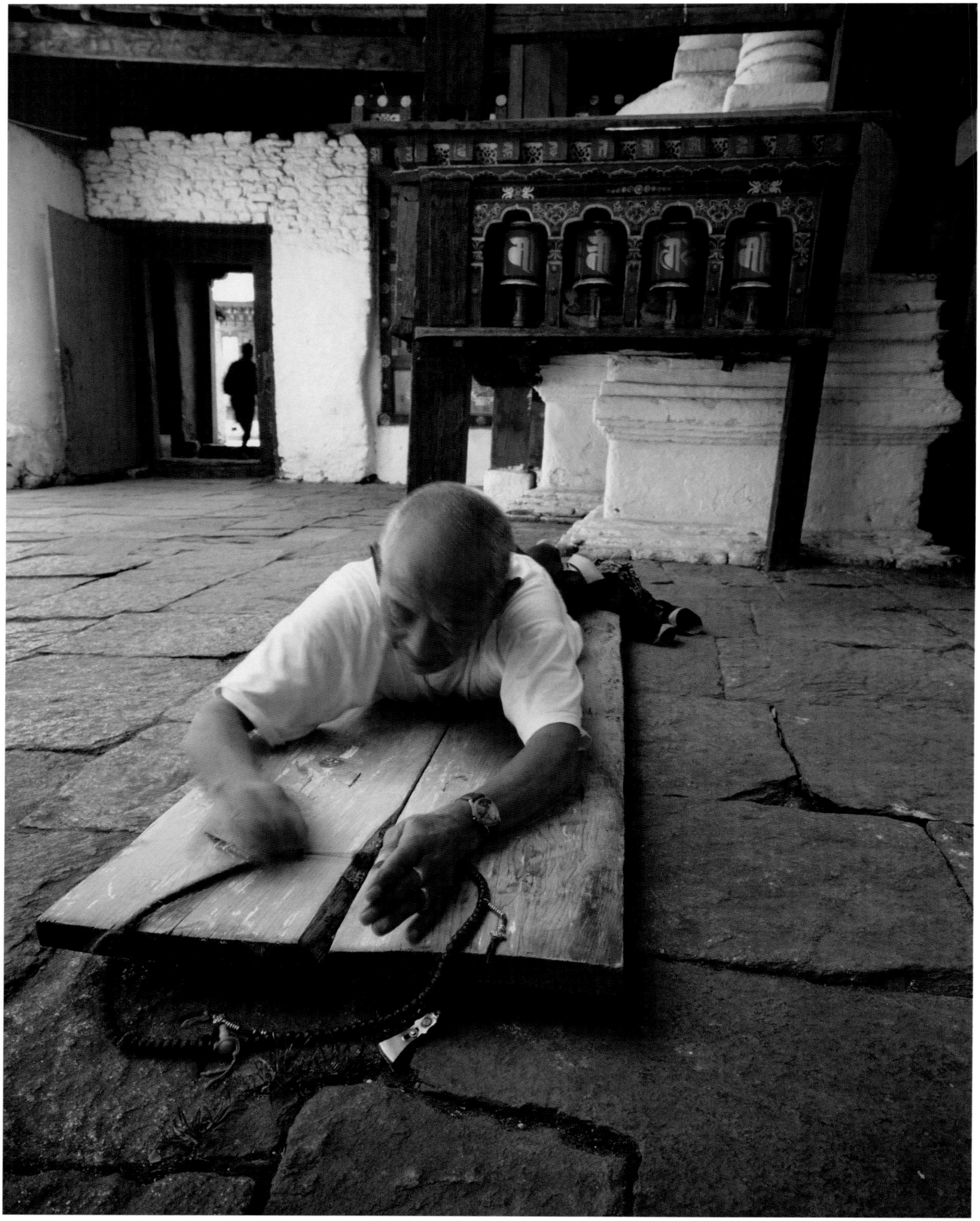